C000255692

They Sleep In Heroes Graves

To Brian
Best Wishes

Gwyn.

They Sleep In Heroes' Graves

The village of Stansted Mountfitchet during both World Wars

Glyn Warwick

First published in 2008
by Warwick Publishing
5 Mary McArthur Place
Stansted, Essex,
CM24 8EB.

ISBN 978-0-9558964-0-8

Typesetting, printing and binding by Repro City Ltd

Introduction

It is not my intention to put forward my views on what took place during the 1914-1918 and 1939-1945 conflicts but only to remember those who served.

This book is about a tiny few who 'did their bit' from the village of Stansted Mountfitchet. Also included are certain interesting incidents, which I stumbled across during my research that happened in and around the village.

At first this book was going to be about those who are named on the Stansted Memorial, sited in the grounds of St. John's Churchyard, but it escalated as I found out more and more about other soldiers connected with the village, whether they were killed or wounded, and also those who were awarded medals for acts of gallantry. My main interest has always been the Great War (World War 1) but hopefully, within this book, I have also been able to do justice to those who lost their lives during World War 2.

I have attempted to find out as much information as possible on all the soldiers mentioned in the book but there came a time when I felt all avenues of research had almost been exhausted. The saddest aspect of researching soldiers from the Great War is that if they were killed then the research is so much easier.

No doubt the day after the book goes to print some kind soul will contact me with additional information and or a photograph. This will no doubt mean a revised version being printed at a later date, hopefully.

Please remember I am not an author, but simply someone who felt it appropriate to write this book. I hope you find it both enjoyable and informative.

I was born in 1959 in Bishop's Stortford and my education took place at Newport Grammar School. Sixteen years ago I moved to the village of Stansted Mountfitchet where I still live and work.

One thing, which has been very prominent during my research is how often the name 'Woodfields' (off Chapel Hill) keeps coming up. It was probably the largest area of housing in the village at the time. Of the losses the village suffered during the Great War many men were from Woodfields (almost twenty families were affected by the loss of their loved ones). The sound of the Postman/Telegraph Boy coming down the street must have been quite frightening.

If anyone, after reading this book, can add any information then I will gladly put it on file for a possible reprint. I am also planning to put all the information and pictures I have onto a website at a later date.

Glyn Warwick.
5 Mary McArthur Place,
Stansted, Essex,
CM24 8EB.
glyn_warwick@yahoo.co.uk

Acknowledgements

Many people have helped me during my time spent compiling this book and I am extremely grateful for all their assistance. Below I have listed many that have helped along the way. Apologies to any names I may have inadvertently overlooked.

My thanks in helping with various aspects of this book must go to the following groups and individuals.

The *Herts and Essex* newspaper archives, National Archives, Imperial War Museum, the Patmore family (especially Val Popplewell, Patrick Patmore and Carole Crosby) for many photographs and allowing me to use Sid's memoirs and personal war diary. Paul Embleton for sharing his early research and photographs from his postcard book *'Around Stansted Mountfitchet'*, Ralph Phillips for his information on soldiers billeted in the village, Chris Baker and his *'Long Long Trial'* website and all the cyber pals from the *'Great War Forum'*.

Sincere thanks to Michael Thierens with his expert help on anything related to the Essex Regiment. Also many thanks to the following, who have helped with information, photographs and other documents and for generally helping me on my journey to find out as much as possible on those from the village of Stansted Mountfitchet; They are, in no special order - Alan Childs, Evelyn Holman, Robert (Bob) Pike, Steve Fuller, John Knight, Andy Pay, Michael Ellis, Des Blackadder, Mike Smith, Jan Van der Fraenen, Paul Reed, Matt Parker, Mary Ecclestone, Bert Van Goidsenhoven, Bill Johnson, Phil Beattie, Martin Harvey, Neil Mackenzie, Stephen Beeby, Steven Broomfield, John Hartley, Kate Dumycz, John Hamblin, Steve Mitchell, Shirley Lawrence, Jacqueline Harrup, Paul Amey, Stuart Norman, Charles Fair, Geoff Stockdale, Trevor Kirby, Andrew Riddoch, Kate Wills, Anne Holdham, Doris Thistle, Janet Townsend and special thanks to Dave Stowe and Chris Noble for there help in locating a picture of **Tommy Brownridge**, a picture we never expected to find.

Also sincere thanks must go to Matt Scoffield for his assistance on producing the front and back covers and my step-father Stan Brownridge for giving me his Uncle Tommy's letters from the Western Front. Also many thanks again to Bob (Robert) Pike for helping me through the final stages.

Finally and most importantly I must thank, with all my love, my wife Rachel, my sons Lee, Joe and George and daughter Megan for giving me the encouragement and allowing me the time to put this book together. Without their unending support I'd still be writing it in five years time! Thanks, love you all.

**'They sleep in heroes' graves,
Each and every one so brave,
Remember them each day,
For the way we live today'.**

*Could I but kneel beside his grave
And shed a silent tear,
Sadly he sleeps in a distant land
The one we loved so dear.*

"They Sleep In Heroes' Graves"

On 4 August 1914, with France and Russia already at war with Germany, the British declared war as the German army marched through Belgian towns supposedly on their way to Paris.

This decision led to men from all over the country joining up in what they believed was going to be a war that would be *over by Christmas*. Those infamous words now ring loud in most history books about the Great War.

A public meeting was held that same week in the Central Hall, Stansted to consider what steps could be taken locally in the present crisis. Mr W.G. Gold presided, supported by the Rev. A.M. Winter (Vicar of Stansted), the Rev. C.W. Holland (Rector of Birchanger), the Rev. A. Cook (Congregational Minister, Stansted) and Mr W.H.S. Tissiman (Vice Chairman of the Parish Council). It was decided the meeting was not for giving opinions but to invite suggestions. A Mr Buck said he had an important suggestion to make. As they were aware, they had in this country a large number of foreigners, some of whom were friendly and some who were their enemies. The latter were beginning to prove themselves as such. A troop train had been fired upon and an attempt had been made to poison that same troop's horses. His suggestion was that the inhabitants of Stansted should form a company of special constables to assist the police. They had not got a very strong police force in Stansted and he suggested that they should pick about fifty men for this task of assisting the police. His suggestion was greeted by a long round of applause.

All over the country, since an appeal by Lord Kitchener for more recruits for his new army, recruiting meetings were taking place. One such meeting took place in the

Assembly room at Stansted Working Men's Club. There were more than 200 men crowded into the room for the meeting which was chaired by Mr Charles Gold supported by the Rev. A.M. Winter, Mr W.J. Bannehr, Mr Gerald Gold, Mr Martin Burls, Mr H. Blyth, Mr A. Bright and the secretary Mr T. Gawthorp.

The Chairman explained that the meeting had been called to consider what steps could be taken to help to obtain recruits for the Army, in view of the crisis. He said *"That great soldier, Lord Kitchener, had appealed for more men and it was for every town and village throughout the Kingdom to loyally respond to the call"*.

The supporting members of the committee all agreed that *"This meeting of the Stansted Working Men's Club pledges itself to do the utmost to get all the recruits it can for Lord Kitchener's Army"*.

Recruits were invited to enrol their names and a list was also signed by employers of labour who undertook to reinstate the men on their return from the war and promised to do all in their power to encourage recruiting. The meeting closed with the National Anthem.

As a result of the meeting seventeen recruits gave in their names and they were conveyed in motor cars to Saffron Walden the following morning where they enlisted for the period of the war. They were given a very hearty send off.

Three days later, on a Sunday afternoon, a further recruiting meeting took place on the Recreation Ground, Stansted, hopefully to obtain more recruits for Lord Kitchener's Army. A speech from Major Taylor (Chelmsford) included the reading of a letter from a Stansted man, named **Gibbs** (from records we find this was **Sapper Stanley Hugh Gibbs,** aged 24, son of Joseph Gibbs of Chapel hill), who had enlisted the previous Wednesday, stating that he was having a right good time and urging other Stansted men to *"hurry up"* and join the colours. Sir Thomas Jackson referred to the necessity of having strong land forces to support our Navy. At the close of the meeting twenty men had come forward and submitted their names. They, too, were conveyed by motor car to Saffron Walden on the Monday where they also joined the army for the period of the war. On Tuesday, the following day, six other Stansted men came forward which brought the total number of recruits from Stansted to forty-three.

This was only the beginning and by the end of the conflict, according to the Roll of Honour in St Mary's Church, Stansted had had over four hundred men involved in the Great War. **The following is the story of only a few.**

The following pictures, of Stansted Scouts, (supplied courtesy of Paul Embleton) were taken in about 1911 in front of Blythwood Dairy, and for me are tinged with great sadness as two of the young boys shown lost their lives during the Great War. They were **Fred TURNER** (see July 1917) and **Donald CARRUTHERS** (see April 1917)

From Left to Right (Names in **Bold** saw service in the Great War) – Back row – Harold Buttery, George Levey, **Ernie Everitt, Tom Levey**. Centre Row – **Austin Reeve, Fred Light, Harold Balaam, Evan Bright,** Cyril Crabb, **Master (probably Walter) Watts, Fred TURNER,** Nelson Griggs, **Ernie Snow,** Leader Mr Jobe, **Willie Everitt,** Wilfred Buttery. Centre seated - **Sid Patmore,** Rev.Willoby, **Donald CARRUTHERS.** Front Row - **Robert Levey,** Tony Gold, **Tommy Johnson.**

Many of these young scouts would have enlisted and served King and Country during the war. **Tom** and **Robert Levey** were the brothers of **Arthur LEVEY** (see November 1916 and May 1918) and **Austin Reeve,** who later served with the Bedfordshire Regiment, was the brother of **Edward Thomas REEVE** (see August 1917). **Sid Patmore** was the brother of **Alfred PATMORE** (See May 1915). Others mentioned elsewhere in the book are as follows - **Ernest Everitt** (see January 1916), **Harold Balaam** (see December 1916), **Evan Bright, Walter Watts** (See March 1918). And the following names can be found on the St John's Roll of Honour, **Fred Light, Ernest Snow and Tommy Johnson.**

Sid Patmore was born in Stansted on March 17th 1895, and from his memoirs (reproduced by kind permission of his family) we get an insight into life in Stansted prior to the Great War and later in the book we will re-visit his memoirs and look at his personal diary when we will find out more about his three years spent on the Western Front with the Royal Garrison Artillery, 112th Siege Battery.

The following are extracts from the memoirs of **Sidney Lewis Patmore**, aged 80, written in his own hand in 1975.

Sidney Patmore

*I was born on March 17[th]1895 and was sent to school when I was aged 2½ years, there were six boys in the family whose names were **Herbert, Frederick, Francis, Alfred, Archie** and myself **Sidney** (See May 1915). I was sent to school at the early age of 2½ because my mother was then a widow and she had to work to provide for all of us, there were no national assistance or widow's pension or family allowances in those poor times so she had to work very hard to make ends meet. At this time we lived in a four roomed house in Woodfields, Stansted. The kitchen was a living room it had an open fireplace there was also a copper and this was covered most of the time with a worktop. The toilet was at the top of the garden at this time. Woodfields had houses on one side and at the other side at Chapel Hill there were four houses. I could sit on the steps at the front door and look over the meadow which reached down to Water Lane, and watch the trains passing, to and from the station. In about 1900 the other side of the road was built on and a year or so later Sunnyside was built so I couldn't see the trains go by anymore. We all went to school, it was known as the National School (Church School), the other school on Chapel Hill was known as the British School called the Chapel School. Mother said the elder brothers had to take pennies to school but by the time I went education was free. Mother got her living by doing various jobs such as going out to do washing at a shilling a day or making boys' trousers at six (old) pence a pair. Boys wore shorts until they started work. She mangled clothes at 2d per basket; she was also a self taught widwife (sic) when she would often be called out in the middle of the night to a confinement or to layout a dead person. She also catered for local dances and would bring a large ham home to boil for the sandwiches and then go and serve the refreshments and come home in the early hours of the morning, we looked forward to the leftovers next day. She worked very hard and when I could understand I felt very sorry for her, she seemed to have good health but she told me before I could remember that she had rheumatic fever and she and her small*

9

children were taken to a Haymeads Infirmary at Bishop's Stortford. This was known as the 'Spike' or the 'Workhouse'. This really hurt her pride, she said when she left school aged 13 years old she was sent to Manuden to be nurse to twin babies and the wage was 6d per week.

I remember going on a school treat to Takeley Forest, being small I sat on the teacher's knee, we went in farm wagons and I saw large urns heated over a wood fire. Tea was poured from large enamel jugs, we took our own mugs and had bread and butter and buns by the lake. The little ones at school were given squares of silk or cloth to unravel this was used to fill cushions and if the children got tired they were allowed to lay their head on one and have a nap. Mother was strict but very fair and she kept us six boys in order in a very remarkable way. I never remember a brother hitting me and she was a very good cook, we had enough to eat, just plain food no luxuries like today, we hung our stockings up at Christmas. In it would be a sugar mouse, a sweet watch which had a paper face and an Orange and some nuts. We did not have Christmas cards and at Easter we only had a chicken's egg. Our clothes though patched were tidy. Mother believed in the old saying a stitch in time saves nine, she also made our shirts. Herb started to work at the local doctors and became a groom and when cars came he was sent to a factory to learn to drive. Fred was also fond of horses and went to Melton Mowbray and became a stud groom for the hunting stables. Frank went to Norman's little ginger beer factory, he had to tie down corks in the stone bottles, then drive a horse van round to the pubs and shops in Stansted and the other villages Alf went to work at New Farm, this belonged to Lord Blyth and was being used as an experimental place to find a cure for tuberculosis, there were lots of monkeys, cows and rabbits there. Alf had to wait on the doctors. One was an Australian he gave Alf a large bean and after over 70 years I still have it, it is as hard as wood and looks and shines like mahogany. Frank went into the army during the Boer War but he was sent to India with the 1st Bedfordshire's. After New Farm closed down Alf went to work at a cycle shop in Bishop Stortford owned by Flo Spearmen in Bridge Street. Her brother Egbert also had one in Potter Street. Flo used to ride a motorbike that was very daring in 1904 (for a woman). Alf left the cycle shop and joined the 5th Royal Irish Lancers. Although Stansted was only a village it had two Churches, three Chapels and three Blacksmiths. The Blacksmith on Chapel Hill was the one I saw the most of as it was on the way to school and in the winter it was good to look over the half door and watch the smith and his striker making horse shoes and see the glowing fire and the sparks flying off the anvil and hear the noise like the ringing of the bell.

Often there would be a lot of hunters waiting to be shooed they would be rugged up against the cold weather. On the corner of each rug would be the monogram of the owner. There were twelve Pubs in the village, a Post Office, and also a Telegram boy. I remember the maker of his bike; it was "Alldays and Onions".

At the bottom of Chapel Hill was Lower Street and there was a large engineering yard owned by T.A. Newman, it was full of Steam Ploughs, Traction Engines, Thrashing Tackles and Steam Rollers. It was quite a sight to see these monsters come hissing out to work, it excited all the children. I remember going to Sunday school with Arch one day, the gates of the engine yard were shut, propped up with a large engine wheel. Arch wanted to have a look inside so he crept through but on his way back the wheel slipped and crushed his big toe, he was in great pain, and someone carried him into the King's Arms pub and sent for the doctor. I was small at the time and don't remember what happened to me.

We used to go to the National School on Sunday mornings and afterwards we were marched up to St Mary's Church, this was a mile each way so we were quite ready for Sunday dinner when we got home and we had to go again to St John's church in the afternoon. Mother would sometimes go to visit her parents at Rickling Green, I would have to go to Sunday school first and then I would run and walk three miles to join her but once there it was worth it. Grandad lived on the green in an old thatched cottage, he had a large garden and he kept a lot of bees so there was always honey for tea and some to bring home. This meant another three miles to walk as there were no other means of transport.

We lived quite close to the Recreation Ground, this was a nice safe place to play and get rid of our energy but once when I was very small a young lady came with a pug dog it took a fancy to one my shoes and ran off with it but I got it back. On the south side of the Recreation Ground was a very fine windmill it was owned by Lord Blyth and when the sun was in a certain direction the shadows of the moving sails fell upon the ground so we would run around with it. We always looked forward to the May fair which was held at the meadow behind the Bell and Feathers pub. Thurstons would be there with the roundabouts and swings and rock stalls. Once they bought along a portable cinema, there were dancing girls on a platform outside to attract people to go inside to see the pictures. If you were lucky enough to have 4d you could ride on the roundabouts for 1d and another 1d for the swings and have fried fish and chips. The fountain at the top of Chapel Hill was a favourite place to meet and sometimes entertaining, I've seen jugglers, acrobats and sometimes a dancing bear. People used to throw pennies on the mat for them. Sometimes a cheapjack (a dealer in cheap merchandise) would set up his stall in the King's Arms Yard selling crockery and tinware, he would shout and throw tea sets in the air but I never saw him break any. Occasionally a street organ would come up Woodfields perhaps with a monkey to amuse and collect the money, sometimes a girl dressed in bright colours and looking like a gypsy, she would dance and sometimes I have seen the women and girls join in the fun. There was no fear of traffic on this narrow road. We moved from our four roomed cottage to a six roomed one on the opposite side of the road, this made it better for mother as she could now take in lodgers. Sometimes there would be telephone linesman or traveling actors or at weekends cyclists from a London Club. There were two halls in the village the Central Hall with its striking clock towers and a Working Men's Club.

When the Empire Mica works closed down a lot of men and women were thrown out of work but one good thing came out of it as the local gentry took over a large room at the top of the factory and started a social club, they fitted one part of it as a gymnastic club with all the apparatus and boxing etc and employed an ex-Army instructor to train a team. When trained they were in great demand at fetes and flower shows etc. The other end of the room was used for dancing and whist drives it was well patronised and the fee was 3d a week. Mother used to supply the refreshments.

It was about this time that the Stansted golf links was started, this included the Castle Hills and reached to Stansted   House halfway to Elsenham. My uncle Ted Woodcock

11

came from Rickling to be the head grounds-man, he and his wife lived in the golf clubhouse and she looked after the luncheons and refreshments for the members. Well now all this had come about it meant there would be jobs as caddies for the boys so when I left school and as work was very scarce I was glad of the opportunity to caddy. It was a fine weather job. All the gentry from miles around came to play, like the families of Sir Walter Gilbey, Lord Blyth, Sir Charles Gold, Sir Thomas Jackson, Sir John Barker and a lot of other notable people. There was a two price system 3d for the young boys and 5d for the big boys, this was the rate for a nine hole round. When you saw a party of members approaching the boys would run to meet them. If ever there were too many boys some were unlucky and dejected, if you were lucky you went with the gent to the driving off place, here was a box of wet sand, the boy had to take a handful and squeeze it to a cone shaped and place the ball on top. The gent would then say mark my ball caddie and he had to watch the flight of the ball till it landed and then make a beeline to it. If it landed on the fairway that was easy but sometimes it went into the long grass called the rough and if you couldn't find it the gent would be very cross. When I was 15 years old the links closed because an 18-hole golf course was started in Bishop's Stortford, Uncle Ted went to live there and was grounds man until he retired. I was now doing a paper round it extended to Bury Farm near Manuden and it was six mornings a week and I had to take the Stortford paper round on Friday nights. The pay was two shillings per week. After that I got a job at Joshua Green's stores to drive a pony trap for an outrider. We went round all the villages. On Monday we went to Tye Green and Elsenham on Tuesday Ugley, Rickling and Quendon, Wednesday Newport and Debden, Thursday Birchanger and Stortford. Green's Stores were wholesalers as well so we also supplied small shops. I liked the job especially in the summer as Mr. Levy would be in houses for some time writing down orders, so I had plenty of time for reading books. My wage was four shillings per week and this was at the time when National Insurance came in. The employer paid a fifth and 4d was stopped out of my pay leaving me which three shillings and eight pence.

One night a not very amusing thing happened, we were coming home from Tye Green when the horse bolted Mr. Levy was driving and the horse got the bit between its teeth, the rein snapped and we landed in a ditch near the Ash pub at Burton End. Then we had to walk the one and a half miles home. No one was hurt not even the horse.

Mother wanted me to get more money so I went to Rochford's nursery to work but at the end of the week they handed me the princely sum of three shillings and 2d so I was 6d worse off than at Green's Stores. I stayed there a while but could see no hope of a rise. I then had a chance to go to work at the Bell and Feathers Pub in Cambridge Road, I had to feed the pigs and chickens look after the customer's horses light the fire and scrub floors but the worst job was washing out spittoons. The pub was open from seven in the morning till eleven in the evening. The pay was five shillings per week and I lived in but I did not like it at all but I stuck it for the winter and then I had another try at Rochford's, this time they gave me seven shillings and 2d per week and I worked there until the1914 war when I went on to work at Chelmsford with my brother Herbert fetching hay for the Army horses. (Sid then went on to describe how much life had changed since he was a young boy living in Stansted). There were no Dustman when I was young, things from the shops didn't have so much wrapping so people were able to *burn all their rubbish. Another thought comes to mind in that there were no letter boxes on the houses in Woodfields, you could hear the postman coming up the road knocking on the doors, this made things better socially as people spoke to one and other and passed the time of day and discussed the latest news. There were postal deliveries three times a day and on a Sunday morning. In the winter the postman had an oil lamp on his belt, so did the policeman. Mother could send a letter all the way to India for 1d. Before I left school me and the girl next door used to walk to Stortford to the International Stores in North Street. It was a coincidence that the girl, Elsie Dixon* (probable sister of **Sidney Louis Dixon**, see January 1919), *and I were born on the same day, we were known as the twins. There was no television or radio in those days, but local celebrities caused a lot of conversation within the village, like Sir Walter Gilbey who lived at Elsenham Hall, he was the wine merchant, he had a lot of property at Elsenham and Hockerill Park, Stortford. His brother declared open the Stansted Fountain in 1871. Sir Walter had a lot of fine horses, he presented six cream ponies to the Royal Family. Lord Blyth lived at 'Blythwood', Sir Charles Gold lived at the 'Limes', Mr. Watney (brewer) lived at Crown Cottage, Sir Thomas Jackson lived at Stansted House and Mr. Fuller-Maitland, Lord of the Manor, was at Stansted Hall.*

*Us six brothers were all in the Army during the war, **Frank** in the Bedfords who was wounded in 1914, **Alf** in the Lancers was killed in May 1915, **Herb** in the Army Service Corps as a driver in France and I in the Artillery (Howitzer Battery) in France and Belgium, **Fred** was a sergeant in the Mounted Military Police in Egypt and **Arch** was Company Sergeant Major in the Royal Engineers, but he was category "B", because of his deformed big toe. He used to take parties of soldiers to France and then returning to England.*

I joined up at the Guild Hall in Colchester and was sent to Yarmouth where the barracks were on the sea front. We were drilling in civilian clothes for a time, (it was Kitchener's Army) these were all volunteers; conscription didn't come in till 1916. I was then sent to Larne in Ireland and on to Lennon Head in Lough Swilly, it was a long old journey, we arrived at Clonmany and had to do the last 8 miles in jaunting cars. We shared barracks with Royal Inniskilling Fusiliers

We will visit Sidney's memoirs again (April 1917 and November 1918) later in the book during his time with the Royal Artillery and the day that a certain General Lord Byng of Vimy entered his dugout but did not recognize Sidney who prior to the war had caddied for him at Stansted Golf Links.

13

Description of Stansted in 1914.

Stansted (or Stansted Mounfitchet) is a village and parish situated on the Roman and modern high road from London to Cambridge, and close to the River Stort, on a tributary of which it stands. It has a station on the main line of the Great Eastern railway, three miles north of Bishop's Stortford and thirty-three miles from London.

The village, one side of which is in the hamlet of Bentfield, principally consists of two streets, and was lit by gas. The church of St Mary the Virgin is a large structure of flint with stone dressings, in mixed styles. The church of St John the Evangelist was erected in 1889. There is also a Congregational Chapel which was erected in 1865, with seating for 500 persons. The Post Office, on Chapel Hill was opened in 1892. The Working Men's Club is a structure of brick and oak timber framing and was erected in 1888. There is also a Central Hall comprising of a lecture hall holding 300 persons.

In 1867 a recreation ground of three acres was given to the village by the late William Fuller-Maitland Esq. Remains of a castle in the village was supposedly built by William Gernon, surnamed Montfichet. Stansted Hall, the seat of William Fuller-Maitland esq. J.P. is a building of red brick with stone dressings and facings in the Jacobean style. It stands in a well-wooded park of about 400 acres. Stansted House is the residence of Sir Thomas Jackson. William Fuller-Maitland was the lord of the manor.

Bentfield End is a hamlet within Stansted and its lord of the manor is R. Cunliffe Gosling Esq. J.P. who along with William Fuller-Maitland were principal land owners. (Sadly both Maitland and Jackson were to lose sons during the Great War)

Another Hamlet is Burton End situated on the eastern side of Stansted.

Schools in the village at this time were as follows.

The Council School, formerly public elementary (boys) built in 1835 and rebuilt in 1862 on land given by William Fuller-Maitland. The school was enlarged in 1912 to accommodate 120 children, and average attendance was about 100. The school master was John Woolley.

Council School (girls and infants), built in 1912 for 216 children. Average attendance was about 140. Miss Irene Woolley was the girls' mistress and Miss E. Staines was the infants' mistress.

A Public Elementary school (mixed and infants), built in 1837 for 260 children. The average attendance was 220 and the master was Frank Dearch.

In charge of the Stansted police station at this time was Sergeant Harry Tucker and at the railway station the station master was Thomas Gawthrop.

The following commercial businesses were listed in Stansted in 1914.

Amey William, Three Colts Public House, Cambridge Road.

Archer Emma (Mrs), Confectioner, Station Road.

Archer Fred Brock, Bell Inn, Silver Street.

Atkins Edwin, Head Gardener to Gilbert Alder, Hargrave Park.

Bannehr Walter J. solicitor, Central Hall, Chapel Hill.

Barclay & Company Ltd, bankers, manager George Foster.

Bass Hugh Henry, farmer, Alsa Lodge.

Bedlow Francis G. blacksmith.

Bloom Frederick, confectioner, Silver Street.

Brett James, blacksmith.

Brockhurst Ada and Louisa, dress makers, Lower Street.
Bunting Ellen Searle (Miss), fancy goods dealer, Silver Street.
Bunting William Charles, seedsman, Lower Street.
Burles Joseph, beer retailer, Lower Street.
Carruthers William, commercial traveller, Albany Villa, Woodfields.
Cayley Frank, physician and surgeon, Woodville.
Central Hall, E.R. Riches.
Chalkley William Noah, Windmill Public House.
Chopping Ernest Henry, taxidermist.
Clarke Sarah (Mrs), laundry, Burton End.
Clarke William, harness maker, Silver Street.
Clarke William, jobbing gardener, Bentfield End.
Cliff George, farmer, Parsonage Farm.
Colman Percy, nurseryman, Elsenham Road.
Conway Lewis, beer retailer, Silver Street.
Dudley H.E. farmer, Bentfield.
Dyer and Young, commutator manufacturers.
Ecclestone George Thomas, chemist, Chapel Hill.
Field Harry, vaccination officer and registrar of births and deaths, Recreation Ground.
Fothergill John, farmer, Burton End.
Francis Joseph Sawkins, watch maker.
Gibbs Joseph, tailor, Chapel Hill.
Goodfellow Sidney, stationer, Station Road.
Gray William, fly proprietors, Chapel Hill
Green's Stores Stansted Ltd, Cambridge Road.
Haggerwood Arthur, horse slaughterer.
Haggerwood John, farmer.
Hall Elizabeth (Miss), district nurse, South View.
Hammond William, seedsman, Recreation Ground.
Hawkins Samuel, baker, Silver Street.
Hayden Isaac, farmer, Elsenham Road.
Haynes Walter Frederick, physician and surgeon, medical officer.
Hendry Paul, land agent to William Fuller Maitland.
Herrington Joseph, greengrocer, Lower Street.
Hicks Thomas, coal merchant.
Hicks Charles, farmer and district surveyor, Bentfield Green farm.
Hudgell Charles, chimney sweep.
Hutley Susan (Mrs), baker, Lower Street.
Jardine Jack, motor garage, Cambridge Road.
Jay Brothers, hauliers, Cambridge Road.
Kitson Laura Eliza (Mrs), basket maker, Cambridge Road.
Kitson Walter J. bee keeper, Cambridge Road.
Levey Alfred, horse dealer, Bentfield End.
Levey Allen, lime burners.
Levey Arthur, bricklayer, Cambridge Road.

Levey George, carpenter and undertaker, Cambridge Road.
Little William George, Barley Mow public house, Chapel Hill.
London Central Meat Company, Chapel Hill.
Mascall Brothers, butchers, Silver Street.
Matthews and Kirk, motor engineers, Cambridge Road.
Mayhew E. and son, fly proprietors.
Muffett Frederick Richard, fishmonger.
Mumford George William, confectioner, Lower Street.
Mumford William, farmer, Down Farm.
Newman Thomas Oswald, agricultural implement manufacturer.
Nicholls Charles, butcher, Silver Street.
Norman Charles Allard, ginger beer manufacturer.
Page Samuel, farmer, Burton End.
Page William, farmer, Bury Lodge.
Pavitt and Cook, insurance agents, St John's Road.
Penny George, hair dresser, Chapel Hill.
Player Mark, shopkeeper, Burton End.
Potter George William, Kings Arms Public House, Station Road.
Pulham Herbert Coulson, nurseryman.
Ramsey William, coach builder, Station Road.
Ratcliff Albert, plumber, Cambridge Road.
Ratcliff Christopher James, plumber.
Ratcliff Ernest Arthur, plumber, Nova Scotia cottage, Cambridge Road.
Ratcliff Mary (Mrs), dress maker, Cambridge Road.
Renfrew Andrew, farmer.
Richardson James, steward to Lord Blyth, Silver Street.
Riches Ernest Robert, clerk to Parish Council.
Robinson Daniel Junior, builder and contractor, Lower Street.
Robinson William, builder, Chapel Hill.
Rogers S.S. and Co. brewers.
Russell, Craigen and Co. cycle agents and repairers, Lower Street.
Ryder George, head gamekeeper to William Fuller Maitland.
Sanders Arthur, grocer.
Savage William, hair dresser.
Smith Arthur, cycle agent, Silver Street.
Smith Spencer, farmer, Hole Farm.
Spalding Walter John, saddler, Silver Street.
Spencer Charles and Sons, corn merchants.
Stansfield Charles William, insurance agent, Cambridge Road.
Stansted Bowling Club, sec. James Brett.
Stansted Club, George Foster sec.
Stansted Water Co. Ltd, E.R. Riches sec.
Tadman Charles Albert, photographer, Chapel Hill.
Tedder Herbert, boot maker.
Thurgood Joseph and Son, farmers, Bassingbourne Hall.

Tissiman William Henry and Son, tailors, Silver Street.
Torey Alfred John, grocer Station Road.
Turner Frederick, grocer.
Turner S. chimney cleaner, Woodfields.
Turner William, beer retailer, Burton End.
Vercoe Reginald, jeweller, Chapel Hill.
Walton Florence Walters (Miss), girls and boys school, New College.
Wareing Joseph, tobacconist, Lower Street.
Waterman Susan (Mrs), beer retailer, Bentfield End.
Welford Albert Ernest, Rose and Crown Public House, Bentfield End.
Winder Richard, beer retailer, Bentfield End.
Working Mens Club, Thomas Gawthrop sec. Z. Baalam, steward.

Throughout this book many of the surnames listed above will appear again as we look at Stansted during the war years.

The population in Stansted in 1911, inclusive of Bentfield End was 2,344. As we know from the Roll of Honour located inside St John's church, over 400 men served for King and Country. This figure, which of course may include some from the outskirts of the village, indicates just how many men were called into active service during the Great War.

During August 1914, Lord Blyth placed all his stables and buildings at Blythwood House (below), Stansted, at the disposal of the purchasing officer, Mr Archie Gold. This was for the collection of horses for the remount department of the War Office.

September 1914

No father or mother saw him die,
No sister or brother to say goodbye.
Not a friend or relation to hold his hand,
But we all hope to meet him in the Better Land.

September saw the first Battle of Marne and the first Battle of Aisne. On the Western Front the Germans continued their push towards Paris, part of the Schlieffen Plan. It was expected that the German army would take Paris, so the British and French troops retreated to positions south of the Seine and Marne rivers. Expecting defeat many Parisians left their homes. On September 6th the French sixth Army launched a counter attack. The Germans manoeuvred their First army to meet the advance, leaving a gap between their First and Second armies. British and French troops pushed into the gap and held off the German counter attacks, forcing them to retreat back to the River Aisne.

Hoping to take advantage of the German retreat to the Aisne, on 13th September the Allies launched a series of offensives against German positions. The Germans however had dug in, creating a range of strong defences. By the end of September it was realised that frontal attacks on the German defences would lead to very high casualty figures and the assault drew to a close. Over quarter of a million French soldiers perished trying to withstand the German forces, a similar number of German soldiers are also thought to have been killed in this early battle. A stalemate had been reached and the French and British now had to consolidate their positions and dig in. Thus began the horrors of Trench Warfare.

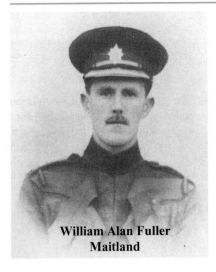

William Alan Fuller
Maitland

The first soldier, remembered on the Stansted memorial, who lost his life, was **William Alan FULLER-MAITLAND.**

William Alan FULLER-MAITLAND was born in Mayfair London on the 13th April 1882. He was the eldest son of William Fuller-Maitland Senior. and his wife the Hon. Evelyn Coulston Fuller-Maitland of Stansted Hall. He was educated at Harrow from 1896–1899 and then at RMC Sandhurst. He joined the Coldstream Guards in 1901 and served in the South African war in 1902. He saw active service in the Cape Colony during the latter part of the South African War, and was awarded the Queen's medal with two clasps. He was with his regiment in Egypt for about five years, and while stationed there he went to the big game country in Central Africa and captured an elephant, a buffalo and many other trophies. Upon his return home from Egypt he hunted with both the Puckeridge and Essex Packs and at the Puckeridge Hunt Point-to-Point races where he won the Light-Weight Cup.

He went to France with his regiment in 1914 and served during the Retreat from Mons and also in the Battle of the Marne.

His details are as follows.

Captain William Alan FULLER-MAITLAND
1ˢᵗ Battalion Coldstream Guards
Died of Wounds 19ᵗʰSept 1914 aged 31

William's name is commemorated on the La Ferte-Sous-Jouarre Memorial, Seine-et-Marne, France.

His family were a very prominent part of the village of Stansted Mountfitchet.

It was his Grandfather William Fuller-Maitland, an art collector, who had Stansted Hall rebuilt when looking for a suitable residence in which to house his priceless collection. The house was designed by Robert Armstrong, who combined Tudor style with nineteenth-century building techniques, in which he included two Adam fireplaces from the old Hall and ceilings created by an Italian artist. Work began in 1871 and by 1876 the mansion was ready, but Fuller-Maitland elder unfortunately died before he could enjoy his new home. The family continued to live at Stansted Hall until 1921.

William Alan FULLER-MAITLAND died of wounds on the 19ᵗʰ September 1914 during The Battle of Aisne. The war diary for the 1ˢᵗ Battalion of the Coldstream Guards states that *on the 18ᵗʰ they moved into the trenches, relieving the Queens Royal West Surrey Regiment, at Troyon Ridge.* It was during this time that **Fuller-MAITLAND** was sustained wounds from which he subsequently died.

Conflicting reports at the time whether he was killed in action or died of wounds can be found in the local *Herts and Essex Observer* newspaper. It was not uncommon for a soldier who may have died of wounds to be reported as having been killed in action as this was often a comfort for their relatives. His father received official notification from the War Office that his son had been killed instantaneously, but the war diary clearly states that he died of his wounds. Just to confuse matters more William was also listed in *The Times* as being killed in action.

La Ferte-Sous-Jouarre Memorial

Mr William Fuller Maitland senior had lost his youngest son Robert three years earlier when he was mauled by an elephant whilst hunting in Africa.

Also in September 1914 another Stansted officer was wounded, he was **Claude Stewart JACKSON** (see October 1917). He was also serving with the Coldstream Guards. The wound, which occurred on September 8th, was caused by a bullet grazing his head whilst in pursuit of the enemy crossing the River Marne. (Letters from his service records suggest it was more than just a graze).

Other Stansted news this same month included an article from the local newspaper which read as follows – Stansted Rovers F.C. will be badly hit if the war continues during the coming football season, the following men having been called up:- **A. Johnson** (Bedfords) , **O. Griggs** (Special Reserve), **L. Smith, B. Robinson** (Territorials) and **J. Hill** (11th Hussars).

October 1914

A loving son, a brother kind,
A beautiful memory left behind,
He proudly answered his country's call,
His life he gave for one and all.

October 1914 saw our soldiers engaged in some of the following actions, The Battles of La Bassee, Messines, Armentieres, Langemarck and the beginning of the First Battle of Ypres.

A Council meeting held at that time heard the Vice-Chairman voicing the feelings of all the members of the Council when he referred to the loss that their Chairman (Mr W. Fuller Maitland Senior.) had sustained by the death of his eldest son, **Captain W.A Fuller MAITLAND**. He proposed that a letter be sent from the Council conveying their condolence and sympathy with him and his family in their bereavement.

Alfred Wootten.

The following soldier, who was living in the village but is not named on the Stansted Memorial but is remembered on the Somersham Memorial, in Huntingdonshire died of his wounds on the first day of this month.

His details are **Private Alfred Wootten, 6995, Coldstream Guards 2nd Battalion, Died of Wounds 1st October 1914 aged 29.** Alfred is buried in Braine Communal Cemetery, Aisne, France. He is named on a special memorial in the cemetery as the exact location of the grave within the cemetery is not known.

Private Wootten was the son of the late Richard and Rebecca Wootten and a husband to Florence (nee Perry). At the time of his death his home was in Woodfields, Stansted where he lived with his wife and two children Alfred Frank (Born 1911) and Florence Pamela (Born 1910). He and Florence were married in April 1909. His military career had begun when he enlisted at Lincoln in 1906 and after serving seven years with the colours was transferred, with exemplary character, to the Army Reserve in 1913. He went to France with the Expeditionary Force in August 1914 and was wounded on 29th September at Troyon during the Battle of the Aisne.

Brigadier General H.W. Stubbs, Coldstream Guards, wrote *"No more faithful, true, and gallant soldier gave his life for his country. He did his duty as a guardsman and lived and died a Coldstreamer"*.

Reports found in the Archive newspapers of the local *Herts and Essex Observer* state the death of **George Vane Secker**, of Stansted, who was killed whilst aboard H.M.S. Hawke. **George** was born in 1892 and details of his connection with Stansted is scarce (other than his mention in the *Observer* local Roll of Honour) which may be a reason for his name not being included on the local memorial.

His details are, **Private George Vane Secker, CH17010, Royal Marine Light Infantry, Killed in Action on 15th October 1914 aged 32.** His name is inscribed on the Chatham Naval Memorial.

H.M.S. Hawke was an old armoured cruiser operating as part of the 10th Cruiser Squadron assigned to the Northern Patrol. She had originally been launched at Chatham in 1891 and was one of the oldest ships still in service. H.M.S. Hawke was being used as a training ship and had many young cadets on board. She had been re-commissioned in February 1913 with a nucleus crew and had come up to her full complement on the outbreak of war in August 1914. On the fateful day she was in the northern waters of the North Sea with a similar ship, H.M.S. Theseus when they were attacked. They were operating on October 15th 1914 without a destroyer screen. Unfortunately they were slower than the submarine U9 which was tracking them. The U-Boat Commander was Lieutenant Weddigen. He missed the Theseus with his first torpedo but unfortunately hit H.M.S. Hawke amidships near a magazine. The detonation was followed by a second terrific explosion, in which a large number of the crew were killed. The ship sank within five minutes and was only able to launch one ship's boat. Five hundred and twenty five perished and only seventy men were saved. They were picked up three hours later by a Norwegian steamer. A survivor said the following *"The Hawke was standing at God knows what angle and it was physically impossible to get the boats out. Every man for himself was the cry and we were over the rails as hard as we could. When I came on top after my plunge I saw nothing but a huge bank of smoke. The Hawke was down, and all around were hundreds of struggling men, hands, arms and faces bleeding, torn in the desperate struggle to get overboard, shouting for assistance. In our boat there were only a few at first, but we rowed round and picked up as many as was possible until we ourselves in the long boat were in danger of being swamped. Hanging about and even when rowing, it was bitterly cold. We waited help, and once the submarine rose not more than 200 yards away".*

However, had they had sufficient time to launch other lifeboats from H.M.S. Hawke, then undoubtedly more would have been rescued by the Norwegian Vessel.

GREGORY D.
GREGORY J.
GREGORY J. T.
GREYGOOSE F.
GRIMSDALE C.
GRIZZELL W. H.
GROOME V. C.
GROVE W. B.
GROVES R.
GROVES W. J.

The next soldier, from the village, to lose his life in the Great War was **Francis GREYGOOSE**, his details are as follows **Rifleman Francis GREYGOOSE 6173 2nd Battalion Kings Royal Rifle Corps Killed in Action 23rd October 1914 aged 31.**

Francis has no known grave and he is remembered on the Menin Gate, Ypres, Belgium, Panel 51/53.

Francis was the son of William and Eliza (nee Burton). He was born in Stansted in 1883, and as far as can be ascertained from census records he had two elder brothers Jonas and Edward, an elder sister Rosina; a younger brother Sidney, and two younger sisters Lucy and Agnes. In 1891 and 1901 he was living at 81 Upgrove Hill (known simply as Grove Hill today). At this time he was working as a nurseryman. During the War **Francis** was living in Tottenham Hale. At the outbreak of war **Francis** was a regular soldier and so became involved from the beginning of the conflict.

For details of the actions in which Francis was involved we are fortunate to have the following extracts taken from the personal War Diary of Thomas William Smith, 6950 2nd Kings Royal Rifle Corps. (These extracts are courtesy of his Grandson Mike Smith.)

October 21st 1914 – *"Left Elverdinge about 10.00a.m and marched to Ypres and stayed about four hours on the roadside and amused the Belgian villagers. We then marched to Boesinghe in the evening and billeted in a convent. The sisters gave us hot coffee as soon as we arrived. They were also busy feeding refugees so they had a busy time. We slept in their schoolroom".*

October 22nd 1914 – *"We got the order to move at once. We marched about four miles to take up position and dug a trench. Digging all night. Had no sleep"*

October 23rd 1914 – *"Made an attack at 6.00a.m which lasted until 3.30p.m. We advanced under rifle fire. Men were dropping out on either side of me. We made for a farmhouse and defended it until 2.30p.m when our people on our right advanced and got round the enemy's left flank and simply routed them. We took their trenches at the point of bayonet. We had a good many casualties but nothing compared to the Germans whose trenches were full of dead. We got over 300 prisoners. I got a watch and a chain off one of them as a souvenir. I shall never forget this day as long as I live. It was a terrible day of slaughter. A pig and a cow were hit by bullets and we had to kill them to put them out of their misery. At 4.00p.m we took up position as support to the North Lancs who took up the new attack and we can hear them at it again. I have just heard that we recovered a few of the Cameron's who the Germans captured. At 9.00p.m we had a very welcome pint of hot tea and settled down for a well earned sleep in our cramped trenches".*

Francis GREYGOOSE was not one of those who settled down to sleep as he had unfortunately been killed during the day's actions and, sadly, now sleeps in an unknown 'Hero's Grave'.

Additional material on the attack on the 23rd October can be found in *The Kings Royal Rifle Chronicles* (2nd Battalion War Records) – some brief details.

At about 3.30p.m the North Lancashires advanced on our right and to the east and although they lost heavily during their advance they succeeded in driving the Germans out of their Trenches. They bolted across the open ground and gave a splendid target to our leading platoons and machine guns.

Later about 10.30p.m, as Major Warre was on his way up to his trenches, he heard his name called in the darkness. He found a wounded Rifleman who had recognised him from his walk and on searching the surrounding ground found five or six other wounded men, whom he was able to send in.

Also during October 1914 another of Sir Thomas and Lady Jackson sons, of Stansted House, was wounded. He was **Captain Julius Jackson** 60th Kings Royal Rifles who was seriously wounded in the groin. His father went to see him at King Edward VII, Hospital, London where his condition was showing progress. His other son, **Claude Stewart JACKSON** (see October 1917) who was wounded by a bullet in September, was now doing well recuperating at Frinton-on-Sea.

23

Two days after the sad death of **Francis GREYGOOSE** another brave Stansted soldier lost his life, he was **Private Frederick WARNER**
Frederick's details are as follows
Private Frederick WARNER 8649
1ˢᵗ Battalion Coldstream Guards
Killed in action on 25ᵗʰ October 1914 aged 23

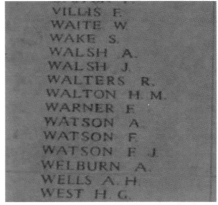

Frederick Warner.

Like many thousands of soldiers **Frederick** has no known grave and is therefore commemorated on the Menin Gate, Ypres, Panel 11.

Many poppy wreaths are laid at the Menin Gate every week. The "Last Post" takes place every night at 8.00p.m without exception.

From the local *Herts and Essex Observer* newspaper came the following. The sad intelligence was received on Tuesday from Colonel Drummond Hay, commanding the Coldstream Guards, that **Private Frederick WARNER**, 1ˢᵗ Coldstream Guards, eldest son of Mr and Mrs F.N. Warner, of Bentfield End Stansted, was killed in action on Sunday October 25ᵗʰ. Accompanying the letter was the following sympathetic message *"The King commands me to assure you of the true sympathy of His Majesty and the Queen in your sorrow, Kitchener"*. **Private Warner** went out with the British Expeditionary Force on August 12ᵗʰ, and had been involved in a number of engagements.

Details of the actions in which **Frederick** died are quite scarce. The war diary states that they were supposed to be relieved by the French during the evening of the 24ᵗʰ October but due to heavy artillery bombardment this failed to happen until the morning of the 25ᵗʰ. We can only assume that **Frederick** was killed during this bombardment and that his body was never recovered during those actions which took place at Langemarck. The battalion was finally relieved by the French during the morning and marched to billets at Zillebeke. Sadly this was one march **Frederick** never took part in.

Frederick was born in Bethnal Green in 1891 and was the eldest son of Frederick Neville, a removal packer, and Caroline Amelia Warner (nee Jarvis). His family moved to Stansted and lived at Bentfield End. He had four younger sisters and a younger brother named Herbert who later in the conflict, at the age of just 17, stopped his work as a butcher's assistant and enlisted in September 1916 when he also joined the Coldstream

Guards, whom he served with until the end of the war seeing action in France throughout 1917.

Frederick was educated at London Council School and became a cycle fitter by

trade. He enlisted in the Coldstream Guards on 17th March 1910 at the age of nineteen and went to France on the 12th August 1914.

As **Frederick** saw action from the outbreak of war he would have been entitled to the 1914 Star, British War Medal and the Victory Medal, often referred to as Pip, Squeak and Wilfred.

Details of Campaign medal entitlement was as follows.

The 1914 Star.

This was popularly known as the Mons Star. This medal was awarded to all officers,

warrant officers, non-commissioned officers, and all men of the British and Indian Forces. It included civilian medical practitioners, nursing sisters, nurses and others employed with military hospitals. Also men of the Royal Navy, Royal Marines, Royal Naval Reserve and Royal Naval Volunteer Reserve who served with on the establishment of their unit in France and Belgium between August 5th 1914, and midnight of November 22/23rd, 1914 were given this particular medal.

The 1914 -15 Star.

A Star similar to the 1914 Star was issued to all personnel, as mentioned above, with certain exceptions, who served in a theatre of war before December 31st 1915 but did not qualify for the earlier star.

The British War Medal, 1914 - 1918.

It is impossible to set out all the details of qualification for this medal, but briefly, the requirement was that a member of the fighting forces had to leave his native shore in any part of the British Empire while on service. It did not matter whether he/she entered a theatre of war or not.

The Victory Medal, 1914 - 1918.

This medal was awarded to all those who entered a theatre of war and presumably took part in the fighting, logistics or medical services. It follows that every recipient of the Victory Medal also qualified for the British War Medal, but not the other way round. 300,000 fewer Victory Medals were required than British War Medals. All three services were eligible. It is not generally known that Victory Medals continued to be awarded after the Armistice, for the British forces who saw action in North Russia (up to October 12th, 1919) and Trans-Caspia (up to April 17th 1919) also qualified.

1914 - 1918 Memorial Plaque – 'Dead Man's Penny'

The next-of-kin of soldiers, sailors and nurses who died while serving during the First World War were presented with a Memorial Scroll, and later a Remembrance Plaque, also known as a *'Dead Man's Penny'*, *"as a solace for bereavement and as a memento"*. The memorial plaques were issued to commemorate all those who died as a result of war service from within the British Empire. Each plaque had the name of the soldier commemorated individually embossed as part of the design. The full name was given without any indication of rank or honours to show the equality of sacrifice of all those who had lost their lives.

Lieutenant Claude Stewart JACKSON (See October 1917) was this month ordered to report for a re-examination as he was still on sick leave since suffering a gunshot wound to his head. The result of the examination by the Medical Board was that he was now fit for light duties at home but must not be detailed to the Expeditionary Force until reported fit for service by a Medical Board.

Quartermaster Sergeant Joseph Burles, of the Queen's Head, Lower Street, enlisted this month at the age of 43, he had already served as a regular soldier for 21 years. He spent the whole of the campaign on the home front where he was involved in the training for both the Royal Field and Royal Garrison Artillery. He was married to Deborah and had two children, Edward and Percy.

Private William Stock 14573 was discharged in this month of October, after only one month's service with the Essex Regiment. The reason given was 'poor physique'. This was not the shortest Great War service I have come across during my research as another Stansted lad, **Private Richard Mascall 962**, Essex Yeomanry was discharged within six days of enlisting. In fairness to him he had previously served in 1913. The reason for his discharge was put as 'Medically unfit for further military service'. His family were part of Mascall's the butchers in Silver Street.

November 1914

Day by day we have missed him,
Words would fail how to tell;
But in heaven we hope to meet him
Evermore with him to dwell

November 1914 saw the continuation of the First Battle of Ypres. Fighting around Ypres would linger on until 22nd November when the onset of winter weather forced a break in hostilities. The combat during this engagement was extremely confusing and unrelenting. After the fight, British survivors were content to say that they had been at "First Ypres", no further information was necessary to explain the horrors they had endured.

Raymond Marker.

The 13th November saw the death of **Lieutenant Colonel Raymond Marker D.S.O. Raymond** was the son in law of Sir Thomas and Lady Jackson of Stansted House and the brother in law of **Claude Stewart JACKSON** (see October 1917).

Lord Kitchener had lost another of his trusted comrades by his death from wounds received in action. Raymond Marker had been previously decorated with the Legion of Honour by the President of the French Republic, with the approval of the King for gallantry during the operations of the British Forces in the battles between August 21st and 30th 1914.

The first news to arrive back home was that he had been seriously wounded. His left leg had been amputated, and his right arm broken. News filtered back from the front that he was going on as well as can be expected in a French Base Hospital at Boulogne, but he later succumbed to his wounds.

For his services in the Great War he was mentioned in Sir John French's dispatches of the 8th October, 1914, and the 14th January 1915. His wounds were received when he was hit by a shell outside the reporting centre of the 1st Army Corps at Ypres on 4th November 1914, but died nine days later. He married the daughter of Sir Thomas and Lady Jackson in 1906 and left a son Richard Raymond born on 18th June, 1908. His details are as follows. **Colonel Raymond John Marker, General Staff, Died of Wounds 13th November 1914 aged 47.** He is buried at Gittasham Churchyard, Devon.

Mr Armitage, at a recent council meeting, said there was a Sergeant of the Lincolnshire Regiment quartered at the scattered home at Stansted who had set his heart on one of the children, aged seven and wanted to adopt her. The matter was adjourned until the next meeting for inquiries.

December 1914

He left his home in perfect health,
He looked so young and brave,
We little thought when he left home,
He never would return.

The short war that had been expected by most parties was not happening. Trenches were dug and across Europe signs of a breakthrough were sought, in vain. December saw further offensives on all fronts.

December also saw the unofficial Christmas truce declared by soldiers along the Western Front. The *"Christmas Truce"* is a term used to describe the brief unofficial cessation of hostilities that occurred between some German and British troops stationed on the Western Front during Christmas 1914. The truce began on Christmas Eve when German troops began decorating the area around their trenches in the region of Ypres, Belgium, for Christmas. They began by placing candles on trees, then continued the celebration by singing Christmas carols, namely *Stille Nacht* (*Silent Night*). The British troops in the trenches facing them responded by singing English carols. The two sides continued by shouting Christmas greetings to each other. Soon thereafter, there were calls for visits across the "No Man's Land", where small gifts were exchanged — whisky, cigars, and the like. The artillery in the region fell silent that night. The truce also allowed a breathing spell where recently-fallen soldiers could be brought back behind their lines by burial parties. Proper burials took place as soldiers from both sides, together, mourned the dead and paid their respect. At one funeral in No Man's Land, soldiers from both sides gathered and read a passage from the 23rd Psalm:

"The Lord is my shepherd. I shall not want. He maketh me to lie down in green pastures. He leadeth me beside the still waters. He restoreth my soul. He leadeth me in the path of righteousness for his name's sake. Yea, though I walk through the valley of the shadow of death, I will fear no evil."

The truce soon spread to other areas of the lines, and there are many stories, some perhaps mythical, of football matches between the opposing forces. Letters home confirm the score of one of these games to be 3-2 in favour of Germany. In many sectors, the truce lasted through Christmas night, but in some areas, it continued until New Year's Day. The truce occurred in spite of opposition at higher levels of the military.

The Parish Room above the Working Men's Club was used as a recreation room for troops billeted in the parish. The arrangements had been made by the Vicar and the Rev. G.W. Howard. A sacred concert was held in the room on a Sunday evening after the usual Church service and a smoking concert was also held on a Tuesday evening.

Fighting during the 1914-1915 winter months seemed to be put on hold as the ground had become so churned up and impassable, that to fight appeared to be a waste of energy. Now it was more time spent in trenches.

Trench Foot was a medical condition peculiar to trench life. It was a fungal infection of the feet caused by wet, cold and unsanitary conditions. It could often turn gangrenous and sometimes result in amputation. Trench Foot was more of a problem at the start of trench warfare. As conditions improved in 1915 it rapidly faded, although a few cases continued throughout the war.

The daily routine of life in the trenches began with the morning 'stand to'. An hour before dawn everyone was roused from slumber by a company orderly officer and a sergeant and ordered to climb up on the fire step, with their bayonets fixed to guard against a dawn raid by the enemy.

Death was always a constant companion to those serving in the front line, even if no raid or attack was launched or no enemy action required defending against. In busy sectors the constant shellfire directed by the enemy could bring random death, whether their victims were huddled in a trench or lying in a dugout.

Soldiers of the Essex Regiment proudly marching through, Norwich, Norfolk.

January 1915

Not dead to us, we love him still,
Not lost but gone before,
He lives within our memory still,
And will for evermore.

Soldiers of the Gordon Highlanders billeted locally, outside the house of Herbert Patmore in Woodfields

Arthur Stanley Law, **John Childs**, **Charles Bradford**, Edward Reginald Sandford and William Sandford, all lads of Stansted were summoned for damaging a stove, basin and glass windows on the property of Mr William Fuller Maitland, at Stansted.

Arthur Law, a farm labourer of Ivy Cottage, Burton End, did not appear as his mother stated he had gone away to join the army. The other defendants pleaded guilty. The house had been occupied by the military for several weeks but the troops billeted there had departed a few days before the alleged break in. From records we know that both **John Childs** and **Charles Bradford** served King and Country later during the war.

From military records it is confirmed the **Arthur Law** went away to join the army. He enlisted in March 1915 only to be discharged three months later. The reason for his discharge read as follows, *"having made a mis-statement as to age on enlistment"*. He had, when enlisted added four years onto his age saying he was 19 when in fact he was only a 15 year old. This was not an uncommon occurrence as many young lads tried to enlist under age especially if they had older brothers already serving. They just felt they wanted to do their bit. This was certainly a possible reason for **Arthur** to enlist under age as his elder brother **Henry James LAW** (see August 1915) was already serving. Unfortunately **Henry** lost his life later in August this year.

The first Zeppelin attack on England during the Great War took place this on 19th January. Two Zeppelins attacked the eastern coastal towns of Great Yarmouth and King's Lynn, killing four civilians but causing little significant damage.

Still recovering from a gunshot wound to his head, **Lieutenant Claude Stewart JACKSON** (see October 1917) notified the war office that his new address would be the Regina Hotel, Wengen, Switzerland. This was agreed on medical grounds to aid his recovery.

Another letter prior to this was sent to the War Office to request sick leave for the coming months of February and March.

Many letters were sent back and forth asking for **Lieutenant JACKSON** to be re-examined by the medical board before any leave could be granted which eventually it was.

February 1915

Gone from us but not forgotten,
Never shall his memory fade,
Fell while fighting for his country,
Lying in a Soldier's grave.

Many troops, like those pictured below, of the Essex Regiment were at training camps in early 1915 in readiness for the move overseas.

Essex Regiment outside their Hut

On 15ᵗʰ February, the first exchange of POWs took place, 110 British and 95 German wounded POWs were released to return home, going via the Netherlands.
On 17ᵗʰ February the first British mine was blown at Hill 60, about three miles south-east of Ypres, by Royal Engineer troops of 28th Division.

Mr Frederick and Mrs Annie Hudgell, of 41 Rochford Cottages, received the sad news that their son **James** had been killed in Belgium. His details are, **Private James Nathaniel Hudgell 7396, Bedfordshire Regiment 1ˢᵗ Battalion, Killed in Action 17ᵗʰ February 1915 aged 29.** He is remembered on the Menin Gate Panels 31 to 33. From the Battalion war diary comes the following. *On the 17ᵗʰ February 1915 orders for relief by 13ᵗʰ Brigade were cancelled. Casualties were two killed. Two bombs were fired at the enemy who at once replied with eight.*

March 1915

If we could have raised his dying head
Or heard his last Farewell
The blow would not have been so bad
To the ones he loved so well

Still desperate to break through the German lines and, convinced that the war could be won relatively quickly a plan was formed that aimed to break through at Neuve Chapelle. A massive artillery bombardment was launched on March 10th before the troops advanced. The German front line was devastated and the four divisions of the British army quickly secured the objectives by taking the village of Neuve Chapelle. The advantage was pressed home though, unfortunately communications broke down and the advance ground to a halt. Commanders were uncertain of exactly what the situation on the front was. This allowed the German reserves to reach the new front lines before any continuation of the attack could be conducted. The allies had advanced across a front approximately two miles wide, but only moved about 750 yards forward.

Since the outbreak of war British casualties had now exceeded the 100,000 mark.

As the war continued Stansted was becoming a huge military transit camp.
(The following information was supplied by local man Ralph Phillips. His Grandfather served later during the war, possibly enlisting under the 'Derby Scheme' see May 1915).
My Grandfather, Alfred James (Jim) Phillips was called up for service when the cream of a generation had been wiped out.
M-415009 Pte A.J. Phillips A S C.
It was thought in the family that he was conscripted under Lord Derby's scheme but I see that that scheme had been supplanted by the Military Service Act of January 1916, which may have been presented to the population in similar terms.
Jim was born on the 13th November 1872, which would have him between 40 & 45 years of age and very near the upper limit for call up. The exact date of his conscription is not known but it is thought later in the war. He left behind a wife, two sons and a daughter.
I have his two medals; I have heard them referred to as one for going and one for coming back. I also have my late father's short account of this time including the military presence in the village. This includes photographs of my Grandfather in training as well as serving in France. There is also a Photostat of one of the cards he as allowed to send home to his wife from France.
He was amongst the lucky ones returning home 1918 with his British and Victory medals. The only time I can remember him mentioning the war was late in life when he was living with my parents and I was at home smoking. He said "I used to smoke in the army but then I got to liking it and gave up!" He was also the longest serving Methodist local preacher, at least locally not giving up the reigns until he was 92.

'Pump Field', an area of many acres in Church Road (the site of the present Council Housing Estate) was rapidly built over with rows and rows of stables for the Artillery, with all concrete floors and link roads, sections for guns and limbers, administration

blocks, huts and guard rooms, with sentries at all approaches which did not deter boys from entering through holes in the hedges.

The horses, guns, limbers and wagons were everywhere constantly coming and going. Half trained horses were continually tearing up and down Chapel Hill in a long stream, often unable to hold back at the bottom of the hill, causing a pile up, drivers and outriders among them. Many wild horses were 'broken in' and trained at New Farm in Gypsy Lane, Stansted, then a modern complex of buildings complete with a racecourse and access to the River Stort. The farm was locally known as "The Monkey Farm" for it was previously a research establishment for tuberculosis. The research being mainly carried out on monkeys and cows until the Great War broke out.

The whole village was full of soldiers. The Alley fields and Brewery Field areas (now built up areas of St Johns Road, St Johns Crescent and Brewery Lane) was covered in bell-tents for the infantry that could not be accommodated in billets. A large number of the men were billeted on the householders. The village was divided into sections for this purpose and a Billeting Officer visited every house in his section to assess the number of soldiers who could be accommodated.

It was based on the floor area of each house, and it was compulsory to accept them. The house of Ralph Phillips family, Montville, was assessed to billet six men, sleeping side by

Soldiers Billeted locally

side in the front room, the other room for our own family. The men were provided with a mattress and two blankets each and expected to sleep on the floor in the allotted space. They had all their military equipment with them, stacked in the hall, packs, webbing, bandoliers of ammunition, trenching tools, greatcoats, rifles, groundsheets, some also had very long swords, all packed in the passage. The Billeting Officer called at infrequent intervals to inspect and hear of any complaints.

The zone we lived in was at first occupied by the 5th Lincolnshire Regiment and later we were re-zoned to have men from the 6th Lincolns. This caused great confusion. The men of the 5th liked their billet and refused to move out. For a time we had a blockade until a day when the 5th were out on parade, the 6th moved in, so when the 5th came back we had both, eleven men all told. To the men it was home from home as far as was possible and the men respected it.

All the time, day after day, week in week out, foot soldiers were incessantly marching, four abreast, along the Cambridge Road to the embarkation points. Each section of men interposed with a horse drawn wagon, whose duty was to pick up the men who fell out from exhaustion, having been pushed to the side of the road until picked up, the column continuously moving along. Every so often a field kitchen would come along, a great boiler on wheels and a few supporting provision wagons to feed the troops on the march.

Mother Alice was a splendid cook. The soldiers ate in, bringing their rations and supplies, twice weekly.

It is a job to imagine the quantity of rations needed and allowed for eleven men. Each group took a sack to the quartermasters stores and returned with it full. Huge 4lb loaves of bread, quantities of potatoes, large lumps of meat, all manner of vegetables and sundries, such as margarine, lard, sugar, salt and condiments. Some had 'Bully Beef' or tins of pork and beans or fish in place of meat. All had tins of condensed milk, fruit, tins of Ticklers Jams (mostly plum and apple) which they heartily disliked, though when made into a jam roly-poly it became delicious, and left a tin or two for our cellar. The' surplus to requirements' which were many, were stacked in our cellar for future use.

We all were fed on beef steak puddings and fresh fruit pies, apple dumplings etc when available , for there were plenty of windfall apples, surplus plums, free during the season, and cheap at any time. The Army Quartermasters stores was next door at St Johns Cottage, just over the wall and many items which were surplus, or difficult to distribute, came over the wall, such as I remember a large 7lb tin of pepper. We also proved to be an acceptable dumping ground for cabbage leaves, damaged or dirty bread, carrots etc. for the chickens and rabbits. These, when converted into table poultry, eggs and rabbit pie were luxurious generally unobtainable for soldiers, going to war, a far cry from an army stew slopped in a billy can. The rabbits were very prolific. The rabbit run covered a large part of the back-yard. There were dozens of them.

The Army paid the householder 6 pence a night for each soldier billeted on them, and a small additional sum for cooking and preparing the rations. This amounted to a very useful sum at the end of a seven day week, bearing in mind that Jim when war broke out was only earning thirty shillings a week.

The food issued to the men was more than adequate for us all. We wanted nothing. We used discarded army blankets on our beds, after a good boiling in the copper. The copper was a large brick built furnace surrounding a ten gallon circular pan, covered with a wooden lid and fired with waste paper and burnable rubbish.

True it was difficult getting around the house while we had eleven men and ourselves. The hall, scullery and every available space was packed with equipment. To us boys it was a great source of enjoyment, we handled the rifles, bayonets etc and spent much of our out of school time with the soldiers, around and in the Alley Fields tents.

Eggs were very valuable at the end and after the war, fetching as much as sixpence each. Alice still kept her hens, Alec and I went to the Millers either to the Windmill or Hicks Mill in Lower Street, to get mixed 'off corn' and middlings for the hens feed. Every day Alice cooked up a bucket-full of potato peelings and scraps, mixed them very hot with middlings to dry them off, then fed the mash to the hens, steaming hot.

The Great War was now over and the soldiers gone. Jim was to be demobilised. It was a time of great rejoicing. The whole village built a huge celebration bonfire on the Recreation Ground complete with an effigy of Kaiser Wilhelm to be burnt. It was still burning tree days afterwards, and Dad Jim cam home with two service medals, the 'British' and the 'Victory'.

Jim – Back Row 5th Left.

36

A letter was received by Miss N. Wells, of Victoria Villa, Lower Street, Stansted, from a member of the Royal Field Artillery. He had been billeted in the village and explained how they had sustained four casualties (two killed and two wounded). The writer also gave an interesting description of the experiences of the men in their journey from the Stansted / Bishop's Stortford area to France. It read as follows: - *"We are now close to the firing line. We left Bishop's Stortford about 9.00a.m. and arrived at Southampton Docks about 3.30p.m. There a surprise awaited us, as, we had to go to a rest camp for a couple of days. Proceeding to the Docks once again on Wednesday we embarked. Even then we were not to sail, as it was not till the Friday about 8.00a.m that we set off. Escorted by a couple of Torpedo boats we then arrived this side of the channel about 12.30p.m. Then a long railway journey all day Sunday till about midnight when we detrained, after which a march by road till about 5.30a.m., when we were introduced to our bedroom – a barn by the way. We have since been under orders to be prepared to move off at a moment's notice. In fact 'Keep Moving' seems to be our motto, as we have had three already. We did not travel 'Saloon' on board the boat – in fact, very much otherwise, as about 140 of us were packed into one of the holds. Cattle trucks were provided for our accommodation on the train, and although not very aristocratic, we did have room to lie down. We took rations on the train for three days, so we were somewhat surprised when we had to detrain. Our rations by the way, have since leaving Stansted been of the typical active service variety – biscuits (cast iron brand), bully beef, jam, cheese, and tea in bulk, which added to hot water makes something wet. Latterly, on rare occasions, once about four days ago, we had a loaf of bread between nine of us. We receive five francs per week pay and on Friday, our first pay day, our fellows made a raid on all the bread in the neighbourhood. They were unable to do so earlier owing to pecuniary embarrassments. As soon as we got off the train we could hear the guns booming, and proceeding to our first billet here we could see the flashes from the guns as the shells were fired, and this, with the searchlights and signalling, made a very picturesque sight. We have been within range of the big guns of the enemy since arriving in this district, but have not been in the trenches yet. Some of the artillery in this Division has been shelled out of their billets and the 5th Leicester's have suffered casualties. Don't know when our turn will come. I have not seen a piano since leaving Stansted. This is a poverty stricken place and I wonder if there is one in the district. Things are rather different here to what they were at Stansted. One thing reminded me very forcibly of 'old times.' That was at the stops during the railway journey in France, when the folks were all clamouring for 'Souvenir-bouton.' We have not been troubled much this way for them as probably the inhabitants here have had a sufficiency of souvenirs military from the Huns. They have been driven out of the district".*

Roy Carruthers, brother of Donald CARRUTHERS (see April 1917) arrived home this month from Burma and is currently training at Aldershot.

Private Alfred Green 3804, Hertfordshire Regiment, aged 19, was discharged this month as 'being medically unfit for further military service'. Private Green was living at 6 Brook Cottage. He had enlisted in November the previous year.

"In memory of our dear old rum.
Born August, 1914. Died March 1915.
Dearly beloved how we miss you,
Now they've stopped our blooming issue.
We will not defeat the Hun
Till they give us back our rum".
Gone, but not forgotten.

The rum ration was issued to the troops in earthenware jars, stamped with the initials S.R.D. (Supply Reserve Depot - not Service Rum Diluted as frequently stated), although soldiers argued that this actually stood for *'Seldom Reaches Destination'* or *'Soon Runs Dry'*.

Lieutenant Claude Stewart JACKSON (See October 1917) was examined as he was recovering from gun-shot wounds to his head. The examination was carried out by Dr Holland who stated *"recuperation in Switzerland would aid his progress, the high dry air of the upper Alps would speed his recovery".* He continued to say *"I have today examined Lieutenant Jackson. I can find no signs of disease but he is not in a normal state of health. He still suffers from headaches and pains over the occipital lobes. His temperature was high and his pulse intermittent, the cause of this I cannot understand. His nervous system is constantly out of gear and he has alternating periods of depression and excitement. There are other reasons which have influenced me in forming the opinion that although this officer could travel to England, it would not be prudent. He certainly is not capable, at present, of doing any responsible work in his regiment. If he was at home he might be loafing about aimlessly in damp, cold, depressing surroundings and not improving his general health".*

April 1915

Killed in action our hearts are sore
For King and Country, we miss him more
His cheerful smile, his loving face,
No one on earth can fill his place.

April 1915 saw the beginning of the 2nd Battle of Ypres. It was used primarily as a means of diverting Allied attention from the Eastern Front, and also as a means of testing the use of chlorine gas.

The German army were the first to use chlorine gas at the battle of Ypres in 1915. Chlorine gas causes a burning sensation in the throat and chest pains. Death is painful - you suffocate! The problem with chlorine gas is that the weather must be right. If the wind is in the wrong direction it could end up killing your own troops rather than the enemy.

On Good Friday a large number of troops who were billeted in Stansted attended the morning service at St Johns Church. The service was taken by Rev. J. Selwyn Sharpe and the collection amounted to £3.12s.9d.

News reached the village that Private **Albert Edward BONNEY** (see July 1916) had been wounded in France.

Private 2079 Walter Harold Spalding, of No 1 Company, 4th Platoon, of the 1st Hertfordshire Regiment, son of Mr and Mrs W. Spalding, of Stansted, writing home states he received a parcel with thanks and that it was "A1" It contained, he says, everything he needed, and the "fags" also were very acceptable as they had all run out of them and it made one really miserable to be out there without a smoke. He adds:- *"I am pleased to say I am quite well and came out of the trenches last night for a few hours, as we got relieved for a few hours after 48 hours in. We are in a desolate spot and nearly everything is ruined by shells. We are in the La Bassee region and I have seen enough sights lately to last me some while, and when the latest casualty list comes out you will see we have been pretty hard hit at this one position, and it makes one's heart ache to see them going. But I suppose we must be thankful we can still tell the tale. I don't suppose you would think it, but there is a certain amount of sport to be had in the trenches. One is always watching for bombs which the Germans send over. You can see them coming and we have to scuttle out of the way and go into our dug-outs. It reminds one of rabbits and then you hear the shells coming and have to lie low and wonder where they are going to burst. Pieces of shrapnel come singing overhead and would give you a nasty crack if they caught you. Then the bullets crack past our ears and make them ring and deafen one for a minute or two. We get some excitement out here, but very risky times as well. One night we were filling sand bags in the open and the Germans kept sending up lights and I think they saw us, for the bullets flew round like rain. One of our mates got hit, but as luck was they were firing too high and most of them flew overhead. It is good sport to watch our aeroplanes. The Germans send little shells up after them* *and it seems as if, they must get hit, but they still continue on their way and I have not seen one fetched down yet, but we seldom see a German aeroplane now, they seem to have been driven right away. One thing I must tell you, when any of our pals are killed out here they are buried with as much respect as if they were in England. At the position we now occupy there is a little patch of ground fenced off, and in it we lay our brave boys and their graves are well looked after and each one has a wooden cross with his name and full particulars on, but we still keep in good spirits and keep smiling".*

Private Spalding had first entered the 'Theatre of War' on the 6th November 1914.

May 1915

Since on the list of those who fell
I read my dear boy's name
He died I know a hero's death,
But Oh, this weary pain,
I never thought when he left home
He would no more return;
That he so soon in death should sleep,
And leave me here to mourn.

The Second battle of Ypres continued throughout May and during this battle was the first use of the new German weapon, poisonous gas. The Germans launched an artillery barrage on the allied lines. It was as this battle was taking place that a cloud of yellow gas began to approach. On seeing this many of the allies left their posts to find cover. This left a gap in the allied line that stretched for some four miles. Spotting this the Germans charged into the gap but, under-estimated the time it took for the gas to disperse thinly enough into the air; they ran straight into their own chlorine gas. The Canadians fought through the night to close this gap. On the first night, the Canadians launched a counter-attack to drive the Germans back. The Canadians cleared the woods, but later had to retire. More attacks that night resulted in disastrous casualties, but bought some time to close the gap.

On May 7th, the Lusitania, a British luxury ocean liner, neared the coast of Ireland. At 2.10 in the afternoon a torpedo fired by the German submarine U-20 slammed into her side. A mysterious second explosion ripped the liner apart. Chaos reigned. The ship listed so badly and quickly that lifeboats crashed into passengers crowded on deck, or dumped their loads into the water. Most passengers never had a chance. Within minutes the giant ship slipped beneath the sea. More than half of almost two thousand aboard died. The dead included over one hundred Americans.

The Germans claimed their reason for attacking the Lusitania was because it was carrying small arms ammunition.

Growing battlefront demand however soon outstripped volunteer numbers and during this month Prime Minister Herbert Asquith appointed Lord Edward Derby, himself an opponent of conscription, as Director-General of Recruitment, tasked with rapidly boosting Britain's volunteer army. Derby's solution was the so-called *"Derby Scheme"*.

This encouraged men to voluntarily register their name on the principle that once registered they would be called up for service only when necessary. As an added incentive married men were advised that they would only be called up once the supply of single men was exhausted.

Announced in a fanfare of publicity the scheme proved unsuccessful however, and was abandoned in December the same year. Excluding men exempted from military service on account of their occupation (e.g. munitions workers) just 350,000 men had volunteered under the Derby Scheme. In its stead the government - now led by David

Lloyd George - introduced the Military Service Act of January 1916, which set down terms for mandatory military service, that is, conscription.

Derby scheme enlisters? - soldiers of the Army Service Corps

Sadly **Alf William PATMORE** was our next unfortunate brave soldier to lose his life at the age of 27. He died of his wounds on 3rd May 1915. His details are as follows.

Private Alfred William PATMORE
7261
5th Royal Irish Lancers
Died of Wounds on 3rd May 1915
age 27

Alfred's grave can be found at Bailleul Communal Cemetery Extension, France. Grave No I.A. 156.

The cemetery is situated in the small French town of Bailleul near the

Alf William Patmore

Belgian border about ten miles south west of Ypres.

Alfred was the son of Elias and Charlotte Patmore, he was born in 1887. During the Great War they were living at 15 Woodfields. The 1901 census has no mention of his father (father died in 1894) only that **Alfred** was living at 136 Woodfields with his mother and three brothers named **Herbert, Archie** and **Sidney**. He also had brothers named **Francis** and **Frederick**.

It is quite possible that **Alfred's** wounds may have been caused from the effects of gas as the day before he died his regiment were attacked by the enemy who used gas. The following

Grave of Alfred William Patmore

extract is taken from the war diary.

May 2nd, remained in dugouts till 5.00p.m when the enemy attacked the first line trenches near St. Julien with gas. A lot of the infantry retired through the regiment

43

*suffering from the effects of gas. The 5ᵗʰ Lancers were turned out and 'A' and 'D'
Companies were ordered to hold the redoubts around Wieltje. (A redoubt was a
defensive fortification, a stronghold.) The Germans concentrated artillery around the
village and redoubts and as a result heavy casualties were incurred. The 5ᵗʰ had 4 killed
and 18 wounded during the action that day.*

This action was known as the Battle of St Julien (The Second Battle of Ypres) which
took place from 24ᵗʰ April to 4ᵗʰ May.

The effects of gas were penned by a Captain in the Royal Army Medical Corps as follows *"Look! On the ground are a score of stretchers, covered with the usual brown rugs, the stretchers are side by side, and on each is a soldier. They seem remarkably quiet. No bandages are to be seen, or sign of dressing of any kind, no blood or wounds. Well may you move to look closer, you look at one man,*

**Alfred with his mother
Charlotte**

and his expression is preoccupied, strained and anxious. He is a little cyanosed (blue at the lips) but his colour is inclined to be ashy, mingling with the bronzing of the skin. His shoulders and shirt are heaving, perhaps 30 or 40 times in the minute, exactly as a fish lying on the bank. You look at the next man and the next and you see to your amazement that they are all suffering with the same thing. And you say' "What, in God's name has happened?" The panting exhausted

Francis Patmore

*forms go on panting. Gassed is the reply. "Good Heavens" you say, "then all these men
are poisoned!" Poisoning it is, and a slow suffocation and the tortures of the damned.
Fine, healthy, strapping young fellows and now without scratch or wound, all poisoned.
All are drowning on shore, surrounded by help and friends. And never a grumble or
word of complaint is heard. They are soldiers. But what can you call those who are
responsible for this fiendish, devilish cruelty that makes the blood boil".*

Alfred (Alf) had enlisted at Bishop's Stortford where he joined the 5th Lancers. He entered the war in August 1914. All of **Alfred's** five brothers served during the Great War but unlike Alfred they were all fortunate enough to return from the conflict. The eldest was **Herbert (Herb) Harry**, born in 1877, who served with the Army Service Corps as a Driver. **Frederick George** was born in 1879 and served as a Sergeant in the Mounted Military Police in Egypt. **Francis (Frank) Edward** who was born in 1881 was a regular soldier prior to the Great War and entered the conflict from the outset with the Bedfordshire Regiment going overseas on the 30th August 1914. Later during that same year he was wounded. **Archie (Arch)**, born 1892, served with the Bedfordshire Regiment 4th Battalion (Special Reserve) which he joined in 1909 and later (according to his brother **Sydney's** memoirs) served with the Royal Engineers. During his nine years service he passed both the school of Musketry and his rifle course. **Archie's** record also states that on the 27th August 1915 he was reprimanded for improper conduct, *"giving beer to a corporal and a private in the sergeants' mess"*. **Sydney Lewis** was born on March 17th 1895 and served with the Royal Garrison Artillery.

Archie Patmore (Alfred's brother) 3rd from the right standing

Frederick Patmore (back right) with comrades in Egypt

Herbert Harry Patmore

Frederick George Patmore

On the 22nd May 1915 the local *Observer* newspaper had the following report in the Stansted Petty Sessions column. This related to two Stansted lads who subsequently joined up and both lost their lives. (Their details can be seen in February 1918 and July 1918)

William HERRINGTON (See July 1918), dairyman of Stansted aged 19 pleaded not guilty to assaulting **Albert John PATMORE** (see February 1918) aged 13 at Stansted on May 10th. The complainant, the son of Horace Patmore a painter, stated that he had been to fetch milk and met the defendant. As he was passing, the defendant kicked two cans of milk out of his hands outside Mr Woodward's, at Mill Field, then kicked him on the leg, hit him with a whip, and went off using bad language. He said he had not been to the defendant's house for about a year. Questioned by the defendant, the complainant said he had not jeered at him and did not accuse him of killing a fowl that was lying in the road. He had not told his little brother to throw paper bags filled with dirt into the defendant's house. Leslie Steed aged nine, said the complainant was telling him something when the defendant evidently thought that complainant was talking about him and coming up to them, knocked complainants two milk cans over, kicked him, and hit him twice across the back with a whip or a stick.

The defendant denied the assault and said he had not had a whip with him.

The Bench fined the defendant 10s. (Ten Shillings or 50p for any younger readers) *Authors note: A very sad tale as both these lads died in 1918.*

Private Walter Harold Spalding, No 1 Company, 1ˢᵗ Hertfordshire Regiment, son of Mr Walter and Mrs Ellen Spalding, Silver Street, Stansted writing home says

"At last I can find time to write and thank you for the parcel and letters which I received quite safe. We have been in action during the last few days and under the most awful shell fire since I have been out here. It was simply hell on earth, and I wonder I am alive to tell the tale, and I can only thank God for bringing me safely through it. I will just explain if the censor will let it pass. The Irish Guards, our dear old mates, were to attack and the object was, I think, a farm which the Germans were holding. No 1 Company of the 1ˢᵗ Herts were the first to support the Guards and as we moved up we came up under shell fire from 'Jack Johnsons' (shells which burst giving out black smoke) and heavy shrapnel. Well we began to lose our men, but we got to the first German trench, then our officer who deserves a V.C, shouted, 'Come on No 1 Company, over the parapet,' and over we went, with German maxims firing upon us, and started to advance across the open country losing men as we advanced. Part of my company got within 50 yards of the farm but had to retire, as we had not enough support to take it. All night and next day we held the trenches, shells continually dropping, and when we were relieved at night our battalion had lost rather heavily. Of two brothers in my section one was wounded and the other killed. One had been out with me all the time. It will, I am afraid, be terrible news for their poor mother. Well, anyhow, it shows that although only 'Terriers' (Territorial force in Hertfordshire) we are not afraid to do our bit, and weren't the Irish lads pleased to see us charge. We get on well with those boys. I expect it will be sad news for the Hertfordshire people when the casualties come to be known, but they will have the satisfaction of knowing that they died doing their duty for King and country, and it is far better that, than stay at home and let the Germans reach England. We have not forgotten the Lusitania yet. Am pleased to hear all are well at home; we are resting now".

A soldier with a Stansted connection, having been born in the village in 1894, lost his life during this month of May 1915. He was **Private Thomas Edmund Chapman 9100, Royal Fusiliers 3ʳᵈ Battalion; Killed in Action 3ʳᵈ May 1915 aged 21**. He was the son of William and Jane Chapman. His family had moved away from the village and were living in Gerrards Cross, Buckinghamshire. **Thomas** has no known grave and is remembered on the Menin Gate at Ypres.

Another brave soldier, not listed on the Memorial, who was living in Stansted at the time of his sad death had the following details, **Private John Green 8383, Essex Regiment 2ⁿᵈ Battalion, Killed in Action 13ᵗʰ May 1915 aged 28**. He has no known grave and is commemorated on the Menin Gate, Ypres, Panel 39. He was the son of William and Phoebe and at the turn of the century the family were living at 21 Brook Road, Stansted.

John was killed during the Second Battle of Ypres during the fighting for Shelltrap Farm (also known as Mousetrap Farm) north of the village of Wieltje.

From the battalion war diary we find that at 4.00a.m the enemy started a heavy bombardment all along the front line from Shelltrap Farm southwards. *At 7.00a.m orders was made to advance and support or retake the farm if it was found to be in enemy hands. At 8.30a.m 'A' and 'B' companies moved off. The attack by these two companies was splendidly carried out with great dash and determination. They were subjected to very heavy artillery fire both high explosive and shrapnel, and on reaching the ridge to heavy machine gun fire, they never faltered in spite of fairly heavy casualties. During the attack the battalion suffered the following casualties, 37 killed, 94 wounded and 49 missing.*

Shelltrap / Mousetrap Farm. *Courtesy of Brigade War Diary, Collections Canada*

Lieutenant Claude Stewart JACKSON returned home in May 1915 and was put on light duties for three weeks.

June 1915

How we miss him, yes how sadly,
None but loving hearts can tell;
But he is at rest with Jesus
He that doeth all things well
(In loving memory of my dear son Alfred Reginald Bush – From his mother
found in the local – Herts and Essex Observer newspaper)

Lance-Corporal Alfred Reginald BUSH 4/6175
Bedfordshire Regiment 2nd Battalion
Killed in Action 16th June 1915 Aged 24
Alfred has no known grave and is remembered on Le Touret Memorial France, Panel 10/11. The memorial is located in the grounds of Le Touret Military Cemetery, Festubert, France.

Alfred was the son of James and Charlotte Bush. He had one brother **James BUSH** (see October 1917) and according to the 1901 census he also had four sisters, namely Clara, Lucy, Minnie and Thirza. In 1901 they were living at Hazel End, Farnham but during the war years the family were residing at Bentfield End Stansted.

On the 15th June 1915 orders were received that **Alfred's** battalion would take part in an attack by three regiments. The action was to commence at 00.30a.m. on the 16th. **Alfred** was killed in action during the following events.
From the battalion War Diaries we find the following details.

On *the 16th June the battalion were in trenches, namely New Cut and Scottish Trench. At 00.17a.m the attack was postponed until 1.30a.m.*

Then at 00.59a.m the attack was again postponed until 05.30a.m. Orders were then received for the battalion to relieve the 2nd Wiltshire Regiment, who were still holding the trenches. The first two platoons were now in position ready for the assault and they were in the front of New Trench and Scottish Trench. The relief of the 2nd Wiltshire Regiment was then carried out. 'B' Company, with its left flank in touch with the Grenadier Guards (20th Brigade), were holding New Trench. Two Machine guns were also in this trench on the left. 'A' Company, who were situated in Scottish Trench, were in touch with 2nd R.S.F. (Royal Scots Fusiliers) on the right and on their left were 'D' Company. 'C' Company and two Machine Guns were in Reserve in New Cut Trench. At 03.55a.m detailed orders for the 05.30a.m attack were received but at 03.58a.m the attack was once more postponed until further orders. At 08.48a.m instructions were received that when the attack was next ordered the battalion was to develop a flank attack along the line. It was uncertain at this time whether the attack was likely to take place or not. Orders were then received that an attack was to take place at 4.45 p.m. The *battalion was ordered to attack from the north and assist the R.S.F. as opportunity offers. The R.S.F. first objective was a German front line trench. At 4.45 p.m. the company advanced in successive platoons from the right. All the platoons entered the Crater at the junction of Sunken Road Trench. The Company came under a considerable volume of rifle and machine gun fire as it topped the lip of the Crater. A spirited fight at close range then took place in the Crater. The company formed a line in the crater as they were not able to push forward on account of the hostile bombs. A Corporal Milne distinguished himself by throwing back all those that landed near him into the German trenches until he was wounded. Lieutenant F. Powell (twice wounded himself) on seeing that his company was suffering heavy losses and some German reinforcements were coming up, and also on account of there being no sign of the Regiment which was attacking on the right or of our bomb throwers then gave the order for the Company to withdraw to their former trenches. This was carried out in good order under the direction of 2ⁿᵈ Lieutenant R.B. Gibson 3rd South Staffs Regiment who was attached to the 2ⁿᵈ Bedford Regiment and was the only officer of the company left. A Corporal T. Green with about nine men was on the left of and slightly separated from the rest on the Company. He saw the Company go back and remained a while longer but seeing he was in danger of being surrounded and that the Germans appeared to be getting ready for a counter attack, he withdrew his men safely, bringing in a wounded man himself, he went out later in the evening and brought some more wounded in. The two Machine guns in New Trench on the left of the line held by our company under Sergeant W. Mart and Lance Sergeant W. Wilson availed themselves of the good targets offered by the Germans in a communication trench. Sergeant Mart was wounded but refused to leave his guns and inflicted heavy losses on the Germans. At least two German officers were noticed amongst those who were killed.*

Approximately forty of **Alfred's** battalion were also killed in action on this day.

Less than two weeks later Stansted had another casualty by the name of **Albert MORETON. Albert** was the first casualty from Stansted who was involved in the campaign taking place at the Eastern front in Gallipoli. His details are as follows –

Private Albert MORETON (Spelt Morton on some research documents) **15980 Essex Regiment 1ˢᵗ Battalion Killed in Action 28ᵗʰ June 1915 aged 20**

As with many soldiers **Albert** has no known grave and is commemorated on the

Helles Memorial in Turkey. The Helles Memorial serves the dual function of a Commonwealth battle memorial for the whole Gallipoli campaign and place of commemoration for many of those servicemen who died there and have no known grave. The United Kingdom, Australian and Indian forces named on the memorial died in operations throughout the peninsula.

There are also panels for those who

died or were buried at sea in Gallipoli waters. The memorial bears more than 21,000 names.

Albert was born in Broxted in 1895. He was the son of Thomas and Eliza Morton of Forest Hall Cottage Stansted. The census of 1901 shows he had a younger sister Ellen.

Albert had enlisted at Saffron Walden where he had joined the Essex Regiment. From **Albert's** Medal Index card we find that he entered the theatre of war (Balkans) on the 10th July and was sadly killed eighteen days later.

From the Essex 1st Battalion History we can find out about the action in which **Albert** lost his life.

The battalion moved on the 27th to a position east of Fir Tree Wood. The last Battle in June took place on the 28th and was designed to shake and hold the enemy on the Aegean Coast line which resulted in a considerable advance of over half a mile. This success and the losses inflicted on the Turks created a feeling of confidence and ultimate success. At 1.00p.m the Essex received orders to attack enemy trenches but it proved to be a task of insuperable difficulty, for the trenches were blocked with our wounded and by our own troops (156th Brigade) coming back. At 4.00p.m an attempt was made to bomb the enemy out by working up the communication trenches, but the outlets were held by snipers. The enemy continued to pour heavy fire on our front line trenches and No Mans land which stretched for 300 yards. The losses included three officers and from other ranks 11 were killed, 49 wounded and 12 missing believed killed. Sadly **Albert** was amongst these losses.

1st Essex Ambushed. An interesting article found in the local *Observer* archives read as follows.

A telegram from Cairo says. *In the earlier fighting in Gallipoli the Turks in the Krithia region penetrated our line at its weakest spot. The 1st Essex Regiment, who were in reserve, were ordered to retake the trenches. They made for a trench on the right of a gully. Soon they heard voices calling "Who are you?" They replied "Essex". Then came the cry, "That's all right; come on Essex". The Essex colonel had only gone a few paces when he was shot in the stomach. He died an hour later. Major Sammut, who had gone with the colonel, met with a like fate. Even at this moment it was not realised that the men had bumped right into Turks, who were only ten yards away, and that the men who had called out "Come on Essex", were Germans. Lance-Corporal Ellingham ran to help the colonel, but was immediately shot. Then Private Staunton, unsuspectingly and unarmed, ran to the colonel. Suddenly realising the situation, he crawled on his stomach, took the rifle from a dead comrade, and shot a Turk near the colonel. The magazine contained this one shot, so all Staunton could do was to lie still and feign death. His pack was found next morning to be in shreds through the passage of bullets. There is no doubt that the first cry "Come on Essex", came from the British, but it was undoubtedly taken up by the Germans.*

From the Stansted Petty Sessions held this month of June 1915 came the following in front of Magistrates F.S.H Judd and the Hon. H Blyth.

Charles Whybrow a fishmonger of Stansted pleaded guilty to driving a coasters barrow in Lower Street without having a lighted lamp attached. P.C Perry stated that

when he called on the defendant to stop he drove his donkey on going at a rate of seven miles an hour. P.C Perry followed him to his house in Woodfields and asked him why he had no light on his cart. The defendant replied *"I saw a Zeppelin coming over and told me boy to blow the light out"*. He continued to say that *"it was like a big cigar and I thought I was doing the best thing"*.
Defendant was fined Five shillings.

Lieutenant Claude Stewart JACKSON (See October 1917) has now been declared fit again for general service.

A Handsome memorial brass has been placed on the wall of the chancel of St Mary's Parish Church to the memory of Captain **William Alan FULLER-MAITLAND** (see September 1914).

It bears the inscription 'In loving memory of **Captain W.A. Fuller Maitland**, Coldstream Guards, Born April 13th 1882, killed in France at the battle of Aisne, September 19th 1914', and upon it are the regimental colours of the Coldstream Guards along with the flags of the allies enamelled in colours.

The following soldier, who was born in Stansted in 1872, was also killed in the Gallipoli Campaign this month. His details are, **Private William Godfrey 313513, Essex Regiment 1st Battalion, Killed in Action 6th June 1915 aged 43. William** has no known grave and is remembered on the Helles Memorial. He was the son of Nathaniel and Eliza Godfrey and spent his childhood days living at Woodfields. Between the 4th and 9th of June the battalion lost 15 officers and over 200 men.

From the war diary came the following account of actions which took place on the 6th June 1915.

At 3.30p.m the enemy attacked our position. They had worked round the left flank of our advanced position and attacked from the rear with bombs. They were driven back once, but the line was eventually forced to fall back. The enemy succeeded in reaching one part of our trench but were eventually driven out by our bombs.

During the afternoon the enemy attempted another attack but were repulsed.

The Bishop of Chelmsford paid a visit to Stansted during June 1915 and addressed a meeting of Church workers in the Parish Room. His Lordship also availed himself of the opportunity of a chat with members of the Bedfordshire Yeomanry on the eve of their departure from Stansted, where they had been billeted for the past three months.

A message found at a local railway station, left there by a member of the Essex Regiment says.

"The person that finds this will know that the good old Essex boys have gone across the water. They are all as happy as larks. They are all going to do their bit for good old England, and we are going to stand together like men and fight like all Britishers ought to. 'England expects every man to do his duty' and I can tell you the old Essex will do their share"

God bless the woman who gives her son
To fight for the country's fame,
God bless the woman who gives her man
For the honour of Britain's name,
When the morning dawns and the fight is o'er
Arms will be opened wide,
To greet the men who have fought the fight –
But the slacker must stand aside.

July 1915

The blow was hard, the task severe,
To part with a brother we loved so dear,
His cheerful smile, his loving face,
No one on earth can fill his place.

On the 30th of July at Hooge, the Germans first used the flame thrower in battle. In the small hours of the 30th July jets of flame from these devices swept across the trenches occupied by companies of the 8th Rifle Brigade. Not surprisingly, the Germans with the advantage of this new weapon (also known as liquid fire) made some gains where it was used. There was desperate fighting with the sides only separated by a few yards. This small area of the line is described even in the Official History as being an area of 'evil reputation'.

Two soldiers, Samuel Quarterman and Alfred Harber, billeted locally were charged with stealing four hens valued at twelve shillings at a hearing at Stansted Petty sessions. They admitted the offence saying at the time they 'were in drink'. The Captain of the Regiment to which they belonged said he had had no trouble whatever with Quarterman and no trouble with Harber until a few weeks ago when he went on the drink. Both soldiers were fined two pounds.

Many soldiers were billeted in the village during the First World War and here they pose with Mrs Dixon and her family in Woodfields, another small street off Chapel Hill.

August 1915

He nobly answered his duty's call
And gave up all for honours call,
We do not know what pain he bore,
We did not see him die,
But this we know he passed away,
And never said good-bye.

Twenty two year old **Henry James LAW** was our next unfortunate lad to lose his life. Like **Albert MORETON** Henry was killed during action in the Gallipoli campaign, they both entered this theatre of War on the 10th June 1915 and as their numbers were consecutive it is quite probable that they enlisted together.
His details are as follows.
Private Henry James LAW 15981
Essex Regiment 1st Battalion
Killed in Action 6th August 1915 aged 22

Memorial to Henry James Law

Henry is remembered on a special memorial in Twelve Tree Copse Cemetery in Turkey.
Twelve Tree Copse is in the Helles area less than a mile from the village of Krithia.
Henry was born in Stansted in 1895 the son of Walter and Jane Law. In 1901 they were living at Burton End, Stansted. **Henry** had five brothers, **Arthur Stanley**, Charles, Frederick, **Horace** and Walter, plus two sisters Alice and Edith. His father was a farm worker. **Henry** had joined the Essex Regiment when enlisting at Saffron Walden. His 21 year old brother **Horace**, a gardener, had previously enlisted in December 1914, joining the Bedfordshire Regiment, but was later discharged as having "flat feet".

Details of the action in which **Henry** was involved and when he was killed are as follows.

On August 5th the Essex were again in the line, having been fore-warned that they would be employed in a big attack. On the 6th the Essex were detailed to attack enemy trenches near Krithia. The artillery opened at 2.30p.m but was immediately replied to by the Turks with shrapnel and high explosive on the British trench system, particularly the reserve trenches which caused many casualties. At 3.50p.m the battalion advanced having two hundred yards to traverse before reaching the enemy's trenches. This movement at first appeared very successful with few casualties but heavy shrapnel fire opened up once more as the men moved forward again. With great gallantry they took the next line of trenches but were then held up by machine gun fire, rifle fire and bombs. The companies were so weak that on the Turks counterattack with both bomb and bayonet they were driven back. At nightfall the battalion had secured as a result of much desperate fighting the corner of the enemy's trench and a connecting trench. Orders were given that these should be held at all cost.

The casualty list for this action amounted to over 50 being killed, 202 wounded and 180 missing, the majority of the missing presumed dead.

Another soldier, who lost his life during the Gallipoli campaign was as follows, **Private Benjamin Macdonald Ryder 20540, Essex Regiment 1st Battalion, Died at Sea 13th August 1915 aged 21.** He was the son of Alice and the late Herbert Ryder and he had spent his childhood days growing up at number 11 Water Lane. **Private Ryder** probably died during the preparations for the landings at Suvla Bay, as records state he Died at Sea. His name is also commemorated on the Helles Memorial.

On 12th August the 1/5th Norfolk Battalion became known as the *"Vanished Battalion"*, as most of them perished in an ill-conceived attack at Suvla.

That they became so famous was due to three factors, firstly, most of them were employed by the British Royal Family at the Sandringham Estate. A second fact was that, officially at least, their bodies were not found. And last but not least, long after the war, a strange story popped up, when two Gallipoli veterans declared they had seen the Norfolk's march into a strange cloud, that engulfed them, then lifted and drifted away, leaving nobody behind.

A telegram dated 21st August to Sir Thomas Jackson read, *"Lieutenant Claude Stewart JACKSON admitted to Red Cross hospital, Le Touquet, on 17th August with a slight injury".*

Private Percy Milton Cottee 12420, Essex Regiment 9th Battalion, of Bentfield End was wounded in the right thigh on the 7th August 1915. He was later, in June of the following year, discharged as a result of the wounds, being no longer fit for active service. Prior to the war he earned his living as a footman.

September 1915

Gone to his peaceful rest,
For him we should not weep,
Since he is now amongst the blessed,
No more by sin and sorrow pressed,
But hushed in quiet sleep.

This month saw the beginning of the Battle of Loos. Despite heavy casualties, there was considerable success on the first day in breaking into the deep enemy positions near Loos. This was the first time the British had used gas in a major offensive.

The Loos offensive began on 25th September following a four day artillery bombardment in which 250,000 shells were fired.

The London Gazette, for September 1915, contained the following announcement: - Commission signed by the Lord-Lieutenant of the county of Essex, **Major Archibald Gilbey Gold** to be appointed Deputy-Lieutenant.

Major Archie Gold, as he is more familiarly known, is the son of Charles Gold, of the Limes, Birchanger, and nephew of Sir Walter Gilbey, and lives at Croft House, Stansted. He married the fourth daughter of Mr Henry Arthur Blyth, of Stansted, and had two children.

Also during this period the funeral took place at St Mary's Parish Church, Stansted, of Mrs Stewart Brown, wife of **Captain Stewart Brown**, 7th Battalion Royal Fusiliers, whose death occurred suddenly in London at the age of 29. She was the granddaughter of the Right Hon. Lord Blyth of Blythwood, Stansted. A large number of beautiful floral tributes were laid upon the grave at St Mary's Churchyard.

A post office telegraph dated 29th September 1915 to Sir Thomas Jackson read as follows.

*"The Military Secretary presents his compliments to Sir Thomas Jackson, and begs to inform him that a report has just been received which states that **Lieutenant Claude Stewart JACKSON** (see October 1917), Coldstream Guards, was discharged from hospital at Etretat to duty on September 20th".*

October 1915

The Lord has taken one we loved
From all his sufferings here,
Into his heavenly home above
We hope to meet him there.

Information was received in October 1915 that three Stansted soldiers were wounded in the recent great forward movement in France. They were Private **Cyril Sampford** 11th Essex Regiment, son of Mr and Mrs W. Sampford, of Grove Hill; **Private William Harbridge** 9th Essex Regiment, son of Mr and Mrs E. Harbridge, of Lower Street; and **Private James Haggerwood 3/3144**, 11th Essex Regiment, son of Mr and Mrs John Haggerwood of Elms Farm, Church Road. **Private Harbridge** who was the son of Edward and Sarah Harbridge was born in Takeley in 1893. Additional information provided by his son, also named William, was that when he returned wounded from France he was hospitalised at Felixstowe and he spent the remainder of his life with shrapnel implanted in his head. When he was finally discharged from the army he went to work as a driver at Daniel Robinson's in Lower Street and was there for over fifteen years. **William's** younger brother **Ernest** was taken prisoner of war later in the conflict. **Private Haggerwood** had sustained gun shot wounds to his back and lower thigh the previous month on 26th September 1915, during the fighting in the Battle of Loos, and was bought back to England where he was treated in a Birmingham Hospital. This was the first of many wounds that **James** received. By the end of the war he had been wounded on no less than five occasions. (see August and December 1916, October 1917 and August 1918)

From local shopkeeper S. Turner, Woodfields, Stansted came the following notice. *"I beg to bring under notice of the inhabitants of Stansted and surrounding villages, that I am now supplying Sunday papers. Orders for any Sunday publication will be strictly adhered to".*

Local arrangements for Flag Day for the French wounded were made by Mrs Archie Gold and Mrs Rowell and the substantial sum of £22.2s.11d was raised.

The following cases were heard at the Stansted Sessions during October.
Lieutenant John Underwood, Royal Field Artillery, was summoned, but did not appear, for driving a motor cycle without a light in Stansted, on September 4th. Sergeant Tucker stated that about 11.00p.m he was on duty on Chapel Hill, when he heard a motor cycle approaching going in the direction of the railway station. There was no light on the cycle either in front or behind. He called to the driver to stop, but he did not do so. Two days later he saw the defendant and asked him why he did not stop when he was requested to, and the defendant replied that he had to get back to camp. A fine of £1 was imposed.

Joseph Chipperfield, licensed victualler, was summoned for serving soldiers during prohibited hours on August 21st. The case was withdrawn on a technical point and the Bench agreed.

2nd Lieutenant Sydney Alder (see January/February 1917) of the 12th Sherwood Foresters was wounded during The Battle of a Loos in October 1915. He later joined the Royal Flying Corps.

Thomas Dare Jackson

Lieutenant-Colonel **Thomas Dare Jackson**, M.V.O., D.S.O. 1st Battalion King's Own Lancaster Regiment, 4th Division, British Expeditionary Force, son of Sir Thomas and Lady Jackson, of Stansted House, has been promoted to the rank of Brigadier General, 55th Infantry Brigade, 18th Division, British Expeditionary Force.

William Tant, straw tier, and Frank Chappell, labourer, were summoned to the Stansted Petty Sessions for trespassing in search of conies on land in the occupation of Mr Walter Seabrook, on October 24th. Complainant said he saw the pair of them at some rabbit holes on his land. Chappell was kneeling down putting a net over a hole and Tant was in the ditch on the other side of the fence. He said to Chappell "*I have caught you at last*" and the latter answered "*It's the first time*". Seabrook asked '*Where is your ferret*' and Chappell replied "*I have not put it in yet*". Tant on the opposite side of the ditch had his head down and witness remarked "*You need not hide yourself Tant, I know who it is*". Chappell then picked up the net and the defendants walked off. In his defence Chappell said a rabbit ran off their gardens into the hole and they went after it.
They were each fine 5s and 4s costs.

October 1915 saw the enlistment of **Private Ernest Charles Whybrow 2667**, Hertfordshire Yeomanry, but after only four months service he was discharged on medical grounds.
'*The complaint from which this man is suffering precludes him from ever firing his musket*'. Simply he had a sight disorder.

60

November 1915
We will not forget you
You gave your all
That we might live.

LIEUTENANT L. J. GIBBS,
Canterbury Infantry Battalion.
Wounded.

Lieutenant Loftus Joseph Gibbs of the 13th (North Canterbury and Westland) Company, Canterbury Infantry Battalion New Zealand Expeditionary Force, has arrived home on convalescent leave after having been wounded in the head and heel by a hand grenade in the Gallipoli Peninsula.

He was the son of Mr and Mrs Joseph Gibbs, a tailor of Chapel Hill, Stansted.

Lieutenant Gibbs left Stansted eight years ago in 1897 for New Zealand. He held a commission in the New Zealand Forces and on the outbreak of war volunteered for active service and proceeded with his regiment to the Dardanelles.

Lieutenant Gibbs was recently 'Mentioned in despatches' for distinguished service on the battlefield. He had joined the New Zealand Expeditionary Force on 21st November 1914 and served with both the Maori (Pioneer) Battalion and the Canterbury Regiment. He was promoted to Captain on 23rd April 1916 and at some stage was an acting Major. **Loftus** was born in Stansted in 1883 and spent his childhood days living in Woodfields.

Albert John PATMORE (see February 1918) was awarded a scholarship this month of November 1915, which was not taken up.

Mr John Carter, a retired farmer, admitted taking game without a license on November 13th, he was accused of shooting a pheasant. In his defence he said *'I thought it was a pigeon'* although at the time when asked if he had a pheasant on him he denied the accusation, but when asked why he had feathers sticking out of his pocket he admitted the offence.
A fine of £2 was imposed.

December 1915

Until death us do join,
But oh! For a touch of the vanished hand
And a sound of the voice that is stilled.

A wide circle of friends and the parishioners of Stansted generally learned with great regret of the sudden death of Sir Thomas Jackson.

At Stansted where Sir Thomas and Lady Jackson and the family have resided since 1903, he was loved by all who knew him, and the deepest sympathy is felt for Lady Jackson and the family in their great and sudden bereavement. Sir Thomas subscribed to everything connected with the Church and parish of Stansted and several old and poor inhabitants found in him a good friend.

Sir Thomas married in 1871 a daughter of the late George Julius Dare by whom he had four sons and four daughters, namely: The new Baronet, **Major Thomas Dare Jackson**, M.V.O., D.S.O., of the King's Own Royal Lancaster Regiment, who gained the D.S.O. in the South African War and was Temporary Brigadier General in France; **Captain George Julius Jackson**, 60th Kings Royal Rifles; **Lieutenant Russell Jackson**, Royal Garrison Artillery; **Lieutenant Claude Stewart JACKSON**, Coldstream Guards; Mrs Tabor, wife of **Major A.M. Tabor**, 3rd Hussars, Mrs Lloyd, wife of **Lieutenant Colonel J.H. Lloyd**, Lancashire Fusiliers, Mrs Raymond Marker, widow of **Lieutenant Colonel R.J. Marker**, Coldstream Guards; and Miss D. St. F. Jackson.

The sad news reached Stansted of the death in King George's Military Hospital, London, of **Private Charles PATMORE.**
His details are as follows.
Private Charles PATMORE 21107
Duke Of Cornwall's Light Infantry 6th Battalion
Died of Wounds 23rd December 1915 aged 19
He is buried in St Mary's Parish Church Stansted.

Charles was the Son of Samuel (Late Coachman to Mr W. Fuller Maitland of Stansted Hall) and Letitia Patmore of Burton End Lodge. He had two brothers Arthur and Gilbert and two sisters Ada and Elizabeth.

The young soldier, who had so nobly given his life for King and Country, was only nineteen years of age. He was an old scholar of the Stansted National School and prior to enlisting on May 4th 1915 he was employed by Mr Fuller-Maitland in the gardens at Stansted Hall.

He proceeded to France on August 3rd, and went straight to the trenches, being selected as one of the bombers in his Regiment. He took part in the battle of Loos and was in the big forward movement on September 25th. In October he was badly gassed, but made a speedy recovery and was soon back in the trenches. On December 8th he was very severely wounded by a shell while in the trenches near the village of Weiltze (The battalion war diary has mention of a shell falling in the front trench). His left shoulder was shattered and his spine injured. He was bought home and admitted to King George's Hospital, but sadly never recovered and died from his injuries on December 23rd.

62

Grave of Charles Patmore

His brother **Arthur Patmore** was also serving King and Country as a Driver in the Army Service Corps.

Charles funeral took place in Stansted, his remains were brought by rail and met at Stansted Railway Station by a gun carriage and bearer party from the 2/7th London Division of the Royal Field Artillery. The coffin, wrapped in a Union Jack, was conveyed on the gun carriage to the deceased's home at Burton End.

The following day the funeral took place at St Mary's Parish Church and was attended by a large number of the parishioners and the Military. His coffin was conveyed by a military bearer party to the entrance of the church where it was met by the Rev. Captain Woottan, Chaplain to the Forces, who officiated. Immediately behind the mourners walked a number of troops, each carrying a wreath, and a bugle party of the Royal Field Artillery. The coffin was placed at the entrance to the chancel during the service, and at the conclusion at the graveside the buglers sounded the Last Post.

The immediate mourners were **Charles** parents, his brothers **Arthur** and Gilbert and his sisters Ada and Lizzie. Close relatives Mr Arthur Lloyd and Mr and Mrs Alfred Patmore and Cousins Miss Dora Herrington and Mr and Mrs E. Reynolds were in attendance. Others present included the butler from Stansted Hall, Mr N. Amber and **Charles'** old headmaster, Mr F. Dearch.

There were dozens of floral tributes from family and friends including one from his sister Ada inscribed *"In loving memory of Charlie, who died a soldier"*, and another from friends which read *"In memory of Charles Patmore another son of Britain, gone to join the throng of those who have done their duty"*.

A week later another young soldier from Stansted became a victim of the fighting and died of his wounds, his name was **Harry PHILLIPS** and his details are as follows.
Private Harry PHILLIPS 1253
Royal Fusiliers 8ᵗʰ Battalion
Died of Wounds 30ᵗʰ December 1915 aged 22
Buried at Bethune Town Cemetery Grave Ref. IV.G.67
Bethune is about twenty miles north of Arras in France.

Harry was the son of George and Ruth Phillips. The1901 census shows he had two elder brothers named George and Charles. He also had four sisters, Maud, Ellen, Ethel and Mary.

Harry arrived in France in the May of 1915 and from the Royal Fusilier's war diaries we find the actions where **Harry** quite probably sustained his wounds.

On Christmas Day at 9.00a.m the 8ᵗʰ Battalion relieved the 7ᵗʰ Royal Sussex in the front line trenches. The 9ᵗʰ Royal Fusiliers were on the left and 21ˢᵗ Royal Fusiliers situated on the right. A mine was blown by the enemy who then occupied the crater and placed machine guns on the forward edge - One other rank wounded.

The following day the battalion tried to bomb out the enemy early in the morning but insufficient time to make full preparation. The rest of the day was spent in the trench preparing for a bomb attack on the enemy who were still holed up in the crater - Two other ranks were wounded.

On the 27ᵗʰ at 5.00a.m we started to bomb the crater ably assisted by a trench mortar battery. The enemy then replied rather feebly for about an hour until their return fire ceased. There were no signs of the crater being occupied when daylight arrived. At 9.00a.m we were relieved by 7ᵗʰ Royal Sussex and we marched to billets at Le Quesnoy.

Then on the 29ᵗʰ we left our billets and relieved the Royal Sussex in the Givenchy Trenches. We then found a fresh mine to the left of Sap 'H' which had been blown by the enemy, little damage had been done. At 2.00p.m the enemy were active all along our front with rifle grenades. Casualties sustained in this attack were one killed and three wounded.

The next day a party of twenty six petty officers and two officers of the Royal Navy arrived. They were being attached for the experience of trench life, they were distributed amongst the companies. The enemy continued to be active with rifle grenades paying particular attention to our right company. Casualties amounted to two killed and six wounded.

Harry's death was recorded in the local newspaper thus.

Died from Wounds. – The casualty list on Monday recorded the death from wounds on December 30th of **Private Harry PHILLIPS**, bomber in the Royal Fusiliers, son of Mr George Phillips, of Water Lane, Stansted. **Private Phillips** was auxiliary postman at Stansted before joining the Forces early in the War, and was a popular member of the Stansted Football Club. He was 22 years of age. Mr George Phillips and Family wish to thank all their kind friends for their sympathy in their sad bereavement.

Part of a stack of oat straw, value £7.10s, belonging to Messrs Rochford, and situated at the Nurseries, was destroyed by fire. About fifteen loads of the straw were saved by members of the London Artillery.

Private Ernest Edwin Matthews 24096 enlisted this month of December and joined the Army Veterinary Corps. Prior to enlistment he was a furnishing salesman living in Water Lane, Stansted.

He was involved for the duration of the conflict and was discharged on 16th May 1919.

The Army Veterinary Corps was well tested in World War 1. There were 2.5 million admissions mainly on the Western Front and 80% of injured animals were treated and returned to duty. An outstanding achievement far exceeding anything previously attained which earned the Corps its Royal prefix on 27th November 1918.

January 1916

Not gone from memory, not gone from love,
But gone to our Father's home above.

During the first month of 1916 news reached the village of the death of **Charles William BROWN** who had been killed in action.

Charles William BROWN was born in Farnham, in 1897, a tiny village situated between Stansted and Bishop's Stortford. He was the son of John and Fanny Brown (nee Milton). At the time of his death he was living with his family in Woodfields Stansted, the 1901 census shows him as having three elder sisters named Annie, Florence and Elizabeth. He enlisted at Saffron Walden where he joined the Suffolk Regiment.

He also had a twin brother named **Robert**, who also lost his life in the war a few months later (**Robert George BROWN** – see August 1916)

Charles details are as follows.
Private Charles William BROWN 20273
Suffolk Regiment 2nd Battalion
Killed in Action on 22nd January 1916 aged 19

Grave of Charles William Brown

Charles is buried in Sanctuary Wood Cemetery Belgium. Grave III.E.1. Sanctuary Wood Cemetery is located three miles east of Ypres (Ieper) town centre.

Sanctuary Wood is one of the larger woods in the commune of Zillebeke. It was named in November 1914, when it was used to screen troops behind the front line. It was the scene of fighting in September 1915 and became the centre of the Battle of Mount Sorrel (2nd -13th June 1916) involving the 1st and 3rd Canadian Divisions.

A brief history of Sanctuary Wood is as follows.

During the second Battle of Ypres Sanctuary Wood became part of the front line. On the 30th of July 1915 the Germans attacked the eastern edge of Sanctuary Wood with flamethrowers.

On the 25th of September 1915 there were attacks on the German positions over the entire length of the wood. Three mines were blown in the south eastern corner. The British were driven back to their lines within ten hours of fighting in which 600 British soldiers lost their lives. Then on the 29th of September 1915 the Germans blew another mine in the south eastern corner of the wood.

During June 1916 the Canadians were pushed out of the wood. The Princess Patricia's Canadian Light Infantry put up a famous stand in the wood, the position was only partly recovered two weeks later due to the loss of Hooge. Most of the wood then became no man's land. And in August 1917 Sanctuary Wood was retaken during the 3rd Battle of Ypres.

There were three allied cemeteries at Sanctuary Wood before June 1916, all made in May-August 1915. The first two were on the western end of the wood, the third in a clearing further east. All were practically obliterated in the Battle of Mount Sorrel, but traces of the second were found and became the nucleus of the present Sanctuary Wood Cemetery.

Sanctuary Wood (preserved trenches) today

A few yards from the cemetery now lies the Sanctuary Wood Trench Museum. This museum was started in 1919 by the grandfather of the present owner, who preserved part of the trench system that remained in what the British Army called Sanctuary Wood. The wood got its name in the First Battle of Ypres in 1914, when men separated from their regiments came to this wooded area - a safe area away from the main fighting, a place of 'sanctuary' - to await rejoining their units.

By 1915, the wood, on the lower slopes of Hill 62, was part of the front line area and remained so until 1917. In June 1916, the Germans attacked and broke through the 3rd Canadian Division who held this sector, and fighting took place within the area of the wood. The wood was captured by the Germans in April 1918, and finally retaken in the Fourth Battle of Ypres.

"Sanctuary Wood was by this time a wood in name only. Such trees as stood were riven and leafless, while their fallen branches added to the maze of wire and trenches beneath. The air was heavy with the sickening odour of decay, so that the whole battered district, even by day, was a place of grisly horror and evil omen".

The following gives an account on how **Charles Brown** lost his life. His battalion were in trenches on 'The Bluff' *(Map of the Bluff below – courtesy of Chris Baker's Website – The Long Long Trail.)*, on the Ypres-Comines canal. On the night of 21st – 22nd of January, just after the battalion had returned to the line, a terrific explosion occurred. The ground shook violently and an immense column of earth shot up in front of the Bluff carrying away the south eastern face of it.

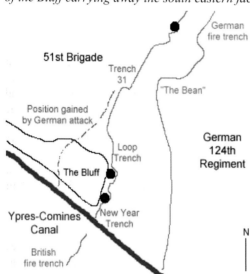

Interestingly the explosion was not followed up by any attack or bombardment. The explosion (a mine of six – seven tons of explosive) caused a crater of 125 yards long, 50 yards wide and 60 feet deep.

Around 100 men were killed in the explosion which took place at 2.15am on the 22nd and one man Sergeant Bragg was awarded the D.C.M. for extricating himself after being half buried by the explosion and digging out four other men, he then proceeded to the crater and remained there all day.

From the war diary the following statement was taken.

The Major General R. Haldane commanding the 3rd Division wished to place on record the behaviour of the 2nd Battalion Suffolk regiment and he went on to describe the above action, finishing with *" several officers and N.C.O s and men of the battalion were conspicuous by their coolness and some behaved with gallantry rescuing their comrades. The conduct of the battalion under these trying circumstances was excellent, all ranks behaving in a soldier-like manner, so held the position, which might easily have become serious, were never in danger".*

The Bluff was an artificial height created by the dumping of spoil when the Ypres-Comines Canal was excavated. In this low-lying area, and being on the northern bank of the canal, it gave a considerable observation advantage to the troops occupying it

The Ypres-Comines canal, running south east from the town, cut through the front lines about 3 miles from the Cloth Hall. This was the position at the end of the First Battle of Ypres and it remained much the same into 1916, the 2nd Battle having not altered things here. Facing the British was the village of Hollebeke; on the left was the hotly-contested ground of Hill 60 and Zwarterleen, and on the right the hotspot at St Eloi. On the northern embankment of the canal, stood the Bluff which gave the British front an unusual observation advantage over the enemy. Equally if the enemy had had the advantage of the Bluff the view across the rear areas of the Salient to Hill 60, towards Ypres and down to Voormezele would have made the Salient very difficult to hold. The mound had to be held.

The German front line fire trench lay some 200 yards ahead of this feature, which the British called the Bluff, and the enemy Grosse, or Kanal Bastion. British trenches ran around the forward base of the Bluff, snaking around the front of the lips of a number of mine craters that had been blown here in October and November 1915, and in January 1916. Communication trenches ran back over the Bluff itself. The canal cutting was steep sided and over 100 yards wide. The trenches continued on the other side of the water, with only a single plank bridge connecting the two banks.

Mr Henry Sanders, a retired builder and George Snow, a drapers assistant, both of Stansted, pleaded not guilty to being in unlawful possession of two pheasants and three rabbits at Stansted Petty Sessions on December 10th. Sergeant Tucker stated that at 6.25p.m he was near Stansted Railway Station and saw the defendants leave the station, having apparently come off the train. He noticed their pockets were 'a bit bulky' and when they were near the *Barley Mow* (A Public House situated on Chapel Hill) he stopped them and searched them under the Poaching Prevention Act. In Mr Sanders inner coat pockets he found two cock pheasants and a rabbit. He then questioned Sanders on how he accounted for them, to which Sanders replied that he bought them from a man on the way home. The defendant Snow, who was in possession of two rabbits and a pocket full of stones suitable for use with a catapult also claimed to have bought them from a man who neither could describe as they claimed it was too dark.

The Bench gave the defendants the benefit of the doubt and dismissed the case.

Three of Stansted's fighting men had been home on short leave during the last few days January 1916. They were Sergeant **Albert Edward Johnson**, 1st Bedfordshire Regiment, who had been at the front in France since the commencement of the War and had taken part in numerous engagements from the battle of Mons up to the present time; **Private Sadler Walter Harold Spalding**, 1st Hertfordshire's (son of Mr W.J. Spalding, of Silver Street), who had been in France for sixteen months and had gone through the whole of the engagements in which the Hertfordshire Regiment had so distinguished itself (he later had spells of duty with both the Royal Field Artillery and the Essex Yeomanry); and **Seaman Ernest Everitt**, son of Mr Arthur Everitt, who was on a destroyer on patrol duty. **Seaman Everitt** had some particularly interesting events to relate. On one occasion, he said, they were patrolling on the East coast when they were sent in pursuit of an enemy submarine which had appeared off the Irish coast. They steamed the 500 miles in the shortest possible time and came upon the submarine unawares. The crew on the submarine had fired two shots at the destroyer, when the skipper sharply turned and cut the submarine clean in two. The destroyer afterwards put into Pembroke, where, he said, everyone was delighted with their performance and they were all hospitably entertained. In the five years **Seamen Everitt** served he made his way from Able Seamen up to Petty Officer, he served on the following ships, HMS Mansfield, HMS Pembroke I, HMS Dido, Attentive II, Woolwich and Prince George. His brother **Seamen William Everitt** also served with the Royal Navy.

69

February 1916

Killed in action our hearts are sore,
For King and Country, we miss him more,
His cheerful smile, his loving fac,
No one on earth can fill his place.

The Battle of Verdun in 1916 was the longest single battle of the Great War. The casualties from Verdun and the impact the battle had on the French Army was a primary reason for the British starting the Battle of the Somme in July 1916 in an effort to take German pressure off of the French at Verdun. The Battle of Verdun started on February 21st 1916 and ended on December 16th in 1916.

A Canadian soldier by the name of **Thomas George Stacke**, who was home on short leave and staying with his parents at Bentfield End, was found lying in a semi-conscious state on the side of the road near New Farm Stansted. He had been for a ride on horseback that afternoon and apparently was returning home when he was thrown. P.C Percival, who was informed, and Mr W. Pomphret, of the Horse Shoes Public house at Hazel End, conveyed the soldier to his home, where, on medical examination it was found he was suffering from concussion of the brain.

    Thomas was killed later in the war (See April 1917) although he is not named on the Stansted memorial.

Three more Stansted soldiers have been home on short leave at this time namely, **Private William Hutley 1247** Royal Fusiliers 8th Battalion, attached to Royal Engineers Signal Section, son of Mrs H. Hutley of Grove Hill; **Private Jesse Miller** (see August 1917) (brother of **Christopher Miller** – see March 1917) 9th Royal Fusiliers son of Mr Miller of Stoney Common and **Private Walter Law** (brother of **Henry James LAW**- see August 1915) Essex Regiment son of Mr W. Law of Burton End.

Private Arthur Luckey, the brother of **Private Ernest LUCKEY** (See August 1918), lost his life during February 1916. He, unlike his brother, is not named on the Stansted Memorial although records show him as living in the village. His details are as follows - **Private Arthur Luckey 16061, Bedfordshire Regiment 8th Battalion 'A' Company, Killed in Action 13th February 1916 aged 30.** He is buried in La Brique Military Cemetery No.2, situated to the north east of Ypres (Ieper), Grave Ref. I. S. 24. His name can be found on the memorial in the nearby village of Birchanger.

    The war diary states that *considerable enemy artillery activity continued throughout the night of the 12th and 13th* and it is most probable that **Arthur** was killed at this time.

70

Pictured above, the Newell Brothers, **William** (left) and **Arthur** (right)

Private William Henry Newell 24558 was, on the 19th of February 1916, discharged from service as being medically unfit. He was suffering from defective eyesight. He had joined up in December 1915 when he joined the Essex Regiment. He was the son of Abraham Newell and they lived in Rochford's Cottages, on the edge of Stansted and Birchanger. He is pictured above (left) clearly wearing the badge of the Royal Fusiliers and also with a wound stripe or possibly good conduct chevron on his left sleeve. Also on his right sleeve are chevrons which denote overseas service of three years, which all adds up to quite a mystery as he was discharged early in 1916, so he must have re-enlisted fairly promptly, quite possibly with a pair of spectacles!

Also pictured above (right) is his brother **Arthur Newell** who served with the Army Veterinary Corps.

March 1916

A year has passed, our hearts still sore,
As time flies on we miss him more,
Thy will be done seems hard to say,
When one we loved was called away.

On the 20th of March one of the village's older soldiers died. He was **Private Henry Levey** who was aged 50. His details are as follows, **Private Henry Levey SS/20024, Army Service Corps, 26th Labour Company, Died 20th March 1916 aged 50.**

He is buried at Boulogne Eastern Cemetery, Grave Ref VIII.D.82. **Henry** was the son of Joseph and Elizabeth Levey and from available records seems to have spent all his childhood and many subsequent years living at Bentfield End. Somewhat surprisingly **Henry** is not named on the village memorial.

The majority of grave markers in Boulogne Eastern Cemetery are flat on the ground due to the soil being sandy, and they are not normal sized, but between about two thirds and half the size of a typical headstone. Because of their location, some of them have been badly weathered, and this has caused some scouring and darkening of the surface of some.

Butchers assistant **Albert Wells**, of 3 Rose Cottages, Bentfield End joined the Essex Regiment this month. He was the son of Henry Wells and was discharged in August 1916 as being 'medically unfit for future service'.

73

April 1916

A year ago, my heart still sore,
Since first the tidings came;
Since on the list of those that fell
I read my dear boy's name.
He died I know a hero's death,
But Oh, this weary pain,
I never thought when he left home
He would no more return;
That he so soon in death should sleep,
And leave me here to mourn.

SILVER STREET, STANSTED.

A slightly later view, c. 1916, looking south in which the soldiers are again prominent. On the right the Windmill pub is selling Fordham's ales. The newspaper placard proclaims the loss of a British destroyer. Next door is Savage's the hairdressers and beyond that is Muffett's the fishmongers.

Four of Stansted's soldier sons, **Privates A. Bass, E. Sayer, G. Watson**, and **W. Shepherd** have been home from the front on short leave during the last few days.

May 1916

Silent and sudden was the call,
Of one so dearly loved by all;
The blow was great, the shock severe,
To lose the one we loved so dear;
None but aching hearts can tell
The pain of not saying that last farewell.

The marriage of Captain **Claude Stewart JACKSON** (See October 1917) Coldstream Guards and Miss Laura Emily took place during May 1916. His brother Brigadier General Sir **Thomas Jackson**, D.S.O., who acted as best man, arrived in London from the front the day before the wedding.

On the final day of this month the Battle of Jutland took place.
The Battle of Jutland is considered to be the only major naval battle of World War One. It witnessed the British Navy losing many men and ships but the verdict of the Battle of Jutland was that the German Navy lost and was never in a position again to put to sea again during the war. Over six thousand lives were lost during the battle.

Private James Haggerwood, Elms Farm, Stansted, 11th Essex, was treated by the 18th Field Ambulance for an injury on his right knee caused by him falling into a shell hole whilst on a working party.

June 1916

Our boy we loved so well is gone,
For King and Country his young life he gave,
And well we know he bravely did his best,
And with our God we leave him now to rest.

News reached the village this month that two of Stansted's soldier sons had been wounded in the heavy fighting which has taken place in France over the last few weeks, firstly **Private Alfred Turner**, son of Mr Frank Turner, of Gall End, and formerly in the employ of Mr H.H. Bass as a milkman and secondly **Private Peter WARWICK** (see September 1917) son of Mr William Warwick, of Woodfields. **Peter** was formerly in the employ of Mr Mascall as a butcher. Both are serving with the Essex Regiment. **Private Turner** was later discharged as unfit for service with wounds to his leg and part of his heel shot away.

The barrage prior to the Battle of the Somme commenced on 24th of June 1916. The expectation was that the ferocity of the bombardment would entirely destroy all forward German defences, thus enabling the attacking British troops to practically walk across No Man's Land. Sadly this was not to be the case as the advance artillery bombardment failed to destroy either the German front line barbed wire or the heavily-built concrete bunkers the Germans had carefully and robustly constructed. Much of the munitions used by the British proved to be 'duds' – badly constructed and ineffective. Many charges failed to explode and still today farmers on the Western Front unearth many tons of these unexploded munitions every year. These finds are known locally as the 'Iron Harvest'.

July 1916

A sudden loss, a shock severe,
To part with him we loved so dear,
Though great our loss, we will not complain,
But trust in Christ at length to meet again.

Battle of the Somme

Intended to be a decisive breakthrough, the Battle of the Somme instead became a byword for futile and indiscriminate slaughter, with General Haig's tactics remaining controversial even to this day.

The British planned to attack on a 15 mile front between Serre, north of the Ancre, and Curlu, north of the Somme. Five French divisions would attack an eight mile front south of the Somme, between Curlu and Peronne. To ensure a rapid advance, Allied artillery pounded German lines for a week before the attack, firing 1.6 million shells. British commanders were so confident they ordered their troops to walk slowly towards the German lines. Some, it was said, even had footballs with them and intended to kick them as they advanced. Then once the German lines had been seized, cavalry units would pour through to pursue the fleeing enemy.

However, unconcealed preparations for the assault and the week-long bombardment gave the Germans clear warning. Happy to remain on French soil, German trenches were heavily-fortified and, furthermore, many of the British shells failed to explode. When the bombardment began, the Germans simply moved underground and waited. Around 7.30am on 1 July, whistles blew to signal the start of the attack. When the shelling ceased, the Germans left their bunkers and set up their positions.

As the 11 British divisions walked towards the German lines, the machine guns started firing and the slaughter began. Although a few units managed to reach German trenches, they could not exploit their gains and were driven back. By the end of the day, the British had suffered approximately 60,000 casualties, of which nearly 20,000 were dead, their largest single loss. About sixty per cent of all officers involved on the first day were killed.

It was a baptism of fire for Britain's new volunteer armies. Many 'Pals' battalions, which comprised of men from the same town who had all enlisted together so they could serve together, suffered catastrophic losses. Whole units died together and for weeks after the initial assault, local newspapers, such as the local *Herts and Essex Observer*, would be filled with lists of dead, wounded and missing.

Stansted, as a village, was fortunate not to lose any of their sons on this day of carnage but two days later on July 3rd bad news reached the village as two of its teenage soldiers, **Walter Frederick GRAY** and **Charles William WARWICK,** had been killed. Both these lads were serving with the Essex Regiment 9th Battalion. There details are as follows
Private Walter Frederick GRAY 24052
Essex Regiment 9th Battalion
Killed in Action 3rd July 1916 aged 18

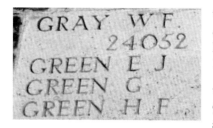

Walter has no known grave and is commemorated on the Thiepval Memorial to the Missing. His name is inscribed on Pier and Face 10D of the memorial.

Walter was born in Stansted in 1898 the son of Walter and Martha Gray. In 1901 he was living at 9 Brook Cottages, Stoneyfield Common, Stansted and at that time had two younger sisters Ida and Dorothy. He enlisted in Saffron Walden and joined the Essex Regiment.

Private Charles William WARWICK 24049
Essex Regiment 9ᵗʰ Battalion

Killed in Action 3ʳᵈ July 1916 aged 19

He is buried at Ovillers Military Cemetery, Grave Ref V11.M.10.

Ovillers is situated in the Somme region and the cemetery is about three miles north-east of the town of Albert.

Charles was born in Stansted in 1897, he was the eldest son of William and Sarah Ann Warwick. In 1901 he was living at 50 Gall End, Stansted. At this time he had a sister Bessie and a brother named Frederick. It is more than likely that as both Charles and Walter's regiment numbers were only three digits apart that they enlisted together in Saffron Walden. They then fought together and possibly died together.

Details of the action of which these two brave boys lost there lives are as follows.

The 9ᵗʰ Essex occupied the line opposite Ovillers on July 2ⁿᵈ. They were in support of the 5ᵗʰ Royal Berkshire Regiment and 7ᵗʰ Suffolks and during the day took shelter in the railway cutting near Marmont Bridge from possible hostile counter bombardment.

78

Orders were received that the Brigade was to attack Ovillers in the early morning of 4th July, but the time was subsequently altered to 3.00a.m on the 3rd, which prevented any thorough reconnaissance.

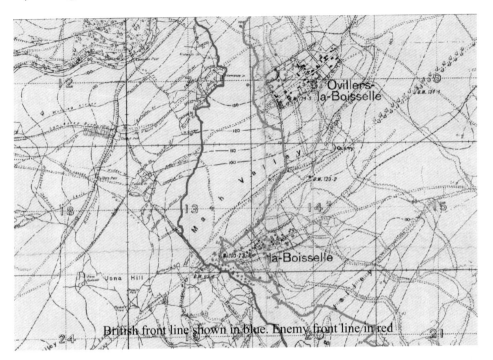

British front line shown in blue. Enemy front line in red

"*The march of the battalion*' wrote a member of the 9th, '*to take up position for their first Somme battle will for ever be remembered by those engaged. Innumerable gun flashes lit the darkness of the night; they seemed endless and as one approached the line, the noise was deafening. After what appeared to be endless marching we reached the trenches in front of Ovillers. They were of hard chalk and with the bad weather not at all easy to negotiate without trench boards. Zero hour arrived when it was raining, and visibility was poor, with bitter retaliation from the enemy*".

At 2.15a.m everything was ready, when a message was received that zero hour had changed to 3.07a.m. The attack took place on time and at 3.20a.m the leading lines of the battalion followed in support. The leading battalions over-ran the enemy's front lines and parties entered Ovillers together with men of the 9th Essex. They had suffered severely whilst crossing the open ground, as they were attacked by enemy machine gun fire from the flanks and the village, and the waves became a series of detached parties under either an officer or N.C.O.

'A', 'D', and part of 'B' Company had advanced in platoon waves, but the lines were not always in touch, due to their damaged condition and the number of wounded, and other details making their way back along the communication trenches. Two platoons of 'B' Company got over the German front line and were then held up at Circular Trench *which overlooked the ground that had been won. At about 4.00a.m.the attack had come to a standstill and the survivors withdrew again.* Over one hundred 9th Battalion Essex Regiment soldiers were killed in action on this day.

Later in July 1916 Mrs C. Bonney received the sad news and particulars of how her youngest son **Albert Edward BONNEY** had been killed in action. **Lance-Corporal BONNEY**, of the Bedfordshire Regiment, was 21 years of age and a native of Bishop's Stortford. Before joining the Army he was a caddie at the Bishop's Stortford Golf Links.

He joined the Militia in 1912 and at the outbreak of war was in South Africa, and on the Regiment returning from that country it proceeded to France in September 1914. His Commanding officer, in a letter to his mother says *"He was a thorough good soldier and feared nothing that came in front of him".* Mrs Bonney had three other son's serving King and Country.

A letter from Corporal C. Griggs a comrade in the same regiment as **Albert** wrote the following

"I will try my best to answer the few inquiries your letter contains and give all the information I can concerning my old and respected comrade. I know the reading of this will be sad and painful, but I assure you, you have the deepest sympathy of all who knew your son. He was respected and regarded by all as a man ever ready to take big risks when circumstances called for it, and it will perhaps make it easier for you to bear when I tell you he did his utmost in a tight corner. I did not happen to be near him at the time but I have a chum who was practically by his side when the shell which laid him low came. We were split up in parties driving the enemy from a wood, and this chum informs me that the spot where your son was killed was certainly the worst position he was ever in regarding big gun fire. A large shell came amongst six or seven men. He saw your son and while another man attended to him to see if anything could be done, my chum was busy getting some badly wounded men to the best shelter available. Your son was killed instantly, so did not linger in pain. The man I mentioned saw Albert's brother, who came over from the Royal Garrison Artillery. He left our camp with a thorough understanding as to the spot and also all the information that could be given concerning his death, and will probably write to you himself".

Albert's details were as follows.

Lance-Corporal Albert Edward BONNEY 10018
Bedfordshire Regiment 2nd Battalion
Killed in Action 11th July 1916 aged 21

Albert's name along with more than 72,000 others can be found on the Thiepval Memorial to the Missing.

The Thiepval Memorial, which was unveiled on 31st July 1932 by the Prince of Wales, can be found just off the main Bapaume to Albert road.

Albert was born in Epping in the spring of 1896 but before the outbreak of war his family had moved to Stansted and were living at Grove Hill. He was the son of Charles and Emily Bonney and had brothers named George and Walter and Sisters called Alice, Daisy, Winifred and Elenora. Albert enlisted in Hertford joining the Bedfordshire Regiment.

As was mentioned in the letter to **Albert's** mother, **Albert** was killed whilst driving the enemy from a wood. From the War diaries we find this area to be known as Trones Wood. The following is an account from those diaries.

On the evening of the 10ᵗʰ of July orders were received that his battalion were to attack Trones Wood at 3.27a.m the following day and attempt to entrench on the eastern side of the wood.

Trones Wood in 1919

Some of the Operation Orders for this attack were as follows.

Intention. On "A" day, and zero hour, both to be published later, the 30th Division will capture the enemy trenches.

Objective. 1ˢᵗ Objective. The King's Liverpool Regiment will assault Dublin Trench. 2ⁿᵈ Objective. A portion of the 20ᵗʰ Battalion King's Liverpool Regt will attack the Briqueterie when Montabaun has fallen.

Dispositions. The 2ⁿᵈ Battalion Bedfordshire Regiment will be in Support. 'A' and 'B' Companies along Grove Avenue and 'C' and 'D' Companies along Grove End Road.

Method of Advance. The King's Liverpool Regiment will advance in four lines, with 100 yards distance between each line. The 2ⁿᵈ Battalion Bedfordshire Regiment will follow the last waves of the King's Liverpool.

Strong Points. The Battalion will establish four Strong Points at once on arrival in the German trenches, and on completion will garrison these strong points.

Cleaners. 'D' Company will detail two Officers and 100 men for this duty into two parties, each of these parties will be divided up as previously, and clean up all trenches. As soon as prisoners are handed over, escorts will return at once and rejoin their parties.

Machine Guns. Two Vickers Guns will be attached to this Battalion.

Lewis Guns. Lewis Guns will work with their Companies.

Signalling. A Signal Station will proceed with each Company. Artillery flags, discs, vigilant periscopes, etc. will remain as in brigade training.

Smoke Candles. When Dublin Trench has been reached the King's Liverpool Regiment will light smoke candles.

Ammunition. Each man will carry on his person 170 rounds and two hand grenades and each bomber will carry ten bombs.

Rations and Water. Water is very scarce and the utmost care must be exercised.

Medical. Battalion Aid Post is established in Cobham Street. Advanced Dressing Station at Bronfay Farm.

Dress. Each man will carry: - waterproof sheet. Pack (without great coat) equipment rifle and bayonet 170 rounds, two mills bombs, one iron ration.

Bombers, Lewis gunners and stretcher bearers will carry: - rifle and bayonet (except 1 & 2 of Lewis gun teams and bombers) 50 rounds (except bombers) Lewis gunners carry 170 rounds. All men will carry a filled oil bottle, pull through and flannelette. Picks and shovels will be carried by all men in proportion of one pick to three shovels.

Wire Cutters. Each man carrying wire cutters will wear a white patch on the shoulder strap.

Communication Trenches. Stanley Avenue and Maricourt Avenue.

Wounded. On no account will they be accompanied to the rear by unwounded.

Retire. This word will not be used.

Great Coats and Haversacks. All great coats will be returned and tied in bundles of twenty and properly labelled. Small kits will be put in the haversack which will be returned properly labelled to Headquarters

Water bottles. All water bottles will be full at ZERO hour.

Secret Maps. No secret maps, papers etc. will be carried by officers or men of this battalion.

Time. All watches will be synchronised at a time to be notified. All messages sent must be timed.

I have listed some of the above Operations Orders to enable the reader to get a feel for the way these attacks were prepared.

Information received was that the wood was only 'lightly held by the enemy' although two battalions had each previously made separate attacks on the wood with severe casualties and both had been unable to establish a footing in the wood.

At 11.00pm on the 10th the battalion moved up the Briqueterie Road to the Sunken Road just east of the Briqueterie which had been classified as the position of deployment for the attack. The battalion was in position by 1.30a.m on the 11th and formed into lines of half companies with a gap of five paces between each man and a distance of about 150 yards between the platoons.

Orders were to attack at 3.27a.m so the leading line started to advance at 3.10a.m heading towards the South Eastern edge of Trones Wood. Under the cover of near darkness the advance was not observed by the enemy until the leading men were only four hundred yards from the wood and it was then that the enemy machine guns opened fire. The enemy quickly got their artillery to work and the battalion suffered many casualties whilst entering the wood. By 3.45a.m the whole battalion had gained the

Trones wood today

inside of the wood but owing to heavy machine gun and shell fire they had entered the wood too far toward the southern end. The companies had further difficulties keeping in touch due to the dense undergrowth which had reduced the visibility down to about four yards. It was found once inside the wood that it was still strongly held and full of trenches and dugouts.

After heavy fighting inside the wood part of 'A' and 'B' companies reached the south east edge and dug themselves in whilst 'C' and part of 'D' company done the same on the south west end edge. At 4.20a.m a party of about forty men, under the command of Captain L.F. Beal and Lieut. H.A. Chamen, reached the north east edge of the wood and commenced to dig in. As there were no British troops holding the northern end of the wood this party became isolated and the enemy could be seen advancing from Longueval. Captain Beal finding his company isolated and nearly surrounded withdrew into Longueval Alley at about 9.00a.m. After several messages had been sent, one finally got through. The party then withdrew back to the South-East corner at about 5.00p.m and joined up with 'C' company who were entrenched there.

83

Great difficulty was experienced with organisation in the wood owing to heavy casualties and the dense undergrowth but the battalion managed to hold its own. By 7.00p.m that evening they had dug themselves in on the south east and south west sides of the wood – All companies were seriously depleted by heavy casualties.

Whilst the men were digging in, strong patrols worked inside the wood collecting stragglers and bombing the enemy in their trenches and dug-outs, they accounted for a great number of enemy casualties.

Earlier in the day 'A' and 'B' Companies were leading the advance and were unfortunate in losing many men while entering the wood. Both Companies much reduced by casualties dug in at the South East corner.

At 11-30a.m a strong patrol of about 40 men endeavoured to work their way northwards along the eastern edge of the wood, but they then encountered fierce opposition from a 'Strong Point' where the Guillemont Road enters the wood. Captain C.G. Tyler was severely wounded and ordered the party to withdraw back to the trench. This trench was held against several counter attacks but at 10.00p.m. the trench was being bombed from three sides and the order to withdraw back to the Briqueterie along the Sunken Road.

The last Company to cross during the advance were 'C' Company under Captain R.O.Wynne. The Company entered the wood by Trones Alley and established itself there.

Further progress was unsuccessful and eventually 'A' and 'B' companies were forced to withdraw but 'C' and 'D' Companies held out against all counter-attacks.

Almost sixty of **Private BONNEY'S** comrades were killed during this one day of fighting.

An overview of the attack at Trones Wood (*courtesy of Chris Baker's The Long Long Trail Website*)

11th 12th July Trones Wood still not captured

By the end of the 10th July Rawlinson and Haig were becoming anxious, for the second step of the offensive, the assault on the German second position, was set for 14th July. But without Trones Wood, it would not be possible to move on Guillemont and Longueval. At 2.40a.m. on the 11th the fiercest British bombardment yet was fired on Trones Wood. At 3.27a.m. the 2nd Bedfords and The 20th King's Liverpool advanced into the maelstrom at the southern end of the wood. There was much fighting as they went but without a decisive result. The enemy were rushing reinforcements into Trones. By great fortune, German orders of a counter attack were found and an intensive barrage was fired on their planned forming up area between Trones and Guillemont, which effectively destroyed the attack. At 10.30p.m. the 17th King's Liverpool entered the wood without opposition and took up a line on the south eastern edge.

On the 12th a line was dug to link up with the Bedfordshire Regiment and that evening an enemy attack on Maltz Horn Trench and the wood was repulsed assisted by British and French shellfire.

Parts of the wood remained in enemy hands and it was not until a greater attack by the British on the 14th that it finally fell.

So was it you who on that fateful day
did make the whistle blow.
For them to raise themselves
above the parapet,
And march into the no-man's land ?
But march they did - and to great cost.

Thiepval Memorial to the missing with over 72,000 names inscribed

Private Charles Griggs, Middlesex Regiment, son of Rebecca, of Burton End was discharged this month. He had served for ten years prior to the war and had re-enlisted in October 1914.

August 1916

Forget them, no, we never will,
We loved them here, we love them still,
Nor love them less because they're gone,
From here to their eternal home.

Mrs Fanny Milton, of 9, Woodfields, Stansted, has received the sad news that her son, Corporal **Robert George BROWN**, Suffolk Regiment, was killed in action by shell fire in France. He was only nineteen years old and before joining up was in the employ of the late T.O Newman. His twin brother, Private **Charles William BROWN** (see January 1916), also of the Suffolks, was killed in action by a mine explosion in January.

Robert George Brown

The Captain of his Company informing Mrs Milton of Corporal Brown's death said *"It is with the deepest regret I have to inform you that your son was killed last night. A heavy trench mortar exploded and blew in the dug out he was in. Our men got him out and we shall bury him tomorrow. He was one of my best N.C.O's, and one of the most popular in the battalion. His cheerful temperament and great heartiness had endeared him to us all. I cannot tell you how grieved I am that he has gone. Your grief must be terrible, but I hope it may be tempered by the knowledge that he did his duty to the end. His memory will always be with us, and we are the poorer for his loss. My sympathy and that of every officer and man goes out to you and yours and may it help you in your great sorrow".*

Letters of similar character had also been received by Mrs Milton from his Lieutenant and the Chaplain of the Regiment.

Mrs Milton had a third son in France **Private Thomas John Brown**, of the Army Service Corps, and three stepsons also in the army, **Corporal G. Milton**, Essex Regiment, **Private H. Milton**, of the Suffolk's, and **Private C. Milton** of the Northamptonshire Regiment.

Robert's details are as follows.

Corporal Robert George BROWN 21352
Suffolk Regiment 12th Battalion
Killed in Action 22nd August 1916 aged 19

Robert is buried in Philosophe British Cemetery, Grave Ref I.H.49, in the Pas de Calais region of France. The cemetery is situated between Bethune and Lens. (See January 1916 for **Robert's** Family details)

Mr William Charles Harritt, farmer and dairyman, of Stansted, was summoned for selling milk not of the nature and quality demanded. An Inspector of Weights and Measures stated that he was in Silver Street and saw a man named Chopping in charge of a milk cart. Chopping said he was in the employ of the defendant. The inspector then purchased a pint of milk from Chopping for two pence. He then told Chopping he had bought it for public analysis.

After much evidence from both sides the Chairman of the bench said they were satisfied that this sample was below the standard and was also quite satisfied that nothing had been done to tamper with it. The summons was dismissed.

About a hundred Soldiers Mothers and Wives were entertained to tea, by Lady Jackson, in the grounds of Stansted House. An address was afterwards given by a lady speaker from London and Lady Jackson also spoke a few words to her guests and mentioned the fact that she had seven sons and son-in-law in His Majesty Forces, which was one better than the best family record among her guests.

By permission of Mr Gilbert Alder, the grounds at Hargrave, Stansted were thrown open to the public and the Widdington Band, conducted by the Rev. J.W. Court, played a selection of music. A large number of the parishioners and residents of the district attended and dancing was enjoyed upon the lawn. A small charge was made for admission and by this means a sum of £9-10s was raised for the Essex Regiments Comfort Fund. A generous donor afterwards gave £10-10s, which bought the total up to £20.00.

September 1916

Weep not for us, our parents dear,
Because we die so young,
It was the Lord who thought it best,
To take us to his home.

The Battle of the Somme continued relentlessly throughout the summer of 1916 and into the autumn.

On 15th September 1916 tanks were first deployed as a surprise weapon in the third phase of the Battle of the Somme, which is known as the Battle of Flers - Courcelette,

The Battle of Thiepval Ridge was designed to coincide with the Battle of Morval by starting exactly twenty-four hours after it. Thiepval itself was a village on a spur dominating the Ancre valley, although the actual front for the battle extended from the Schwaben Redoubt to Courcelette.

Beginning on 26th September and after three days of intense bombardment, four assault divisions attacked along the 6,000 yard front. On the extreme right the Canadians, shielded by a creeping barrage, made their first objectives north of Courcelette. The adjoining 11th Division, attacked northwards and quickly overran the unrecognisable pile of rubble that was once Mouquet Farm

Day two of the attack saw the capture of the German fortress at Thiepval. Thiepval village had been an objective on the first day on the Somme campaign, and had repeatedly defied British attempts to capture it.

Successful British operations concluded on 28th September with the capture of the Schwaben Redoubt, north of Thiepval, another first day objective that had been the site of fierce fighting by the 36th Ulster Division.

During September 1916 four more of Stansted's brave boys were wounded. They were **James Haggerwood** 3/3144 of the 11th Essex Regiment, **Henry Walter Prior** (See July 1917) 26962 9th Essex Regiment, **George Henry CARTER** (See July 1917) 10th Essex Regiment, and **J. Treslove** 13659 Essex Regiment who joined the Oxford and Bucks Light Infantry later in the campaign having first entered the war with the Essex in July 1915.

Also wounded during action was **Lieutenant Richard Fuller Maitland**, second and only surviving son of Mr W. Fuller Maitland, of Stansted Hall. He was wounded in the knee in France.

This was the second occasion in which **Private Haggerwood** had been wounded, this time he sustained shrapnel wounds of the hip on August 21st last. Although the 11th Battalion had actually been relieved the previous day a working party had five killed and eleven wounded when they were hit by a trench mortar.

The following soldier, who died on the 12th of this month, was, **Private Frederick Charles Sizeland G/14576, Royal Sussex Regiment 2nd Battalion, Died of Wounds 12th September 1916 aged 25**. We know that **Frederick** was born in Birchanger but is listed as the son of Alfred and the late Mary Anne Sizeland of Stansted. He is buried at Heilly Station Cemetery, Mericourt-L'Abbe, Somme, France. **Frederick** is remembered on the Birchanger Memorial. **Frederick**, when he enlisted at Saffron Walden, originally joined the Essex Regiment.

Private Frederick Sizeland died from wounds he received on the 9th September

Frederick (seated on left) with the Essex Regiment

when his battalion attacked a German trench in High Wood. 2nd Sussex casualties on that day were 43 killed in action and 146 wounded with over 60 more missing.

Private Frederick Bloom, aged 21, of Mill Road Stansted was discharged from service this September in 1916. He was no longer fit for service after suffering severe gun shot wounds of the neck during his 6 months at the front line in 1915. At the time of his wounding he was with the Suffolk Regiment. Prior to serving he ran a confectioners shop in Silver Street, Stansted.

October 1916

Around the flag of Britain,
He nobly took his place,
And fought and died for England,
The honour of his race.

It took almost eight months for the wife of Lance-Corporal **Joseph HAGGERWOOD** to finally find out that her husband had been killed in action. She received a letter in July of the following year confirming his death. **Joseph** had initially been reported wounded and subsequently missing but no details of his whereabouts could be found.

After enlisting in Saffron Walden he had gone to France with the British Expeditionary Force in May 1915 and was wounded in the shoulder early on in the campaign. He made a good recovery in hospital in London and afterwards proceeded to the Dardanelles. Following the evacuation of the Dardanelles he went to Egypt before finally returning to France.

Joseph left a widow, Emma Ellen (nee Carter), and five Children. He was the son of John and Eliza Haggerwood of the Elms Farm Stansted. He was born in 1877 in Stansted and was bought up living in the *Dog and Duck* public house, he was part of a very large family and research shows he had four sisters Agnes, Ellen, Mary and Minnie and seven brothers Arthur, Charles, Frederick, Henry, John, **James** and Edward.

Joseph's details are as follows.

Lance-Corporal Joseph HAGGERWOOD 3/3482
Essex Regiment 1st Battalion
Killed in action 12th October 1916 aged 40

Sadly **Joseph** is another of our brave soldiers who has no known grave and is remembered on the Thiepval Memorial to the Missing.

The following are the actions **Joseph** was involved in when he lost his life.

On October 4th the battalion moved by train to Poperinghe as a move had been expected. Then on the night of the 9th they were transported in buses to relieve part of the 37th Brigade in the firing line. They marched up to the support line through Delville Wood into Gird Trench, Pioneer Trench and Bull's Road. On the 11th they moved into the firing line in readiness for an attack alongside the Royal Newfoundland Regiment.

'W' and 'X' Companies were in the firing line in front of Gueudecourt, 'Y' and 'Z' companies were in support in the Sunken Road. 'W' and 'X', behind our barrage, advanced at zero hour, 2.05a.m, and took their 1st objective of the first line trenches. There they were reinforced by half of 'Z' company. The remainder of the battalion swung left to achieve an objective not gained by the Suffolks. They came under heavy shell and machine gun fire, which halted their advance, and they tried to dig into old shell holes. There they remained until 5.30p.m when they retired and re-organised on the original front line.

Meanwhile 'W' and 'X' Companies had mopped up the dugouts of their first objective killing 300 Germans and capturing about 60. They then moved onto the second line, but about halfway were pinned down by very heavy fire from the front and flanks. At this time a group of about fifteen Germans came up from a dugout showing signs of surrendering but as two Essex officers approached them a German jumped on one

90

officer and shot him with his revolver. Others assisted and the enemy were killed. Under heavy fire the Companies gradually retired to their first objective. At nightfall the battalion held the original front line and the Newfoundlanders retained the first objective. Later a German counter attack was beaten off. The battalion had lost over 80 men during this days fighting.

Less than a week had passed when another of Stansted's soldiers lost his life. He was,

Walter E Saggers

Private Walter Ernest SAGGERS 43615
Essex Regiment 9th Battalion
Killed in Action 18th October 1916 aged 26

Walter, like so many others, is also remembered on the Thiepval Memorial. He was the son of Frederick and Agnes Saggers. He had a brother Frank and two sisters, Kate and Lilian. They all lived at 3 Cambridge Road Stansted and his father earned a living as a farm labourer.

Walter lost his life during an attack on Bayonet Trench which took place on the morning of the 18th October.

The battalion was to attack Bayonet Trench, which lays north-west of Gueudecourt, at 3.40a.m. Each company had two platoons in the first wave and the remaining two in the second wave. The ground was in very heavy condition after the continuous wet weather and the men were suffering from a long march, from Flers in the adverse conditions. At 3.40a.m, under protection of a barrage, the two waves went over. Very quickly the leading men were within 50 yards of the German line. 'C' company on the left gained its objective without difficulty but the other companies 'A', 'B' and 'D' were held up by intact barbed wire. The officers sought gaps in the wire but were being picked off by German sniper fire. 'A', 'B' and 'D' companies were unsuccessful in their attempt and were forced to retire and 'C' company under fire from both flanks had to follow suit.

A fellow soldier in **Walter's** battalion wrote *"It was pouring with rain, and, heavily equipped as we were, the going was very bad. Slipping and sliding, covered with mud, we arrived in the front line absolutely worn out. The crowning blow came when each bomber was handed a box of twelve Mills bombs. Already overloaded, it seemed impossible to carry more. Nevertheless, we ranged ourselves in No Man's Land ready for zero hour. A more dejected crew would be hard to find. We were beaten before we started. We attacked with the opening barrage, but we were held up by machine gunfire and uncut wire. Little progress was made, although some managed to gain a footing in the German line. Finally we retired to our own trench. It was not yet light. We had no idea of whether the enemy would counter attack so we built and manned a bombing stop, only to find, by the light of day, that instead of the enemy being on the other side, it was men of one of our other companies. The bombing section of 'C' Company still held the position, which was forward, until the afternoon, when we found that the remainder of the battalion had been withdrawn, Leaving the Berkshires holding the line. After* *consultation with a Berkshire officer, we decided to retire. This we did in the only way we knew. Having only travelled it at night time we found that it was very exposed by day and we were subject to heavy fire. However we scraped through and reached our rendezvous".*

Over twenty of **Walter's** battalion were killed in action on this day of fighting.

On the 15th of this month, **Private Cyril Sampford** 13211 11th Essex Regiment was reported missing. He was the son of William and Catherine Sampford of Grove Hill, Stansted. **Private Sampford** went out to the attack with a Machine Gun Section but none of the party returned. He was nineteen years of age and was formerly employed at Messrs Green's Stores. He was previously wounded in September 1915. From all records available it would appear that **Cyril** survived the war and was probably taken prisoner. (See December 1916 & 1918) **Private Sampford** had entered France during August 1915.

Cyril Sampford

Details from the war diary for the 11th Essex enlighten us on the actions that took place on the day **Private Sampford** was captured. They are as follows.

At 5.35a.m. his company attacked, there first objective was a trench central to Mild Trench and the second was a point in Cloudy Trench, both north east of the Gueudecourt area. The objectives were reached but owing to the failure of the attack on the right the Germans bombed down the trench which was our first objective and the men at the second objective were surrounded and were not seen again.

The casualties for that day were three officers killed, two missing and four wounded. Other ranks killed were 13 with 76 wounded and 75 missing. The battalion then consolidated the position held and were relieved that night by the 14th Durham Light Infantry. On relief they proceeded to bivouacs in Trones Wood. Sadly **Private Sampford** was one of those listed as missing but subsequent news was positive, he had been taken prisoner and not killed.

An officer described these actions. *This period was about the most trying I went through during the war. The Somme fighting was done under great physical and mental strain. The ground was so heavy and muddy, cut up by shell-holes, that to walk any distance over it was fatiguing; in addition, we were continuously under shell-fire day and night, as we were living in old German trenches and so were properly taped.*

Another Stansted soldier listed as wounded this month was **F. Trigg** 14635, 10th Essex Regiment. He was later discharged with his Silver War Badge in January 1918.

Private Charles Henry Bushell 40855 Royal Fusiliers, aged 37, of 2 Rochford's Cottages was on the 14th October 1916 diagnosed at the front as suffering from 'Shell Shock'. He was subsequently transferred 'home'. Later he was awarded the Silver War Badge and discharged from service. Prior to enlisting he had worked at the Rochford's Nurseries. He had been serving overseas since July 1916.

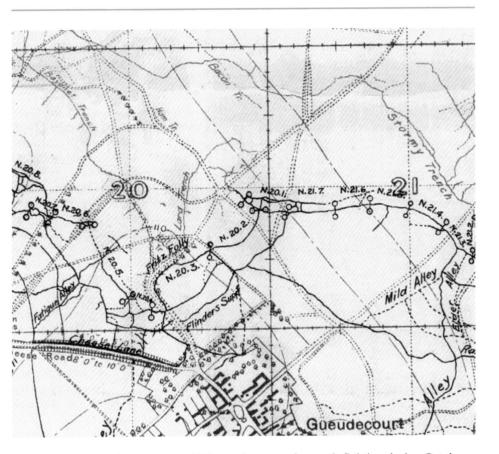

Above – The Guedecourt area which was the scene for much fighting during October 1916 for many battalions of the Essex Regiment.

November 1916

We do not forget them; we love them too dearly,
To e'er let their memory fade like a dream,
Tears often start and the heart mourns sincere,
Grief often dwells where it seldom is seen.

Grave of Arthur Levey

One of Stansted's gallant soldier sons from overseas, who nobly responded to the Mother Country's call, has made the supreme sacrifice. **Pte Arthur LEVEY**, eldest son of Mr Arthur Levey, of Cambridge Road. **Private Levey**, who was 34 years of age, left Stansted in 1906 and went to Australia but was always well remembered by a large number of local folk. In 1914 he joined up in Sydney and was attached to an infantry battalion of the Australian Expeditionary Force. The sad news of his death was conveyed to his father by the Chaplain of his battalion in the following letter;-
" *Dear Mr Levey, - You may have already heard of the death of your son, **Private A. Levey**, and I write only to add some details. The battalion of which I am Chaplain were in the front line from November 7th to the 10th and your son was killed by shell fire on the night of November 9th, outside Headquarters. An original member of the battalion, he had proved his worth and was highly spoken of by his officers and popular with his Company. His loss is regretted by us all. Of him, in his gallant response to duty, it can truly be said 'He being dead yet speaketh,' since his life was witness to the fact that the true man holds honour and justice above life itself. With sincere sympathy. Yours very truly, W.N. Higgins".*

A description of the conditions that **Arthur** and his comrades found themselves in can be found in an extract from the War diary at the time. *"There was no overhead cover, other than that which could be "scrounged" from odd places for use as company or post headquarters or by spreading the men's waterproof sheets over vertical holes scooped in the trench wall. The trenches themselves in many places were feet deep in*

94

mud, in which men were frequently bogged and had to be dug out with shovels, often after much labour. No hot food could be supplied, although hot tea was brought up in petrol tins. The troops in consequence had to carry on with dry rations, frequently fouled by contact with the mud. Communications with flank companies and the supports was difficult and hazardous, runners preferring to walk along the top of trenches at the risk of being sniped, to the slow exhausting process of ploughing through the gluey slime on the trench bottoms".

Arthur's details are as follows,

Private Arthur LEVEY 598

Australian Infantry A.I.F (Australian Imperial Force) **18th Battalion**

Killed in action 9th November 1916 aged 34

Arthur is buried at Bull's Road Cemetery, Flers, Somme, Grave ref III.H.18. Flers is a small village about five miles north east of Albert.

Arthur was born in Deptford London in 1882, the son of Arthur and Susan. On the 1901 census we find him living with his aunt and uncle on the Cambridge road. Research has found that **Arthur** had three brothers, Edgar, Thomas and Robert, plus a sister named Annie.

Service records for soldiers who served in the Great War were largely lost during the blitz of World War Two with only a 30% chance of them being available but for those who served in the A.I.F. they are easily available. From **Arthur's** service records came following information.

Arthur, a bricklayer prior to joining the Australian Imperial Force enlisted on 25th February 1915. He was 5'3" tall and weighed 135lbs; he was of fair complexion with brown hair and had a birth mark on his left buttock. He joined the 18th Battalion 5th Brigade 'B' Company.

In August 1915 he went to Gallipoli but was evacuated sick in December 1915. He reported for duty again in January 1916 and went to Tel-el Kebir Egypt. In March he moved to France, and in the August, two months before he was killed he was given 21 days field punishment Number 2. A brief description of the field punishments given to soldiers was as follows.

Field Punishment Number 1 consisted of the convicted man being shackled in irons and secured to a fixed object, often a gun wheel or similar. He could only be thus fixed for up to two hours in twenty-four, and not for more than three days in four, or for more than twenty-one days in his sentence. This punishment was often known as 'crucifixion' and due to its humiliating nature was viewed by many Tommies as unfair. Field Punishment Number 2 was similar except the man was shackled but not fixed to anything.

News of another Levey reached the village. He was Corporal **George Levey** Essex Regiment, son of Mr George Levey Junior, of Cambridge Road has been wounded in the thigh and right hand and is now in a Birmingham Military Hospital.

Maurice Bright

News also reached Stansted this November 1916 of an award of the Military Medal to **Sergeant Maurice Bright**. **Sergeant Bright** is the son of Mr and Mrs A. Bright, of Woodfields, Stansted, and was formerly footman in the employ of Colonel D.J. Proby, Conservative M.P. for Saffron Walden. The award came for conspicuous bravery while scouting on the battlefield.

William HERRINGTON (see July 1918) was listed this month as having been wounded during the fighting in France as was **George Bonney 40147**, Essex Regiment, who was the brother of **Albert Edward BONNEY** (see July 1916).

Another Stansted lad who left the village for Australia lost his life during November 1916. He was **Private Richard Hutley**, son of Eliza and the late Charles Hutley, who had been living at 140 Cambridge Road before leaving for Australia. He had enlisted on October 8th 1915 and first entered the front line in August 1916. His details are as follows. **Private Richard Christopher Hutley 4427, Australian Infantry, A.I.F. 26th Battalion, killed in action 14th November 1916 aged 19**. He has no known grave and is remembered on the Villers-Bretonneux Memorial. Villers-Bretonneux is a village eleven miles east of Amiens on the straight main road to St Quentin.

On the 14th November 1916 the 26th Battalion was the right hand battalion of the 7th Australian Brigade attacking at Flers. The 26th Battalion was tasked with attacking the Maze. Zero hour was at 6.45am; starting with an artillery bombardment followed by the infantry advance three minutes later. The 26th got into the Maze trenches, but was driven out by a determined counter-attack. It was one of the last actions of the Battle of the Somme, and was a complete failure.

Richard's brother **James Edward Hutley** was also killed later during the war (see April 1918)

December 1916

Our thoughts they often wander to an honourable but unknown grave,
Your dear name is often spoken in the home you died to save,
Our hearts are still united with the same fond love for you,
And loving thoughts are cherished of one so brave and true.

Trooper Percy Robert Church, a Son of Mr Phillip Church, of Linden House, Stansted, has been invalided from the Somme and is now in a hospital at Reading Suffering from dysentery. **Trooper Church**, who prior to the war spent some time in the Colonies, enlisted soon after its outbreak and joined the Australian Contingent, 25th Battalion 'A' company, with whom he first saw service in Egypt, afterwards at Gallipoli, and later on the Western Front.

He had joined up on in February 1915 but had suffered with bad health during much of his service and was discharged on 9th October 1917 having contracted dysentery whilst serving in Gallipoli. His discharge papers stated that he was of very good conduct and character. **Percy** was 43 years old at the time of his discharge and would have received the Silver War Badge - The Silver War Badge (SWB), sometimes erroneously called the Silver Wound Badge, was authorised in September 1916 and takes the form of a circular badge with the legend "For King and Empire-Services Rendered" surrounding the George V cypher. The badge was awarded to all of those military personnel who were discharged as a result of sickness or wounds contracted or received during the war, either at home or overseas. Percy's was numbered A13811.

December 1916 saw **Signaller Harold Balaam**, Essex Yeomanry, son of Mr Z. Balaam, steward of the Working Men's Club, home on ten days leave after eighteen months service in France. During his time in France he had passed as a first class signaller having first entered this theatre of war in June 1915.

The village received more news of one of its missing sons. Mr and Mrs Sampford, of Grove Hill, have had their great anxiety allayed by the receipt of a postcard from their son, **Private Cyril Sampford** (see October 1916), Essex Regiment, stating that he is an unwounded prisoner of war in Germany. **Private Sampford** had been missing since an engagement on October 15th 1916 and the postcard was dated October 22nd. No address was given on the card but **Private Sampford** promised he would write home again soon.

A communication was received stating that **Private James Haggerwood**, Essex Regiment, son of Mr J. Haggerwood, farmer, of Elms Farm, Church Road, had been wounded in the knee in France. His brother, **Lance-Corporal Joseph HAGGERWOOD** (see October 1916), Essex Regiment, has been missing since an engagement on October 12th, and no further information obtained on him. Letters have been sent to the War Office, and also to his commanding officer but his whereabouts still remains a complete mystery.

James's wounds occurred on the 2nd of this month whilst with the 11th Essex in the front line trenches. He was bought home and hospitalised at Keighley War Hospital.

News reached the village this month of December 1916 that **Private Stephen Stanley STAINES 27961** (see February 1919) Suffolk Regiment had also been wounded as has **Private Sidney Harvey 5944**, Essex Yeomanry.

George Ernest Reynolds

The sad news reached the wife of **Private George Ernest Reynolds** that her husband had been killed in action. His details are, **Private George Ernest Reynolds 31874, York and Lancaster Regiment 6th Battalion, Killed in Action 13thDecember 1916 aged 34.**

His grave can be found at Hamel Military Cemetery, Beaumont Hamel, Somme, France Grave Ref. II.D.31. At the time of his death he was living with his wife Susannah at Mill Hill, Stansted. His sad death occurred when an explosion near the regimental cookhouse killed him and four others.

George's name can be found on the nearby Bishop's Stortford Memorial.

January 1917

They died at their posts like soldiers brave,
They answered their Captains call;
They sleep far way in heroes' graves,
For their country's cause did they fall.

The Stansted War Working party met every week during 1916 on Wednesdays in the Friends Meeting House, between the hours of 2.00p.m and 4.00p.m. They made 4,059 garments most of them for hospitals, and a few which have been given to soldier's at home on leave and in special need. The parcels have been mainly sent to Cambridge, Saffron Walden, and Colchester, but also some to Bishop's Stortford, Roydon and Hoddesdon. Also several large bundles were sent to Mesopotamia where supplies were urgently needed. Most grateful letters of thanks were received from all. Mufflers, socks or mittens were sent to all Stansted soldiers and sailors whose addresses were sent in.

Later this same month a telegram was received by Mrs Alder, of Hargrave, Stansted, from the Secretary of the War office, to the effect that unofficial information had been obtained about her grandson, **2ⁿᵈ Lieutenant Sydney Alder**, of the Royal Flying Corps. He had been reported missing on the Western Front in France since Thursday, January 25ᵗʰ, and was now wounded and a prisoner of war in Germany. The telegram was as follows: - *"Beg to inform you that information has been received from an unofficial but apparently reliable source that **Lieutenant Sydney Alder**, Sherwood Foresters and Royal Flying Corps, is wounded and prisoner of war. Secretary War Office".*
2ⁿᵈ Lieutenant Alder was given a commission in the Sherwood Foresters soon after the outbreak of the war and was wounded at the Battle of Loos on September 1915. On recovery he joined the Royal Flying Corps in January 1916, and proceeded to France again that June. He has done good work in the Flying Corps on the Western Front. He was unable to attend the funeral of his uncle, Mr Gilbert Alder, on January 4ᵗʰ but was subsequently granted ten days leave and only returned to France four days before the date of his capture. On that day he went out with several other airmen over the German lines, when they were attacked by enemy planes. **Flight-Lieutenant Alder** for some reason seemed to lose control of his machine, but when near the ground his machine seemed to right itself, and although his fellow airmen could not see exactly what happened they believed that he had been taken prisoner. (see also February 1917).

News of another soldier being wounded reached the village during January 1917, he was **Lance-Corporal Walter Shephard** 12238, Bedfordshire Regiment who later in the war was in the Labour Corps.

February 1917

Softly at night the stars are gleaming,
Over a silent grave,
Where there sleepeth, without dreaming,
One we loved but could not save.
But the hardest part is yet to come,
When the heroes all return,
And we miss amongst the cheering crowd,
The face of our dear one.

Another overseas son, who is commemorated on the Stansted Memorial, was the next to lose his life this February. It was **Arthur GRAY** who was the son of Alfred and Elizabeth, of The Gatehouse, Stansted Road, Stansted. **Arthur** was born in 1891 and had three brothers named Edward, Francis and Thomas, and a sister Sarah. His brother **Francis** was also a soldier with the Australian Infantry.

Arthur had gone to Australia where prior to enlisting had served for six months in the police force. He enlisted on the 14th January 1916 and joined the 41st Battalion 'D' Company. His details are as follows,

Private Arthur GRAY 873
Australian Infantry, A.I.F 41st Battalion
Killed in Action 14th February 1917

Arthur is buried at Cite Bonjean Military Cemetery, Armentieres. Grave Ref IV.E.34

Armentieres is a town in the Department du Nord, on the Belgian frontier, about 10 miles north-west of Lille.

From **Arthur's** service records we find he was 5' 11" tall with brown eyes and black hair, he left Australia bound for Plymouth on 18th May 1916 and arrived on 20th July 1916. Before heading for France **Arthur**, it would seem from his service records, had some disciplinary problems. Firstly he was deprived of his Lance-Corporal stripe and forfeited two days pay for being absent without leave from midnight on 7th October 1916 until 6.00a.m on the 9th. Then on 15th October he was absent from roll call and received seven days C.B (Confined to Barracks). Finally he was absent without leave again between the dates of 1st and 8th November, this time he was given twenty-eight days pay forfeit and twenty-one days field punishment.

On 30th December 1916 **Arthur** left Folkestone and proceeded overseas to France. Less than two months later he was killed. The following was written by a fellow soldier 951 J. Randall – *"Arthur was in 'D' Company, 14th Platoon. He was hit through the heart by a bullet – it happened at Armentieres on February 14th. He was on patrol at the time. He was killed instantly. I saw him hit. He was buried in the cemetery about two miles from Armentieres. His grave had a cross with his name, number etc. I saw his grave".*

And from 2nd Lieutenant D. Gates came the following message,

"I was officer in charge of a party sent out on 'Wiring' duty at Armentieres on February 14th 1917. This man was with me and I saw him fall shot through the heart by a bullet

100

and killed instantly. Ground was held. I arranged his burial at Armentieres Military Cemetery. His mates provided a cross with his name and number inscribed on it. I saw it placed over the grave. A chaplain read the service. His mates and many of the men of his company attended".

From a pal in his Platoon Private 834 P.C. Carroll who wrote -

*"I saw **Gray** killed by a rifle bullet through the heart about 10.00p.m on the 14th February when out wiring in front of our trenches near Square Farm about two miles from Armentieres. He was buried in the Australian section of the cemetery at Armentieres. Our platoon erected a cross of imitation marble and we put a railing round the grave. We made it one of the best looking graves in the cemetery. He and I went into camp together in Queensland and came over in the ship "Demosthene". He was thought a great deal of in his platoon".*

Halt Thy tread is on heroes' graves, Australian lads lie sleeping below; Just rough wooden crosses at their heads To let their comrades know. They'd sleep no better for marble slabs, Nor monuments go grand, Thy lie content now their day is done In that far-off foreign land.

101

A postcard was received this month from **2ⁿᵈ Lieutenant Sydney Alder**, Royal Flying Corps, son of the late Mr Sydney Alder and grandson of Mrs Alder, of Hargrave Park, stating that he is a prisoner of war in hospital in Germany, and giving a few particulars of his marvellous escape from death. He says *"We both had a marvellous escape, as all controls were shot away and we fell three miles. The machine was smashed up, but I only got a badly smashed ankle and a knock on the eye"*.

2ⁿᵈ Lieutenant Alder was the pilot of FE 2d A34 of No 20 Squadron R.F.C. on 25ᵗʰ January 1917, with Lieutenant R.W. White as observer. While on a reconnaissance mission, they fought enemy aircraft over Menin. A34 was seen going down out of control, but recovered before making a forced landing.

Oberleutnant Karl von Grieffenhagen of Jasta 18 was credited with the victory after he claimed shooting down "Vickers A34" (the Germans usually described all British 'pusher' aircraft as Vickers) over Bousbecque; it was the first of his two victories. An anti-aircraft battery, FkB336, also claimed to have brought down A34.

(The Royal Aircraft Factory F.E.2 was a two-seat pusher biplane that was operated as a day and night bomber and as a fighter aircraft by the Royal Flying Corps during the First World War)

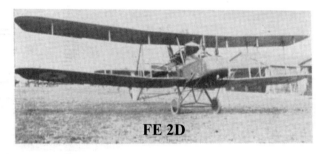

FE 2D

Sydney's younger brother **Stanley** had also enlisted for the duration of the war with the Army Service Corps but was discharged in March 1917 due to severe back problems.

Local girl Miss Hilda Newman married **Lieutenant Maurice H Wood** of the Royal Flying Corps at St Mary's Church Stansted. The Rev. E. Goodchild officiated. They had met when the bridegroom was billeted in the village whilst with the Lincolnshire Regiment. Unfortunately tragedy struck two months later when the groom lost his life on the Western Front. (See April 1917)

John King, a hay tier, of Bentfield End, Stansted, was summoned on an adjourned case for not sending his son to school regularly. His wife appeared and admitted it. Mr H.A. Levey, School Attendance Officer, stated that the boy was 11 years of age, and had not been to school since last November. He had seen Mrs King about it, and she replied that the boy was assisting his father with his work. The Magistrates Clerk read a letter from the defendant stating that as labour was so scarce, due to the amount of Stansted lads away at the front, he could not get anyone to help him and was obliged to have the boy stay away from school for that purpose. The boy, he said, was nearly 12, and was the eldest of six children. The Attendance Officer said the boy was not old enough for exemption. Supt Boyce stated that there was a previous conviction for a similar offence. On that occasion the defendant begged the sergeant to pay the fine for him, so that he did not have to go to prison, and the sergeant did so, but the defendant still owed the sergeant 4 shillings of the money. The Bench fined the defendant 10 shillings.

The death occurred at Bassein, India, of Mr Edwin Lawrence Read, chief officer in the British India Steamship Company, only son of the late Mr Read, and of Mrs E. R. Read, of Boldel, Stansted who succumbed after an operation on February 23rd 1917. The funeral took place at the Cemetery at Bassein, the burial being conducted by the Rev. C.W. Lyne. The captain of his ship and brother officers followed the Union Jack covered coffin and a large number of wreaths were laid upon the grave. The deceased who was in his 30th year, was educated at Perse School, Cambridge, and had for the previous 14 years been in the Merchant Service. Since the outbreak of war he had been engaged on useful and strenuous work for his country.

The only son of Mrs Sarah Elizabeth Bush, of 33 Rochford's Cottages, between Stansted and Birchanger, died on the 18th of this month. He was **Private John Henry Bush 31563, Essex Regiment 13th Battalion, Killed in Action 18th February 1917 aged 19.** John is commemorated on the Birchanger Memorial. He has no known grave and is remembered for his part on the Thiepval Memorial, France. **John** lost his life along with four others of his battalion.

John Henry Bush

Another brave soldier to lose his life this February 1917 was **Private William Nathan Fordham**. **William**, the son of William J. and Eleanor Fordham, was born at 75 The Cottage, Bentfield End, Stansted. His family later moved to Rickling Green and then on to Little Chesterford. **William's** name is not on the local memorial. His details are, **Private William Nathan Fordham 35190, Suffolk Regiment, 8th Battalion, Killed in Action 17th February 1917 aged 37.** His grave can be found at Regina Trench Cemetery, Grandcourt, Somme. Grave Ref VI. D. 3.

The actions in which **Private Fordham** was killed are from the Unit Histories, as follows.

The advance to Miraumont began on the 17th February with the attack being delivered at 5.45a.m. These operations, known officially as the actions of Miraumont, but euphemistically to the 8th Battalion as the Battle of Boom Ravine, were carried out under very trying conditions. The frozen ground had recently thawed converting it into a complete bog.

The battalion gained its objectives quickly in spite of stubborn fighting in front of the uncut wire. The battalion casualties for this action amounted to 130 with over 30 killed.

Private John Meadows, Middlesex Regiment, 11th Battalion, was wounded on the 6th of this same month. He suffered gun shot wounds to the right knee which subsequently led to his discharge later in October 1917. **Private Meadows** lived at 9 Brook Cottages, Stoney Common and was 35 years of age.

October also saw the enlistment of **Albert Francis Watson 234318**, age 31, of Mill Hill Cottage, who joined the Labour Corps 458th Employment Company. His service was all on the Home Front and he was invalided from service at the end of 1917.

Private Joseph Childs TR10/53746, 102nd Training Reserve Battalion, Middlesex Regiment, was discharged from service this month as suffering with a 'mental deficiency'. He was the brother of **Alfred Henry CHILDS** (see July 1917) and **Charles Childs** (see April 1917). His address is listed as Wilderness Lane, Burton End.

From his nephew I have been told that he suffered from *Shell Shock* and was treated at Severals Hospital in Colchester. Prior to the conflict he worked on a farm for Messrs Renfrew.

Shell Shock was a term used later during the Great War to describe the psychological trauma suffered by men serving on the war's key battlefronts. Sent home to recover, many shell shock victims recovered over time, whereas many others continued to feel its effects for years afterwards.

March 1917

We never knew what pain he had,
We never saw him die;
We only know he passed away,
And never said good-bye.

The March 1917 Roll of Honour memoriam (above) was in remembrance of Private **Joe DEBMAN** beloved son of Mr James and Mrs Lydia Debman, who lost his life in Belgium on 24th March 1917 aged 34 years. **Joe** had a brother Ernest and four sisters named Ethel, Florrie, Henrietta and Kate. Born in Stansted in 1882, his family lived in Bentfield End Stansted. **Joe** lived in Harlow and prior to enlisting worked as a groom to Mr A.S. Bowlby of Gilston Park.

Private JOE DEBMAN
(Royal West Kent Regiment),

Joe's grave at Dikkebusch Cemetery

Joe's details are as follows.
Private Joe DEBMAN G/18737
Queens Own Royal West Kent Regiment 11th Battalion
Killed in Action 24th March 1917 aged 34
Joe is buried at Dickebusch New Military Cemetery, Dikkebus Belgium. Grave ref AA.22. Dikkebus is a village situated south west of Ypres (Ieper).

From the battalion war diary we can find the action **Joe** was involved in on the day he was killed.

His battalion were in the Trenches and at 4.30p.m the enemy intensely bombarded the left of our line, chiefly with minethrowers, (minnenwerfer known to the Tommies as 'Minnies, probably the most disliked of all the bombs to which they were subjected in the sector) for two hours, effectually destroying it. A small raiding party came over at dusk but only succeeded in obtaining a wounded man's pay book. It is believed that this was part of a planned large raid and that our artillery was successful in dispersing the greater number of the raiders. They suffered twenty-one casualties from the bombardment, four O.R's (Other Ranks) killed, one officer and sixteen O.R's wounded.

Private Guy R. Bass, eldest son of Mr and Mrs H.H. Bass, of Alsa Lodge Farm, has been recommended by the Brigadier General and his commanding officer for a commission. During March 1917 he was at home on leave prior to joining an Officers Training Corps. Before the war **Private Bass** was with the Society of the Sacred Mission at Kelham College, Newark, in preparation for the ministry. Soon after the outbreak of war he joined the Queens Royal West Surreys and proceeded to France at Christmas 1915, being afterwards attached to the Machine Gun Corps. He was wounded in the hand by shrapnel in the Battles of the Somme last July. He also had a brother in France with the Army Service Corps, Mechanical Transport.

This month the marriage took place between **Private Percy R Church**, third son of Mr Phillip Church of Stansted, and Miss Constance Mary Wood. **Private Church**, who belongs to the Australian Forces, had seen service in Gallipoli and the Western Front.

Another Stansted soldier **Private L. Hammond**, Coldstream Guards, son of Mr W. Hammond, of the Recreation Ground, has been gazetted (noted in the London Gazette) 2nd Lieutenant in the Royal Warwickshire Regiment.

William Middleditch, a carman, and Edward Harbridge, a porter, both of Stansted, were summoned for gaming with dice on the licensed premises of the Barley Mow Inn, Chapel Hill, Stansted. The land lady had stated that she did not know gambling was going on, but that she had cautioned Middleditch about it before. In every public room in the house hung a printed notice 'Gambling is Prohibited'. Some people called the game they were playing 'Under and Over' and the soldiers called it 'The Mud Hook'. The defence stated that Middleditch held a position of responsibility and bore an excellent character and this was the first time he had been in trouble. He also said he knew nothing about the game until it was introduced to Stansted by the soldiers who were billeted in the village. The Bench said it was a serious thing to have gambling in licensed houses and the least they could do was to fine each of the defendants 14 shillings.

2nd Lieutenant Percy Frederick Finch, of the Honourable Artillery Company, eldest son of Mr and Mrs Frederick Finch, of Park Road, Stansted, was recently awarded the Military Cross. The supplement to the London Gazette of March 26th states that *'he led his men to the attack with great dash and succeeded in capturing his objective. He set a fine example of courage and determination throughout'*.

2nd Lieutenant Finch enlisted in the Honourable Artillery Company as a private and went to France in 1914. He was wounded at Hooge in 1915 and afterwards returned to England and was given a commission in his own Regiment. He received the ribbon this month but the Cross was not presented to him until his return home to England.

Percy Frederick Finch

One of many pubs in Stansted in 1915, the Barley Mow was converted to a private house in the 1960s. The writer states, 'This is one of the principal streets, about ten minutes' walk from the camp,' so he was clearly a soldier billeted nearby, perhaps on his way to the front. The high entrance steps were said to have been the downfall of many a patron at closing time.

Widespread sympathy was felt, this month, for Mr Harry and Mrs Mildred Chester, of Broom End, (at the time the Chester's were listed living in Birchanger but it is situated today within the boundaries of Stansted) in the death of their elder son, **Lieutenant Harry Keppel Chester**, of the Essex Regiment. The deceased officer was 22 years of age. He was educated first at Ludgrove, under Mr G.O. Smith, the well-known footballer and athlete. At the age of 13 he gained a third place in the scholarships at Eton. He remained at Eton until 19, and when he left was second captain of the school. In October 1913 he took the first place in the open scholarships at Kings College, Cambridge. He then joined the Officers Training Corps at Cambridge and had completed a year when the war broke out. He was then given a

Harry Keppel Chester

commission in the Essex Regiment, being gazetted full lieutenant. But it was represented to him and another young officer that such junior full lieutenants could not go on active service, and they both applied direct to the War Office and got themselves re-gazetted second lieutenants. **Lieutenant Chester** went with his battalion to Gallipoli in August 1915 and was only two days off duty the whole time. For some time while in Gallipoli he was acting captain in command of a company. At the evacuation of Gallipoli he went with his battalion to Egypt and in April 1916 was gazetted to full lieutenant. He came home on leave in September 1916 and returned to his Regiment in the following month.

Harry Keppel Chester's details are as follows, **Captain (posthumous commission) Harry Keppel Chester, Essex Regiment 1/5th Battalion, Died of Wounds 28th March 1917 aged 22.** His grave can be found at Deir El Belah War Cemetery, Israel, Grave Ref. C.80.

A bit more about **Chester** from the Unit history is as follows

*'The enemy continued to shell the Wadi, and we continued on our way by platoons. The leading platoon of 'A' company was caught by a shell which wounded Willmott, the company commander in the head, severely wounded C S M White and **Chester**, the platoon commander, and caused several other casualties among the rank and file. It also killed several of the Lewis gun mules. The guns and ammunition were off loaded and brought on by hand. Poor **Chester** died the next day, mourned by officers and men alike. He was never a barrack-square soldier, but probably had more brains than anyone else in the battalion, having had a brilliant career at Eton, which promised great things - alas, never to be realised. A little hesitating in his manner and careless in his outward appearance, he had nevertheless the heart of a lion and a true sympathy for his men which earned him alike their affection and their esteem'.*

Lieutenant Chester was an exceptionally good classical scholar and gained many prizes both at Eton and Kings College. He was keenly interested in social reform and in the Boy Scout movement and he had a very promising future.

Harry Keppel Chester is commemorated on the Birchanger Memorial.

On the 26th March the following soldier died of his wounds. He was **Private Christopher Miller**, the youngest son of Walter and Eliza Miller, of Brook Cottages, Stoneyfield Common. This area of Stansted was at the time part of the Civil Parish of Birchanger but today is part of Stansted. This is probably why **Private Miller** is not named on the Stansted Memorial, but is listed on the Birchanger Memorial, although **Walter Frederick GRAY** (see July 1916) who was living next door to him has his name inscribed on the memorial in Stansted. At the time the memorial was erected it was up to the families of the soldiers to decide whether they wanted the name inscribed or not.

Christopher Miller

Christopher's details are, **Private Christopher Miller 32376, Essex Regiment 11th Battalion, Died of Wounds on 26th March 1917 aged 22.** He is buried at Bethune Town Cemetery, France, Grave Ref VI.C.36. Bethune is situated twenty miles north of Arras.

He had four older brothers, William, **Jesse** (see August 1917), Charles and Bert, three of who were also serving, and two sisters Grace and Katie. **Christopher** originated from the village of Takeley and prior to enlisting in the army at Warley where he joined the Essex Regiment, he worked at Rochford's Nurseries.

On March 24th the battalion were involved in raiding enemy trenches. From the War Diary comes the probable actions in which **Private Miller** received his wounds.

Four companies, each with two officers and eighty other ranks took part in the operations with the object of taking two German positions on their first and second lines. Two waves of two companies each were formed, the first wave being assembled in our Front Line and the second wave in our Support Line. Each wave was commanded by a Company Commander in addition to the officers. Each wave advanced in two lines. Two Lewis Guns went with the first wave to guard flanks in 'No Man's Land' and three Lewis Guns went with the second wave to guard the flanks and centre. The tasks were for the first wave to take the first German Line and the second wave to take the second German Line passing over the first wave. A bombardment by Heavy Artillery and Trench Mortars prior to the attack had smashed up the enemy front and support trenches and the wire offered no obstacle to the assault. The 18 pounder barrage was excellent and all ranks had the utmost confidence in our Field Artillery. About an hour before zero-hour the enemy opened up upon our Front and Support lines, which were packed with men. Both these trenches were blown in in several places, causing nearly forty casualties including ten killed. The result of this was a certain amount of disorganisation which was quickly tackled by the young Officers and N.C.O's who throughout showed a magnificent spirit and this was reciprocated by their men. Zero hour came and both objectives were gained at the allotted times. The spirit of the Company Officers and Men who had been sitting in the trenches under heavy bombardment was splendid. At zero they were up and off like a pack of hounds. Very little resistance was encountered in the first line and the Germans that were there ran into dugouts and refused to come out. Their support line had been absolutely knocked in by our Heavy Artillery and there was no sign of life there.

April 1917

We think of him in silence, no eye can see us weep,
But even in our aching hearts, his memory we shall keep,
Not here but in a better land, some day we'll understand,
We never thought his time short in this world to remain.

Another of Stansted's gallant young soldier sons made the supreme sacrifice in April 1917. Private **Donald CARRUTHERS**, fourth son of Mr and Mrs William Carruthers, of Woodfields, Stansted, and nephew of Mr E. Carruthers, chairman of Bishop's Stortford Urban District Council. The deceased enlisted as a trooper in the Royal Bucks Hussars eighteen months previously, when he was a little over seventeen years old and was only 18 years and eleven months old at the time of his death.

On December 13th he and an intimate (sic) friend were transferred to the Oxford and Bucks Light Infantry and the following day proceeded to France.

Donald Carruthers

The sad news of his death was received by his parents in a letter from his friend. The letter written on Easter Sunday contained the following extracts: *"I regret to say that poor **Don** was shot through the throat during an attack on Good Friday. He passed peacefully away in my arms. We were both together at the time. Another man in front of us was shot through the leg. Our Captain was killed at the same time and in another company we lost four officers out of five.* (This as a statement cannot be confirmed as research shows only one officer of this battalion was killed). *The machine gun fire was terrific. Goodness only knows how I missed them, exhausted with the pack and marching. I had to crawl back. I cannot say whether Don will be buried by us or by the Germans, as he is between the lines, but we shall do it if at all possible".*

We know that **Donald** has no known grave so unfortunately his body was never recovered from no man's land on that awful day. His body would have remained between the lines and sadly that was to be his 'Hero's Grave'.

Two of **Donald's** brothers were also serving, namely **Private R. L. Carruthers**, Royal Army Medical Corps, who has been in France nearly two years. And **Second Lieutenant W.F. Carruthers**, London Regiment. The latter went through the campaign in German South West Africa and then volunteered for service in France, where he was wounded on September 15th. He has now recovered and returned to his regiment.

Donald's details are as follows
Private Donald CARRUTHERS 203455
Oxford and Bucks Light Infantry 2nd/4th Battalion
Killed in Action 7th April 1917 aged 18
Donald who as stated has no known grave is commemorated on the Thiepval Memorial to the Missing.

He was born in Stansted in 1898 and had older brothers named William, Roy and Keith. His parents were named William and Margaret and his father worked as a draper's assistant.

From the war diary it would appear that **Donald** was killed during the night between the 6th and 7th of April as his battalion attacked enemy trenches but without success. Eight other ranks including Donald were also killed.

Donald Carruthers

The battle of Arras ran from the 9th of April, through to the 16th May 1917. The Battle of Vimy Ridge was one of the opening battles of this offensive. It is also considered a major event in Canadian history for the primary role the Canadian Corps played in the attack.

On April 14th at Monchy-le-Preux the Essex 1st Battalion alongside the Royal Newfoundland Regiment, with the 2nd Hampshires and 4th Worcesters in support, prepared to attack the high ground to the east later known as Infantry Hill. The attack was launched at 5.30a.m under a 'creeping barrage', which was a slow moving artillery barrage acting as a defensive curtain fired over the heads of the infantry following closely behind. It commenced 200 yards from the enemy's front line and lifted 100 yards every four minutes. There were machine gun barrages on the flanks and four mobile machine guns also accompanied the assaulting troops. It was a misty morning, with the wooded ground wet and heavy from recent rain and snow. The 1st Essex rapidly advanced and within an hour was reported to be digging in and had taken a handful of prisoners. The Germans had retired from Shrapnel Trench as soon as the barrage had opened.

However when patrols were sent forward to ascertain the enemy position it was reported back that large masses of German troops could be seen, obviously preparing a counter attack. From that moment the situation rapidly became critical. Heavy enemy artillery fire had been opened up on Monchy, which was almost levelled within a few hours. The fighting was obstinate and men of the 1st Essex and Newfoundland suffered severely. Although practically destroyed as battalions their resistance broke the offensive of a German division. From 7.30a.m onwards no messages arrived at battalion headquarters nor did any more wounded report at the aid post. The truth was that the Essex had been annihilated. The Essex went into action with 31 officers and 892 other

ranks, of who at the end of the day 17 officers and 644 other ranks were reported to be either killed, wounded or missing. The Royal Newfoundlanders reported 487 casualties out of 591 officers and men employed.
Of the 203 Essex men who became prisoners very few were not wounded, and 16 of them later died in Germany. One hundred of the Newfoundlanders were taken prisoner and with the 203 Essex men this agreed with the official German statement that they had captured 300 on that bloodstained hill.

   Reuben LAW was one of those taken prisoner. Born in Ugley in 1887, the son of Reuben and Esther Law and was one of the 1st Essex, having enlisted in Saffron Walden, taken prisoner during the above attack and who subsequently died as a prisoner of war. He is listed as having been at Mulheim Ruhr which was a military hospital north of Dusseldorf.
Reuben had a brother George and sisters Ann, Esther, Charlotte and Lillian.
Rueben's details are as follows.
Corporal Reuben LAW 28790
Essex Regiment 1st Battalion
Died 24th April 1917 aged 29
He is buried in Cologne Southern Cemetery Germany. The cemetery lies within a large civil cemetery known locally as Koln Sudfriedhof and is about 3 miles south of the centre of Cologne, on the Honigerweg. It was used during the war for the burial of more than 1,000 Allied prisoners, as well as German servicemen.

Grave of Rueben Law

113

Another of Stansted's brave sons was taken prisoner during the same month, **Private G/43670 Charles Reuben Childs** son of Rueben and Lydia Childs was captured on 28th April in Oppy Wood on the Arras front and was taken to a Prisoner of war camp in Germany. He was serving with the Middlesex 17th Battalion, 'C' Company (Known as the 1st Football - Many professional football players, joined the 1st Football Battalion of the Middlesex Regiment.) when he was captured. His parents have since received communications from him stating he was well but he asked for food to be sent urgently. **Charles** elder brother **Arthur Henry CHILDS** (see July 1917) known as **Harry** lost his life a few months later. **Charles** was born in 1893 and was a Cowman by trade. After the war he mentioned the day he and a sergeant had to go out into no-

Charles Reuben Childs

mans land to bring back a wounded officer, he said that the sergeant was given an award but he received nothing.

The following is the entry taken from the 17th Battalion war diary the day that Charles was taken prisoner.

The battalion marched from Roclincourt on the evening of 27th and formed up in its battle formation on the front allotted, opposite the wood and village of Oppy. The forming up was carried out without hitch and in perfect silence in spite of the heavy shelling of the front area. The attached 2nd South Staffordshire Company formed up also in their respective places either as moppers up or strong point parties and the carrying parties also provided by the 2nd South Staffs formed up in the rear. They were in touch with the 13th Essex on the right and 2nd Highland Light Infantry on the left. The battalion was formed up on a four Company front and in three waves, each wave having its own Moppers up immediately behind it. The five Vickers guns attached to the battalion took posts, two behind the right flank and three behind the left flank of the last wave. These guns were allotted duties of covering the flanks during the advance until they should have reached the strong points which they were destined to garrison. The two Stokes mortars had instructions to move up behind the right flank. The order of Companies from right to left was 'D', 'C', 'A' and 'B'.

At 4.25a.m our barrage came down and at 4.33a.m the leading wave entered the enemy front line trench. The wire was found to be perfectly cut and the trench was practically empty. The battalion pressed forward behind the creeping barrage and the first objective was reached with only a few casualties. Shortly after the advance commenced the commanding officer of 'A' Company noticed that the battalion on our left had either lost touch or had been unable to make progress. He therefore placed a Lewis gun section and some bombers in the enemy front line trench with instructions to block the trench and prevent any movement by the enemy against the left flank. The right flank during the advance to the 1st objective appears to have kept well in touch with the 13th Essex. Fighting became much heavier on reaching the line of the first objective, very heavy machine gun and rifle fire being opened from the houses in the village. Capt Parfitt of 'D' Company had been specially charged with the consolidation of the first objective and this was taken in hand by the first wave, while the remainder pressed on to the second objective. Very heavy fighting now ensued on the right flank, but on the left the German trench running from north – south was reached. The fighting had now become so serious that both the 2nd and 3rd waves were fully involved in the struggle for the second objective while the first objective was still being consolidated. Up to this juncture reports from wounded men and reports by runner had been received confirming the capture of the first objective and of the struggle for the second objective, but owing to the hostile shelling all reports were somewhat late in making in reaching Battalion HQ and the situation on the left did not seem clear as although 'A' Coy were known to have gained ground, a report came in from the Highland Light Infantry on our left to the effect that they were hung up by fire in the Sunken Road in the neighbourhood of the Crucifix. A senior officer was now sent from Battalion HQ to clear up the situation on the left and to locate a suitable forward position for Battalion HQ to move to. It was now nearly 8.00a.m and a few minutes later a report came in from the officer in command of 'A' Company, the left Company, to say that the enemy was working round both his flanks. The only available reserve inside the battalion, namely the 'Moppers Up' of the 1st objective (who had reported the completion of this task) had already been sent forward to strengthen the right in the hope that the second objective might still be reached. Captain Edwards, the officer, who had been sent out to clear up the situation found that the enemy had pressed down in strength from the North both down the German front line trench and by the Crucifix Road on the flank of our two left Company's, and had driven them back through the wood to the enemy front trench. Here these two Companies were making a stand, but had by now maintained very heavy losses. The enemy also appears to have counter attacked against the front and right flank as well and had succeeded in re-entering the wood and getting in between the troops consolidating on the first objective and those who had been driven back to the Oppy Trench. The enemy had also worked up the Oppy Trench from the south and were bombing up from that direction also. All communication with the remnants of the troops in the 1st Objective was now cut off and runners who attempted to get through to the troops still holding the Oppy Trench were either killed or wounded.

Lieutenant Colonel Martin, 13th Essex Regiment commanding, sent forward a Company of 1st Royal Berkshires to endeavour to relieve the situation, but they could not get beyond the OB line. The remnants of the two Companies still holding onto Oppy Trench finally exhausted all their bombs and when reduced to about ten men all told made a dash for the OB line. One officer and three men succeeded in getting through. The troops on the first objective were not heard of again until a wounded officer with news succeeded in making his way back during the night. His evidence made it clear that these troops had fought till they were practically exterminated by the superior pressure of the enemy; the few survivors surrendered. The few remaining men of the battalion with some of the Staffs carrying party remained for the rest of the day in the OB line until relieved at night by the 23rd Royal Fusiliers.

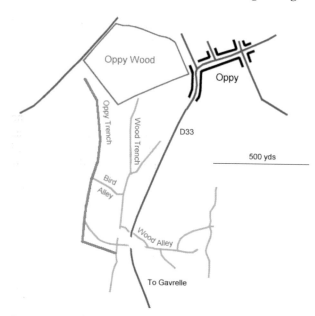

Of the troops that went over the top that morning only one officer and forty-one unwounded men eventually found their way back. Three wounded officers and 106 wounded other ranks were able to get back in the early stages of the fight. Had the flanks remained secure it is believed that the first objective could have been held against counter attack and possibly the second objective would have been gained in its entirety. In view of the strength of the enemy in the village, this was doubtful.

As it was, the sudden onrush of the enemy from both flanks combined with their vigorous counter-attacks was disastrous and it enabled them to re-occupy the wood. In the confused nature of the fighting it was impossible to know where to ask for fresh artillery barrages to be placed.

This was now the end of the fighting for **Private Charles Childs** as he was to spend the rest of the conflict as a prisoner of war, which was perhaps fortunate for him as over one hundred and thirty of his 17th Middlesex battalion comrades lost their lives on this fateful day.

Letters were also received this same month stating that two Stansted soldiers had been seriously wounded. **Private George Arthur Amey**, Northampton Regiment, of Bentfield End (son of the late Mr Joseph Amey), has been wounded in his back/hip and is now in the Countess of Lyttleton Hospital in London. He spent 15 days in hospital before being moved to a convalescent home.

Lance-Corporal Harry Turner, Queens Royal West Surrey's, of 1 Clarence Villas, Cambridge Road had been wounded in the thigh and was in hospital in France. He was the son of the late Mr James Turner, of Vicarage Cottage, and of Mrs Turner of Clarence Villas. Harry was gardener to Mr E. L. Burton, of Spencer Close, and having joined up in June 1916, proceeded to France in November. This was the second time **Private Turner** had been wounded.

Mrs Turner has four other sons serving, namely, **Bombardier George Turner** Royal Field Artillery, who was severely wounded in September 1916 but later returned to duty, **Gunner Thomas Turner** also with the Royal Field Artillery, **Private Archie Turner** Devon Regiment and **Private Herbert James Turner** who was serving with the Middlesex Regiment.

Another brave soldier with a connection to the village who lost his life on 9th April 1917 was **Thomas George Stacke**. **Thomas** is not named on the village memorial but his details are as follows. **Private Thomas George Stacke 6269, Canadian Infantry, Western Ontario Regiment, Killed in Action 9th April 1917 aged 23**. He was the son of Mr and Mrs Stacke, of Rose Cottages, Bentfield End, Stansted.

Thomas was born on 31st January 1894 and joined the Canadian Expeditionary Force on 31st August 1914.

Thomas's name can be found on the Vimy Memorial.

The Vimy Memorial overlooks the Douai Plain from the highest point of Vimy Ridge, about five miles northeast of Arras on the N17 towards Lens. The memorial is signposted from this road to the left, just before you enter the village of Vimy from the south. The memorial itself is someway inside the Memorial Park, but again it is well signposted.

After the war, the highest point of the ridge was chosen as the site of the great memorial to all Canadians who served their country in battle during the First World War, and particularly to the 60,000 who gave their lives in France.

Vimy bears the names of 11,000 Canadian servicemen who died in France - many of them in the fight for Vimy Ridge - who have no known grave.

Henry William Sanford

Three more brave soldiers with a Stansted connection lost their lives during this month of April, the first two (**Private Henry William Sanford** and **Private Harold Charles Childs**) mentioned are remembered on the Birchanger Memorial.

The first of these was **Private Henry William Sanford**, son of **Henry** and Edith Sanford. **Henry** was born in Stansted in 1884 and had four brothers Albert, Arthur, Edward and Leonard and four sisters Alice, Annie, Florence and Minnie. Prior to enlisting, at Saffron Walden in June 1916, he had been employed at Messrs Rochford's Nurseries.

Henry's details are as follows, **Private Henry William Sanford 28386, Northamptonshire Regiment 7th Battalion, formerly 31208 Suffolk Regiment, Killed in Action 8th April 1917.** He is buried in Aix-Noulette Communal Cemetery Extension which is situated about eight miles south of Bethune on the main road to Arras.

Henry had been reported to have been killed by a German sniper on Easter Sunday.

From the War Diary for this day we find the following – *A fine day. Our artillery shelled the enemy heavily all day. The enemy retaliated at intervals during the night.* The diary makes no mention of casualties but as it was reported that **Henry** had been killed by sniper fire we must assume that this happened some time during the day.

Private Harold Charles Childs, son of Arthur and Martha Childs, of 46 Stoney Common, Stansted, was the second of the three to be killed, losing his life just days before his twenty first birthday. He was born in London in 1894 and the family later moved to Elsenham. Harold had brothers named Arthur and Victor and a sister Beatrice. **Harold's** details are as follows, **Private Harold Charles Childs 19300, Essex Regiment 11th Battalion, Killed in Action 18th April 1917 aged 20.** Harold's grave can be found in Philosophe British Cemetery, Mazingarbe. Philosophe lies between Bethune and Lens.

Harold was killed by the explosion of an enemy's shell which buried him in his dugout. It was described in the battalion war diary thus – At 2.00a.m on the 18th a party of 1st Leicester's raided German trenches opposite our Left Front Company and captured one prisoner.

Harold Charles Childs

Our casualties from the retaliation were two killed and one wounded. Sadly **Harold** would have been one of the two killed from the retaliatory shellfire from the enemy. Details found in the local newspaper were as follows, found under the title of 'Stansted Soldier Killed by a Shell' –

News has been received by Mr and Mrs Arthur Childs, of 46 Rochford's Cottages, of the death on the Western Front through the bursting of an enemy's shell, by which he was buried in his dugout, of their son **Private Harold Childs**, Essex Regiment. The deceased soldier who was within a few days of his 21st birthday, had been in the Army two years, for the last six months he had been engaged as a stretcher bearer. In civilian life he was employed at Messrs Gold Bros.' Nurseries at Elsenham. Writing home to the deceased's mother, his captain says, in the course of his letter - *"Your son was killed last night and it has filled us all with the greatest grief. He was killed instantly by a shell, so did not suffer at all. He was an excellent soldier and one of the most popular men in the company. He was buried in a cemetery nearby".*

Finally this month Stansted lost another of its sons with the death in action of **Private Alfred William Henderson**, of Lower Street, Stansted, son of Mr Frederick Henderson, and son-in-law of Mrs Ridgewell, of Isolation Hospital-lane, Saffron Walden. He was first reported as missing but was subsequently reported as being killed in action on April 28th. **Private Henderson** was formerly in the service of Lord Peel and afterwards employed at Messrs Rochford's nurseries at Birchanger, then for the previous two years was the Prudential agent for Stansted. He joined up in October 1916 and went to France on January 1st 1917. He had only been there three weeks when he was granted leave to return home for a few days (he returned to France on January 26th) his wife Fanny having been taken ill and removed to an institution where she was still a patient at the time of her husband's death.. Alfred had two children aged five and one month.

Alfred's details are as follows, **Private Alfred William Henderson, 32349 Essex Regiment 13th Battalion, Killed in Action 28th April 1917 aged 32.** He has no known grave and is remembered on the Arras Memorial Ref Bay 7.

Alfred was born in Poplar and enlisted in Saffron Walden where he joined the Essex Regiment. For whatever reasons **Alfred's** name is, surprisingly not found on the Stansted Memorial.

Details from the war diary for the 28th are as follows. (Also see the 17th Middlesex Battalion war diary, earlier in this chapter)

At 2.00a.m. the battalion were formed up in their jumping off positions without any hitch in spite of heavy shelling. Companies were organised into three platoons, one platoon of each company representing the first 3 waves each wave consisting of two lines. The first line was bombers and riflemen and the second line with lewis gunners and rifle bombers. Moppers up for each wave were formed up in the rear of its second line. Carrying parties and garrison for strong points were formed up in rear of the last wave. An enemy trench was gained with the Highland Light Infantry, the 17th Middlesex and the Royal Marine Light Infantry. At 4.25a.m our own barrage started and at 4.38a.m the first wave crossed the enemy's front line trench. The extreme right of the battalion was held up by uncut wire and lost heavily from machine gun fire in endeavouring to get through it. At this period touch was entirely lost with the Royal

Marine Light Infantry on our right. It was maintained between the 13th Essex and 17th Middlesex but was lost with the Highland Light Infantry who were on the left of the 17th Middlesex. At this point a party of German bombers attacked our right flank. Heavy machine gun fire and rifle fire took place from Oppy village and large numbers of the enemy were advancing down the Sunken Road at the Crucifix. At 5.50a.m the 17th Middlesex were heavily attacked and large numbers of the enemy advanced through Oppy Wood and reoccupied part of the German front line. A senior officer was sent forward to clear up the situation about 7.30a.m but did not return, and no messages were received from him. The heavy fighting continued and at 9.00a.m the troops were ordered to fall back, hold and consolidate the German front line. Small detached parties only succeeded in doing this and were unable to cope with the enemy who were then holding the trench. All the officers of this battalion had become casualties and the majority of the non-commissioned officers and what was left of the battalion was quite disorganised and exhausted. Small parties held out but eventually retired to the old British line running from shell hole to shell hole at dusk. Over 120 soldiers of the 13th Essex were killed in action during the fighting on this day.

The husband (see February 1917) of Mrs Hilda Wood (nee Newman) was killed this month whilst serving with the Royal Flying Corps. His Details are as follows **Lieutenant Maurice Herbert Wood, Royal Flying Corps 59th Squadron** (formerly 4th Lincolnshire Regiment) **Killed in Action 13th April 1917. Maurice's** name can be found on Arras Flying Services Memorial. The Memorial commemorates nearly 1,000 airmen of the Royal Naval Air Service, the Royal Flying Corps, and the Royal Air Force, either by attachment from other arms of the forces or by original enlistment, who were killed on the whole Western Front and who have no known grave.

Maurice Herbert Wood

Lieutenant Wood was flying as observer in RE 8 A3190 of No 59 Squadron, piloted by Capt James Maitland Stuart (formerly 1st Battalion, Royal Inniskilling Fusiliers), as escort to a photographic reconnaissance mission when they were shot down near Vitry-Brebieres on 13th April 1917. The enemy victory over aircraft A3190 was credited to Rittmeister Manfred von Richthofen of Jasta 11; it was the 41st of his eventual 80 kills.

The 13th April (in the month known as 'Bloody April' to the Royal Flying Corps) was a terrible day for No 59 Squadron. The unit, based at La Bellevue aerodrome at the time, lost 5 aeroplanes, with all 10 crew members being killed.

Lieutenant Wood is commemorated on the Stamford School War Memorial and the main town memorial. Prior to the war he was a "master" at Stamford Grammar School having been educated at London University.

He landed with the 4th Lincolnshire Regiment in March 1915, and was promoted and mentioned in despatches during his time at the front. On 27th April 1917 the Stamford Mercury newspaper records him as appearing on a wounded list but in October 1917 the newspaper carried an article recording the changing of his status from missing to killed.

At this point we will re-visit the memoirs of **Sidney Patmore** as sometime during this month the following occurred, in **Sidney's** words.

At an observation post in France I was with an officer, I was sitting by the telephone, when a Sergeant came into the shack and said "the army commander to see you" and in stepped Lieutenant General Sir Julian "Bungo" Byng (pictured left) (Lord Byng of Vimy), he spoke to the officer and looked through his binoculars at the German positions, then went on his way. He didn't know that one of his ex Boy Scouts and golf caddy was huddled beside the telephone. I told the officer about it, but of course a private soldier cannot approach a General, anyway it was an interesting encounter knowing I had caddied for him on the Stansted Golf Links about eight years earlier.

When I was at an observation post with an officer we were on equal terms and would talk about anything (between messages) except it would be "yes sir" or "no sir". The officers were very good. One thing made an impression on me, it was on Easter Monday 1917, the Battle of Arras, when in the morning I watched the Bengal Lancers go by on their beautiful horses, but a day or two later, I saw a lot of them dead in front of the old barbed wire. I thought back to my brother Alf (**Alfred PATMORE** May 1915) lying in a grave. My first Christmas in France was spent digging cable trenches for the Royal Engineers, in Delville Wood on the Somme front.

I remember being sent on a refresher course at a signalling school and just before it finished I contracted scabies, this was due to filthy conditions and lice. I was sent to a hospital in Doulens, the treatment was to scrub the patches with a stiff brush and rub in a blue ointment. The rest and the food were very acceptable. In the next bed to me was a German prisoner and he was treated the same as us. We used to play cards and draughts together. I went to 3 rest camps whilst I was in France, they were Ambleteuse, Wimereux, and St Valery-sur-Somme, these were well known resorts.

I shall always remember my old chum Sid Naylor and the way we first met, he was a signaller and had been sent out as a reinforcement, we were sitting in an old barn and started to talk to each other, asking where each came from, he was from Hull. After a while he undid a parcel he had brought from home and produced a large pork pie, he cut me a large chunk, it seemed like a miracle as army rations were eight men to a loaf. From then on we looked after each others personal belongings when one of us was on duty. We had each others home addresses so if anything unpleasant happened , like wounded or killed, one could write home to wife or mother. But I am happy to say we survived. These are some of the places we had Battery positions in, Sailly-au-Bois, Albert, Bouzincourt, Arras, Messines, Ypres, Mailly Maillet, Beaulencourt, Haulchin Maing, Aulnoy, Saultain, Valenciennes and Mons. One unpleasant job I think about was when a telephone line was broken by shellfire, lines were often laid on the ground over fields, but were put on poles over roads. To find the break you picked up the line in your hand at the Battery or Observation post and walked along until you found the break, we had a torch but only used it when absolutely necessary in case of drawing fire from the enemy. I always dreaded it in case I fell on top of a dead body as they often lay about for a long time and the stench was awful.

Private Harry Turner 40245, Queen's Royal West Surrey Regiment, aged 29, returned home during April 1917 after suffering severe gun shot wounds to his right thigh. He lived at Clarence Villas, Cambridge road, Stansted and was married to Minnie and they had one daughter, Evelyn. In December 1917 he was discharged due to his wounds. He had seen action on the western front between the months of December 1916 and April 1917. Prior to enlisting **Harry Turner** was employed as a gardener.

May 1917

The stately ships sail on,
Far away over the hill,
But oh for the touch of a vanished hand,
And the sound of a voice that is still.

News reached the village of Stansted that **Frederick Alfred MUMFORD**, son of Mr Arthur and Mrs Salome Mumford, of Water Lane Stansted, had been killed in action. Known as **Alfred** his details are as follows

Private Frederick Alfred MUMFORD 19224
East Surrey Regiment 1ˢᵗ Battalion
Killed in action 8ᵗʰ May 1917 aged 19

He has no known grave and his name is commemorated on the Arras Memorial. The Arras Memorial is in the Faubourg-d'Amiens Cemetery, which is in the Boulevard du General de Gaulle in the western part of the town of Arras. The cemetery is near the Citadel, approximately a mile due west of the railway station.

Alfred was born in Stansted in 1898. He had four brothers Arthur, Harry, James and John, and two sisters, Alice and Kate. At the time of enlisting **Alfred** was living in Wandsworth Surrey and joined the 1ˢᵗ Battalion of the East Surrey Regiment.

The following is an account of the action **Alfred** was taking part in when he met his death.

A good deal of rain fell during the night of the 7ᵗʰ/8ᵗʰ May 1917 and more the following morning. As dawn appeared, the Germans delivered a strong attack on the village of Fresnoy but three times in the space of two hours were beaten off by the machine guns and rifles of the East Surreys and Gloucester's. The enemy fire then abated for a while and it appeared they may have given up attempts to take the village, when, at 6.30a.m an intense bombardment burst on the whole of the left flank (which the East Surreys were helping to hold) followed by an infantry assault. Due to the heavy rain at the time and a thick mist the S.O.S. signals were not seen by any of our gunners. A little later the East Surreys, on the right of the 95ᵗʰ Brigade, were attacked and their left flank was being exposed. They were compelled to fall back to the trenches east of Arleux and then reserve troops were sent up, but by this time the Germans were firmly in control of the village.

A counter attack was planned where the wood and village of Fresnoy were to be attacked on the evening of the 8ᵗʰ and the original line to be re-established. The East Surreys, part of the 95ᵗʰ Brigade were to be in the centre line of attack with the 13ᵗʰ Infantry brigade on the right and the 2ⁿᵈ Canadian Division on the left. The advance was to be made under a cover of creeping barrage of artillery but the assault was broken up by enemy artillery fire as it was assembling and the planned attack was put off until the following day.

Over one hundred of the East Surrey 1ˢᵗ Battalion lost their lives, along with **Alfred** on this day in May.

123

At the Stansted Petty Sessions this month.

Charles Gray, innkeeper, of Henham, was summoned for permitting George Luckey to consume intoxicating liquor on his licensed premises after the hours of 9.00p.m and George Luckey was also summoned for consuming the liquor during prohibited hours. Both defendants were each fined £2 and 10shillings and sixpence costs.

On the 12th May **Captain Percy Herbert Burton** the brother of Ernest L. Burton of Spencer House, Stansted, died of wounds received the same day. He was aged 49 years and served in the Royal Army Medical Corps. He is remembered on the Arras Memorial.

His details are, **Captain Percy Herbert Burton, Royal Army Medical Corps and Royal Fusiliers 2nd/4th Battalion, Died of Wounds 12th May 1917 aged 49**. He was the son of Joseph and Eliza Sarah Burton and the husband of Minnie Emma.

Harry White 10724, 11th Essex Regiment, was listed as wounded this month. **Private White** had joined the overseas campaign in the August of 1915.

Private James Carter, the son of Thomas and Agnes Carter, of Woodfields, Stansted, was killed in action during this month. His details are, **Private James Carter 149975, Labour Corps 5th Company, killed in action on 23rd May 1917, aged 22 years.** Prior to joining the Labour Corps he was serving with the Norfolk Regiment. He has no known grave and is commemorated on the Arras Memorial to the Missing. **James's** name, like a few others, was not put forward to be included on the Stansted Memorial.

June 1917

We shall never forget him, though his grave we can't attend,
But think of him always, more or less to the end.
God sent him and lent him us, for a short time,
By walking in faith we shall meet him again.

Private George W Bonney, brother of **Albert E BONNEY** (see July 1916), was listed as missing in June 1917. No news of his death is recorded so it appears he would have become a prisoner of war in Germany. (See July 1917)

The casualty lists for this same month contained, among the officers killed in action, the name of **Captain Joseph William Mayersbeth** of the Australian Infantry. Captain Mayersbeth was an ex-scholar of Stansted Church of England School and was brought up by Mrs F. Bedlow of Stansted. **Joseph's** details are as follows, **Captain Joseph William Mayersbeth, Australian Infantry 48th Battalion, Killed in Action on 12th June 1917 aged 25 years.** His name like so many others can be found on the Menin Gate. A year prior to his death **Joseph**, as a Lieutenant, had a court martial against him for drunkenness and fighting with a private. For this he was reprimanded but his conduct must have improved somewhat as he went on to become a Captain. An extract from the diary of Captain G.D. Mitchell MC, D.C.M., 48th Battalion was as follows.

At the time of writing they were in the vicinity of Messines. *"June 12th. I soon discovered a concrete blockhouse and dived in. There were several bunks in it. Soon I was on one and sound asleep. The other company officers were in the adjoining one. Many shells landed outside. The blast shook the place. Then the tragedy happened. Captain Mayersbeth dashed in with blood pouring from a hole in his chest. An artery had been cut and there was no possible compression point. I pressed on top of the wound, and the bleeding went on internally. He was doomed. He knew it and said so. I knew it and could not deny it. Such futility would not be right. He said goodbye to his wife, Goodbye to his boys. He asked for absolution, recited a prayer and died like a brave man.*
Night came. We buried the Captain and another man who had been killed".

As it states that they buried **Joseph** it was most likely his grave was lost in subsequent actions as today he has no known grave.

A number of children and their parents and others, all living in the Stoney Common area, were summoned for stealing and receiving wood stakes, the property of H.M. War Department. The names of the defendants were as follows: Edward Roberts, 12, and William Roberts, 9, schoolboys, and their father Griffith Roberts; Gladys Reed, 12, Edward Reed, 9, school-children, and James Reed, their father; Kathleen Sugars, 13, school-girl, and widow Elizabeth Sugars, her mother; Ellen Jackson, 13, school-girl, and Clara Turner, 26, married woman; Ethel Watson, 13, school-girl, and Ellen Watson, 40, her mother; Rosie Jackson, 11, school-girl; Ellen Mitcham, 50, married woman.

Lieutenant Davey appeared to prosecute on behalf of H.M. War Department. Sergeant Tucker made enquiries and visited a number of persons where the children told him they had taken them from the Camp Field, but most felt there was no harm in taking them. Some said the soldiers had told them to pick up pieces of the broken wood and take them home to their mothers and the children naturally did so. Philip Richards of the Royal Engineers identified the wood as the property of the War Department, and said it had been used in the North Stable field. On being charged the children admitted taking the wood, but the parents denied receiving it knowing it to have been stolen. Lieutenant Davey said the authorities had no wish to press the case against the children, but they particularly wanted the pilfering from these stables stopped. The Chairman said, having regard to what the Military Representatives had said, the Bench decided that the children be bound over for six months. As to the parents receiving the wood, the Bench looked upon it as a serious matter and fined the adults 5 shillings and 15 shillings each.

Private Charles Stansfield 27786, Essex Regiment, was listed among the wounded soldiers. Later in the war he joined the Royal Army Medical Corps.

Private Samuel Richard Clarke 41314, Royal Irish Rifles 10th Battalion, was accidentally wounded on the 25th June 1917. Whilst holding the line he came out of the orderlies dug out when one of the corporal's in the dug out who had picked up a German hand grenade and whilst examining it accidentally pulled the button out. A piece of shell went into **Private Clarke's** thigh. He was taken to Bailleul where the shrapnel was removed and then onto Boulogne. Prior to the war he was a footman at Stansted Hall. The wound had ended **Samuel's** service as he was discharged later in November.

Details of another teenage soldier connected to the village who died of wounds are as follows. **Private Charles Frank Shaw 36863, Machine Gun Corps (Infantry), died of wounds 25th June 1917, aged 19.** He was the son of Mr and Mrs F.E. Shaw, of Rochford's Nurseries.

July 1917

The dearest place on earth to him was
'Home, Sweet Home,'
He's now at rest, his work well done,
'In Home, Sweet Home'.

Arthur Henry (Harry) Childs

Five of Stansted's brave soldiers lost their lives during July 1917, the first was **Harry Childs**.

Mr and Mrs Rueben Childs, of Burton End Stansted, received information that their eldest son Private **Harry (Arthur Henry) Childs**, Essex Regiment, had fallen in action on the Western Front. A friend in the same company stated that he was killed by a shell adding *"He was respected by all his mates all of whom send their sympathy"*.

Harry joined the army, enlisting in Saffron Walden, in March 1916 and left for the front about three months later. In civilian life he had been employed by Mr Wm. Page, of Bury Lodge Farm and formerly by Mr J.W. Bolton, then of Bassingbourne Hall Farm. His brother **Charles Childs** became a prisoner of war (see chapter April 1917).

Harry was born in Stansted in 1887 and had two other brothers George and **Joseph** (see February 1917), he also had four sisters Susan, Ethel, Lavinia and Minnie.

Harry's details are as follows.
Private Arthur Henry (Harry) Childs 26995
Essex Regiment 2nd Battalion
Killed in action 8th July 1917 aged 30
His grave can be found in Happy Valley British Cemetery, Fampoux, France. Fampoux is a small village about 5 miles east of Arras. The cemetery is named after a long valley which runs eastward from Orange Hill where British troops fought their way during early April 1917.

The war diary states that on the day of **Harry's** death they were *in the reserve position* and gives us no additional information regarding the circumstances of his death.

Grave of Arthur Henry Childs

Three soldiers who were together in the Northamptonshire Regiment were officially reported as missing since another battle on the Western Front on July 10th. They were **Private Archer Monk**, (brother of **William MONK**) of Lower Street, Stansted, **Private Frederick Charles TURNER** also of Lower Street and **Private Wheeler** of Manuden whose elder brother Reginald (Killed in action on 17th February 1917 serving with the 11th Battalion of the Rifle Brigade) was killed in action some time ago. All three were just nineteen years of age. **Privates Monk** and **Wheeler** were formerly employed at Messrs Green's Stores and **Private Turner** was with his father in business in Lower Street. A letter from an officer of the regiment suggested that as all the men in their platoon were missing they may have been taken prisoners.

Unfortunately this was not the case for **Frederick TURNER** as he was killed during the actions of that day, July 10th 1917.

Those actions, known as The Battle of Nieuport or Battle of the Dunes, were as described below (courtesy of Chris Baker's Long Long Trail Website).

Nieuport Memorial

F.C. Turner

On the 6 July 1917, the Marines Korps Flandern began a desultory artillery bombardment, which continued for the next three days. Fog and low cloud prevented detection of the German build-up. Then, at 5.30am on the 10th July, the massed German artillery, including three 24cm naval guns in shore batteries, and 58 artillery batteries (planned naval gunfire support from destroyers and torpedo-boats was cancelled), opened up on the British positions. Mustard gas (Yellow Cross *) was used for the first time in the barrage.

* During the First World War, a yellow cross was painted on gas shells to identify their contents. Yellow cross gas shells contained the volatile liquid dichlorethyl sulphide, more commonly known as the blistering mustard gas. Although it had a death rate of just one or two percent, the gas was considered an effective weapon because it usually disabled rather than killed outright. Panicking and incapacitated soldiers are more of a hindrance to the enemy then dead ones.

All but one of the bridges over the Yser River were demolished, isolating the 1ˢᵗ Battalion Northamptonshire and 2ⁿᵈ King's Royal Rifle Corps. Telephone communication was also cut. The German bombardment continued throughout the day. The British artillery attempted a counter-barrage but several guns were knocked out and the German infantry were well protected. At 8.00p.m, the Marines Korps launched the infantry assault, by which time the two British battalions had suffered 70-80% casualties. The German Stormtroopers attacked down the coast, outflanking the British. Their attack was then followed by waves of German Marines, supported by flamethrower teams to mop up dugouts. After a gallant defence, the British battalions were overwhelmed. Only 4 officers and 64 other ranks managed to reach the west bank of the river Yser. Nearly eighty other ranks were killed during this action.

Frederick's details are as follows,
Private Frederick Charles TURNER 27723
Northamptonshire Regiment 1ˢᵗ Battalion 'D' Company
Killed in action 10ᵗʰ July 1917 aged 19
Frederick's body was never found and he is remembered on the Nieuport Memorial, Nieuport, West Vlaanderen, Belgium.

The following statement found in the war diary summed up the days events in which **Frederick** was killed. *This was a disastrous day of intense enemy shelling on all areas. The advance Companies of the King's Royal Rifle Corps and Northampton's had been moved into a network of trenches and posts on the east bank of the broad estuary of the River Yser. The only way of crossing was by one of a few narrow plank bridges. The enemy first cut off all communication with these exposed positions by laying down a very heavy curtain of artillery fire, then advancing in strength using bombs. The enemy action was completely successful and it virtually wiped out all British troops on that side of the river.*

Mrs Annie Banks, of Stansted received official news from the War Office, that her husband, Private **Edward BANKS**, had been killed in action in France on July 26ᵗʰ. Until recently they had been living in Allens Green, Sawbridgeworth, the deceased having in civilian life been employed as gamekeeper to Mr G.S. Streeter, of Thorley.

He was born in Birchanger in 1879. He was the eldest son of James and Harriet Banks. He had six sisters, Edith, Jane, Kate, Elizabeth, Ellen and Eva. He also had two younger brothers Thomas and Harry. In 1901 he was living in Bishop's Stortford and working as a gamekeeper, he enlisted in Sawbridgeworth, where he joined the Bedfordshire Regiment.

Edward's details are as follows,
Private Edward BANKS 202698
Bedfordshire Regiment 2ⁿᵈ Battalion
Killed in action 26ᵗʰ July 1917 aged 38

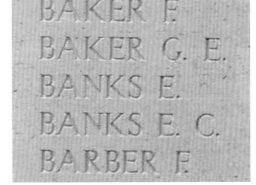

Edward's name can be found on the Menin Gate, Ypres, Belgium. Panel 31 and 33. **Edward** was killed in action during the Third Battle of Ypres, his battalion were involved in the line at Zillebeke and reserve at Chateau Segard which are south east of Ypres. The 2nd Yorkshire Regiment and the 18th Manchester Regiment carried out raids in front of this sector with successful results.

Edward's battalion suffered casualties of eleven killed and nineteen wounded and we must assume that Edward was among one of those, it was possible he was killed whilst returning to Chateau Segard under the command of Company Sergeant Major R.Kirby as this party were knocked out by an enemy shell near Bedford House and six men were killed and five died of wounds.

On the last day of July Stansted soldier **William Thomas MONK**, (brother of **Archer Monk**, who was missing – mentioned earlier in this month) son of Mr and Mrs George Monk, of Lower Street, Stansted, was killed in action.

Private William Thomas Monk
Killed in Action

Private Archer Monk
Missing

The parents of the Monk brothers received letters from officers of both their regiments speaking in high terms of their sons, both of whom were Lewis gunners, and extremely keen and efficient.

William's details are as follows
Private William Thomas MONK 36407
Royal Berkshire Regiment 6th Battalion 'C' Company.
Killed in Action 31st July 1917 aged 26.

Like many of our brave soldiers **William** has no known grave and his name is inscribed on the wall (Panel 45) of the Menin Gate.

William was born in Stansted in 1891. His father George worked as an Engine Driver, his mother was named Selina and he had a brother called Archer and a sister named Ida. In 1901 they were all living at 71 Bentfield End before moving to Lower Street in Stansted.

MAY P.
MEARS H.
MEARS S.E.
MILLS F. J.
MONK W. T.
MOORE B.
MORRIS P.C.
MOTH F. J.

From the War Diary of the 6th Royal Berkshire Regiment we can learn more about the circumstances of **William's** death.

Battalion were in position at Zillebeke.

At 3.05a.m. the battalion reported present in the assembly area. A message was sent to Brigade Headquarters to this effect.

At 3.50a.m. - Zero hour.

At 5.00a.m. The Brigade reported that the Blue line had been captured.

5.50a.m. - Patrols under the command of 2nd Lieutenants H.R. Hooper and G.H. Tigar were sent forward to get in touch with 17th Manchesters.

At 6.50a.m. The Black line was unofficially reported as being captured.

At 7.15a.m. The battalion moved from the assembly area in Artillery formation towards forming up the line.

At 8.30a.m. The battalion were passing through Sanctuary Wood. Fairly heavy machine gun fire and artillery barrage was directed against the battalion. No Manchester's were met up to this point and the captured trenches did not appear to be garrisoned.

At 8.45a.m. The Jackdaw Reserve Trench was reached. Owing to enemy machine gun fire from Ypres Menin Road and Surbiton Villas the battalion advance paused. The advance resumed and the line of the Ypres-Menin road was made good.

At 9.00a.m. The attack on the Black line determined on and was commenced by rushes under cover of rifle and machine gun fire.

At 9.50a.m. In spite of strong opposition and without assistance from our own Artillery which was unaware of the situation the line at Jargon Switch and Surbiton Villas was captured. Touch was gained with the Lincolns.

At 10.10a.m. A British barrage opened behind the line of resistance holding up the battalion. Efforts to advance were stopped by rifle and machine gun fire from the Jargon Trench Line.

At 10.30a.m. A Consolidation of the line at Jargon Switch, East of Surbiton Villa, enabled touch to be made with the Suffolk's.

The work of consolidation was very difficult owing to hostile machine gun fire and aeroplane's dropping bombs on the troops consolidating.

At 3.00p.m. The enemy were seen massing for a counter attack in Glencorse Wood. An S.O.S. barrage was called for and Artillery opened fire and the attack did not materialize.

The remainder of day was fairly quiet but the enemy kept up continuous shell fire on the

consolidated troops and Battalion Headquarters on Ypres Menin Road.
At 8.30p.m. Orders for relief were received. Details were arranged direct with the
battalion with relief orders attached.
At 12.00 midnight the relief commenced and was completed at 2.50a.m on August 1st.
The battalion then withdrew to Dickebusch.

William along with over fifty of his comrades, were killed in action on this day.

An article, at the time, about the two brothers appeared in the local *Herts and Essex Observer*, it was as follows.

ONE SON KILLED, ANOTHER MISSING.

Mr and Mrs George Monk, of Lower Street, have during the last few days received sad news with regard to both their sons. Their younger son, **Private Archer Monk 27740**, was in the Northamptonshire Regiment, and he has been missing since the battle on the Western Front on July 10th, when his regiment suffered heavy casualties. A letter received form a Lieutenant in his regiment read as follows:

*"Dear Mrs Monk,- I am very sorry to have to tell you that your son, **Private A. Monk**, has been missing since an action on July 10th. All of his platoon who were in action are missing, so I have no news to give you. We know that the Germans took some prisoners, and so I hope he may be one. He was one of my best Lewis Gunners, who are generally the best men of a platoon, and I feel very cut up about losing him. I hope you will not worry too much, and my sympathies are with you. I hope your loss will be just temporary. I was not up the line at the time, so I can say no more".*

Private Archer Monk was 19 years old at the time and was apprenticed at Messrs Green's Stores. He was just out of his apprenticeship when he joined the army on August 25th 1916 and went to France in the December of that year. He was born in Stansted in 1898.

Following closely on the above letter they also received the sad news of the death of their elder son **William Thomas MONK**. He had joined the Hertfordshire regiment on August 30th 1915 and went to France almost a year later, being afterwards transferred to the Royal Berkshires. A letter from a Captain of his regiment read as follows,

'Dear Mrs Monk, - I am afraid I have to tell you of the death of your son in action on July 31st, during the most recent British advance to the east of Ypres. He was killed instantaneously, so suffered no pain. I knew your son very well and feel his loss very much. As anyone from this battalion will tell you, our best men are always Lewis Gunners and your son was one of these. In spite of his bad eyesight, he was extremely keen and efficient, and it is the loss of such men we find it difficult to replace. Please accept my own sympathy and that of all his company and I hope that you will soon see the fruits of your sacrifice in a lasting peace for all Europe'

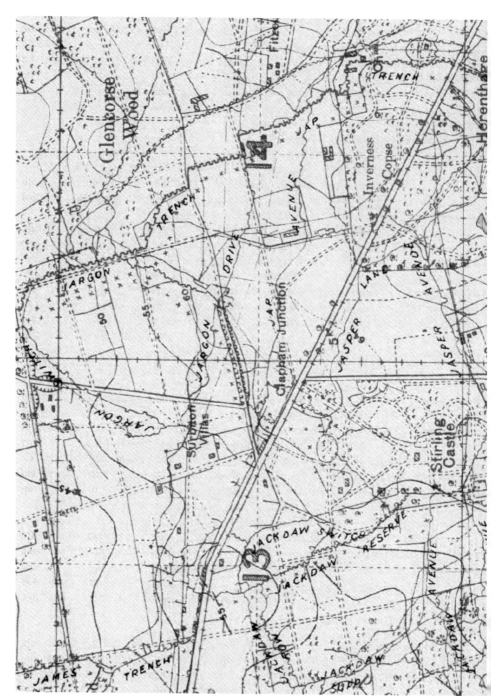

Trench map of the area dated 1st July 1917.

134

On the same day that **William Thomas MONK** had been killed, the village mourned the loss of another young man. It was **George Henry CARTER,** the son of Smith and Fanny Carter of Burton End, Stansted. **George** was born in Stansted in 1893 and had a younger brother John and sister Dora. He enlisted at Saffron Walden where he joined the Essex Regiment. **George's** father Smith worked as a Horse keeper.
George's details are as follows.
Private George Henry CARTER 14582
Essex Regiment 10th Battalion 'D' Company
Killed in Action 31st July 1917 aged 25
George is remembered on the Menin Gate, Ypres, Belgium, Panel 39.

From the 10th Battalion War Diary and the Unit History we learn of the action which led to the sad death of **Private George Henry CARTER** during the Third Battle of Ypres.

July 31st was fixed for the attack, by which it was hoped that our troops would succeed in establishing themselves on the crest of the high ground east of Ypres on which a strong flank could be formed for subsequent operations.
Gun barrage opened at 3.50a.m. Three minutes later the enemy brought down a light barrage on our forward area followed by gas shells into Zillebeke. At 5.00a.m 'B' and 'C' Companies commenced to move from their positions north of Zillebeke Lake. At 7.00a.m they moved off from Ritz St area following the 6th Royal Berkshire Regiment and the 8th Suffolk Regiment respectively. HQ and 'A' and 'D' Companies commenced to move from Railway Dugouts at 6.50a.m. They moved to Ritz St area and HQ was established. While 'B' and 'C' Companies were moving the enemy was placing a heavy barrage overhead. When they had crossed the Ypres–Menin road it was found that the Berks and Suffolks had halted after coming under hostile machine gun fire. The two battalions were now face to face with the enemy and it was evident that the line had not been taken. The 6th Royal Berks with 'B' Company (10th Essex) and the 8th Suffolks with 'C' Company (10th Essex) then attacked the enemy. On the left the Berks made a short advance during which 'B' Company captured one gun. On the right the Suffolks and 'C' Company forced the enemy back but were held up by a strong point. Machine gun and rifle fire continued throughout the day, the day that devoured many men including **George**.

Mrs E. Hutley, of Tye Green, Elsenham, received a letter from her husband, **Private Ernest Hutley,** Essex Regiment, who was reported missing in April, stating that he is a prisoner of war in Germany. **Private Hutley's** parents live at Grove Hill, Stansted, and prior to the War he looked after the fire engine for the Stansted Parish Council and was for 14 years in the employ of Mr A Ratcliff, plumber and house decorator, of Cambridge Road.

Mr and Mrs Charles Bonney, of Grove Hill, Stansted, received a letter from their son, **Private George William Bonney**, Essex Regiment, who had been reported missing since April 28th, stating that he is a prisoner of war in Germany. He states in the letter that he is in the best of health and that he had previously written to them two letters and two postcards, none, of which, however had been received. Some of his old chums, he said, are with him including **Private Charles Childs** (see April 1917), of Burton End. He urgently asked his parents to send him a parcel of food.

The girls and teachers of the Stansted Council School have collected weekly during the past month a box of 180 eggs and forwarded them to the London Central Depot for the wounded soldiers.

Local Hero

It is my opinion that all those who served King and Country during the Great War were heroes. Some also went that little bit further and showed extreme bravery and courage. For some of those soldiers awards for gallantry were given. One of those men, from our village, was **Henry Walter Prior** who was awarded the D.C.M. (Distinguished Conduct Medal). This is his story.

Henry was born in Stansted in 1896, the son of Walter, a foreman at the brickworks, and Rosina Prior of 90 Upgrove (now Grove Hill). He had three sisters named Lucy, Ellen and Hilda and a brother Leslie Henry. **Henry** had enlisted into the Essex Regiment, and joined the 9th Battalion.

26962 Pte. Henry Walter Prior (Stansted, Essex),
Essex Regiment 9th Battalion
'For conspicuous gallantry and devotion to duty during a hostile bombing attack. To check this he piled up ration bags, and sitting behind them fired over 100 rounds at the enemy, forcing them to build a bomb-stop. He then built a bomb-stop, which he held all day, and his action saved the whole of his platoon and enabled them to get back to our lines. His gallantry and determination were beyond all praise'.

From The Essex Unit History came the following account.
The Essex went into the front line on July 7th. In the early morning of July 11th the enemy opened a heavy bombardment with trench mortars upon the front and support lines and fifteen minutes later they put down a barrage of all calibers, under cover of which they attacked Long Trench in force, preceded by a bombardment at the same time making a demonstration against Hook Trench. Working parties had been out that night digging the trench and connecting it with the front line. It was some 300 yards in front of Monchy and was being prepared so a much and more tenable position could be held. Before daylight the working parties returned, with the exception of No 12 platoon, 'C' Company, which was left to hold the unfinished section or northern end of the trench

with outposts between that point and the 'Hook' of Hook Trench. About 5-30a.m. the German bombardment opened, followed by an attack in force. On the right the 6th Buffs (East Kent Regiment) were preparing for a raid, so that the enemy effort was met and held. The move out on the left came against the forward posts held by No 12 platoon, one section of which was either killed or wounded, including the officer. The remainder of the platoon took position in a small unfinished slip trench, about 100 yards in front of the regular front line. Lance-Corporal Mobbs did brilliant work in stopping the hostile advance, lying on the parapet with his Lewis gun and firing until it jammed. Whilst trying to put it right he was shot through the head and killed. When the enemy were within forty yards of the position the party made an effort to regain the front line, but only two were successful, the remainder being shot down as they left the trench. The artillery and machine guns stopped the advance when within thirty yards of the slip trench. The enemy then tried to get forward by bombing up Long Trench, but a fire screen of ration bags was made at all junctions of the trench with the slip trench, and there **Private Henry Walter Prior** *and Private H. Savill held them at bay, assisted by Corporal George Pitches* (who was before and during there time together on the Western Front a very close friend of Henry's). From George's regiment number being 27963 which is only one digit from Walter's it's fairly certain that they had enlisted together.

An article in the local *Herts and Essex* newspaper conveyed the news of **Henry's** D.C.M. to the village, it read as follows.
'Stansted Soldier Wins the D.C.M.'
  His parents and friends in Stansted have been gratified this week to learn that **Private Henry Walter Prior**, Essex Regiment, eldest son of Mr. and Mrs. Walter Prior, of Chapel Hill, has been awarded the D.C.M. for distinguished service and devotion to duty on the battlefield. Writing home to his mother, **Private Prior** says: *"You will be pleased to hear that I have got a D.C.M. for what happened on your birthday (July 11th). The other two men had got their Military Medal when I went into hospital and I did not know till I got back whether I should get a medal at all".* **Private Prior** is 20 years of age and has been in France some fifteen months. He was wounded by shrapnel in the left shoulder about three months ago. Before joining up he was a baker in the employ of Mr. A. Sanders, of Lower Street

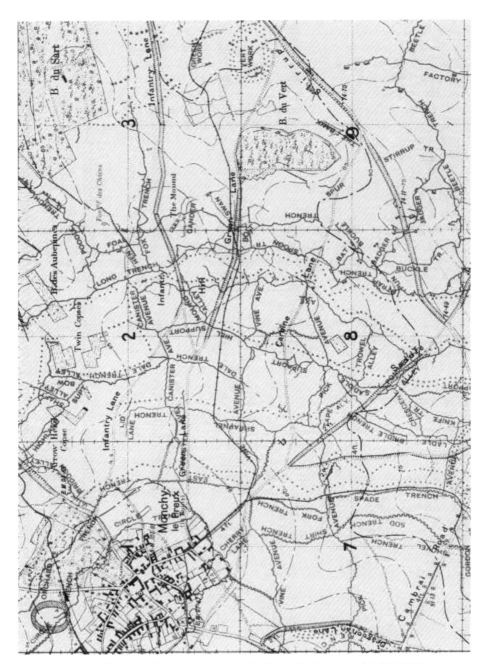

Trench Map of the Area where **Private Prior** won his D.C.M.

138

Private Henry Walter Prior D.C.M. with two of his sisters.

Another award for bravery came to light this month as news that **Corporal Frederick Haggerwood** of the Australian Light Infantry, son of Mr. and Mrs. A. Haggerwood, of Grove Hill, Stansted has been awarded the Military Medal for bravery and conspicuous service on the battlefield. He was formerly a scholar of the British School at Stansted and was remembered as a dairyman in the parish. He went to Australia in about 1910 and joined the Australian Forces early in the War. In a letter to his parents he says

"You say you would like to know what I did to get the medal. We had to follow the New Zealanders close up and when they took (censored) we had to go 1,000 yards further on, and I can tell you some fight. We lost heavily but Fritz suffered worse, in fact the Fritzes laid about like dead flies. I shall never forget it as long as I live. When the New Zealanders had reached their objective, one officer and eight of us were picked out to run a tape in front of them for our battalion to line up and give them directions. Well, the officer and two others started the job and in less than ten minutes the officer and one of the men were killed and the other man wounded. I and a corporal took it on and did the job and got the battalion lined up in their places and never got a scratch. The Corporal was recommended for a V.C. and I for a D.C.M., but they gave us a Military Medal each. I have been made a full Corporal as well, so that is something. We were there for three days. On the last day a shell came close to a shell hole I was camped in and a piece hit me on the leg, but it was only a small cut. I went to the dressing station to get it dressed and while I was there a shell went right where I had been camped and blew everything there to pieces, so I was lucky. You can guess how lucky I was when I tell you that there were 36 of us in the platoon when we went in and only five of us came out all right. The others were either killed or wounded".

From the Australian archives we find that the award was for bravery and coolness under fire at Messines during an attack on Owl Trench on 7th June 1917. **Private Haggerwood** was one of the scouts who under Lieutenant Murray were detailed to lay tapes in *'No Mans Land'* to guide our troops (A superb account of this action can be found in the book *'Somme Mud'*) This work was successfully accomplished under very dangerous and difficult circumstances. Subsequently **Private Haggerwood** guided two platoons to their objective.

This was the first day of the Battle of Messines.

At 03.10a.m on Thursday 7th June 1917, the British Second Army under General Sir Herbert Plumer started an attack which in three hours resulted in the capture of the whole of the Messines Ridge on the South side of the Ypres Salient.

The attack effectively began on 3rd June when the preliminary bombardment intensified, and was kept up until 2.50a.m on 7th June. By this time, 100,000 men of the Second Army were lying in position waiting to attack. The weather was clear with a bright moon. The sudden silence spooked the Germans who started firing flares in an effort to find an explanation. Twenty minutes of tension packed waiting culminated in a loud bang, followed seven seconds later by a continuous series of huge explosions which tore at the German front line and threw the watching British, who stood 400 yards away, off their feet.

The British rose from their trenches under cover of the renewed barrage of every gun available. Nine divisions of infantry advanced through the clouds of smoke and dust and within minutes, the whole of the German front line was in British hands. Three hours later, the whole of the Messines Ridge was taken. The success of the assault was in large part due to the explosion of nineteen mines tunnelled under the German front line

From **Frederick's** service record the following information about him can be found. He was named **Frederick Isaac Haggerwood** the son of Arthur Haggerwood, of Grove Hill, Stansted. He joined The A.I.F. on 17th August 1915 aged 29 years. He was 5'8" tall and weighed 146 lbs with a dark complexion, grey eyes, and brown hair.

A brief history of **Frederick's** service was as follows:-

He embarked at Sydney 22nd December 1915 and was taken on strength of 45th Battalion on 6[th]March 1916. On 10[th]September 1916 he was admitted to hospital sick. He was appointed Lance-Corporal on 27[th]April 1917 and temporary Corporal on the 14[th]June 1917. On the 23[rd]June 1917 he was made a full Corporal which was the day he earned his Military Medal. He was again admitted to hospital, sick, on the 26[th]October 1917 and subsequently hospitalized in England on the 2[nd]November 1917 when he was suffering from Myalgia and was discharged from hospital 21[st]Jan 1918. He was wounded by a gun shot to the thigh 20[th]May 1918 and admitted to the general hospital in Portsmouth where he received treatment for the gun shot wound on the 30[th]May 1918. He was granted one months leave of absence without pay from 6[th]August 1918. **Frederick** rejoined his battalion on the16[th] October 1918.

On the 14th of July the following soldier died of his wounds, his details are, **Private Nelson Levey 73843, Labour Corps 124th Company, Died of Wounds 14th July 1917 aged 33**. His grave can be found at Dozinghem Military Cemetery, Poperinghe, West-Vlaanderen, Belgium. Grave Ref I. C. 14. **Nelson** was born in Stansted, in 1884, and grew up with his parents Alfred and Isabelle in Woodfields. At the time of his death **Nelson's** company were in the Poperinghe area. **Nelson** had enlisted at Bishop's Stortford where he originally joined the Queen's, (Royal West Surrey Regiment) 47347.

August 1917

We are left to mourn the loss of one
We should have loved to save,
Beloved on earth, regretted gone,
But remembered in his grave.

The sad news this August that came to hand was that **Rifleman Edward John REEVE**, son of Edward, a boot maker, and Charlotte Reeve, of the Common (Stoneyfield Common) Stansted, was killed in action on August 14th. Before the War **Rifleman Reeve** was for fourteen years clerk to Mr E. Rochford , first at the Birchanger nurseries and afterwards as his private secretary at Loughton, where he enlisted and joined the Queen's Westminster Rifles (16th London Regiment). He left a widow, namely May, whom he had married in 1914 and an infant child, a daughter Dora. Two of his brothers were also serving King and Country, **John**, in the Herts Regiment and **Reginald** (known as **Austin**), who was with the Bedfordshire's. He also had sisters Hilda and Ellen. **Edward** was born, in Balsham Cambridge, in 1886 and in his young days was an errand boy.

Edward's details are as follows
Rifleman Edward John REEVE 555037
London Regiment 1st/16th Battalion Queen's Westminster Rifles
Killed in Action 14th August 1917 aged 31
Edward has no known grave and is remembered on the Menin Gate, Ypres, Belgium. Panel 54

    Edward's battalion details on the day, and day before, his death were as follows.

On the 13thAugust 1917 the battalion were in trenches. The plan was to push the line forwards 100 yards towards Glencorse Wood. Six posts were to be established three each by the Queens Westminster Rifles and the Queen Victoria's Rifles. There was heavy intermittent shelling throughout the day. During the night they were ordered to establish the posts in

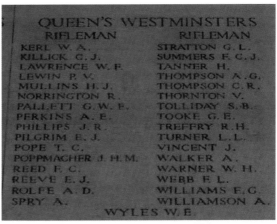

Glencorse Wood (See earlier Trench map July 1917) 100 yards from our front line. Operations were ordered to start at 9.00p.m. At that time our heavy guns were shelling close to our front line trenches on the right. This delayed the start of 'A' Company but on the left 'B' Company got their posts out. At 9.07p.m. the enemy put down a heavy barrage on our front line, but this did not interfere with the left company posts. The right company, however, could not move owing to our own heavies and protective barrage was later called for by lamp signal which was immediately put down.

143

On the 14*th* heavy enemy shelling continued again throughout the whole 24 hours. In the evening the battalion was relieved by 2*nd* Londons (Royal Fusiliers) and they proceeded to trenches at Halfway House. **Edward's** battalion suffered approximately 75 casualties on this day of which 24 were killed.

Edward John Reeve

Mrs Crockford, of 12 Sunnyside, Stansted, had an intimation that her husband, **Private Albert Henry Crockford**, Suffolk Regiment, (brother of **James Walter CROCKFORD** see May 1918) has been wounded in the left thigh and right leg and is now going on well in Upper Edmonton Hospital.

By invitation, this August, of Lady Jackson the summer treat in connection with the Church Sunday Schools was held in the grounds of Stansted House, and despite the unsettled weather the children had an enjoyable time. They mustered in the school yard and walked in procession to Stansted House, Mr H. Bass conveying the younger ones in a wagon. The proceedings opened with a cricket match between eleven girls and eleven boys, and resulted in a win for the boys. Various sports and games were arranged and swings also provided entertainment. Refreshments, consisting of buns and lemonade, were served, and afterwards a programme of keenly contested sports was carried out. At the close hearty cheers were accorded Lady Jackson, The Vicar and Mrs Goodchild, and the teachers and helpers.

William George Rayment

Another brave soldier lost his life, he was **William George Rayment**. **William** and was the husband of Francies Clara Rayment whom he lived with in Woodfields, Stansted. **William's** details are as follows.
Private William George Rayment 40467. Royal Dublin Fusiliers 9th Battalion, (formerly Bedfordshire Regiment), Killed in Action 16th August 1917 aged 36.

William has no known grave and is remembered on the Tyne Cot Memorial, Panel 144 to 145.

William is not named on the Stansted memorial although records show his wife was residing at Woodfields. From our research he may have had more connections with Much Hadham. He was the son of Mrs Mary Masclow, of White Horse Hill, Chislehurst, Kent.

Over 150 of the 9th Royal Dubliners were killed on the fateful day as they attacked enemy strong points such as, Bremen Redoubt, Borry Farm and Vampire Farm.

The brother of **Private Christopher Miller** (see March 1917) was killed in action this month, his details are, **Private Jesse Harry Miller 1259, Royal Fusiliers 9th Battalion, Killed in Action 9th August 1917 aged 32.**

Jesse Harry Miller

Like his brother he is remembered on the Birchanger Memorial, the family having lived at Brook Cottages, Stoneyfield Common, situated today on the edge of the village of Stansted. **Jesse** has no known grave and his name can be found on the Arras Memorial.

It is thought that **Jesse** was killed when the enemy put down a heavy barrage in retaliation for an earlier attack.

Private Jesse Miller had been on active service since June 1915.

Another soldier with a connection to the village but not named on the local memorial is **Private Henry Milton** who sadly lost his life. His details are, **Private Henry Milton 201187, Essex Regiment 4th Battalion, Died 11th August 1917 aged 37**. He is buried in the Baghdad (North Gate) War Cemetery, Grave Ref. XXI. E. 30.

Usually when a soldier is stated as Died, rather than Killed in Action or Died of Wounds, it means he died of illness or disease etc. **Henry** was born in Farnham, Essex, the son of Thomas and Emma Milton and the husband of Phoebe, of 6, Brook Cottages, Stoneyfield Common, Stansted.

On the 22nd August the following soldier was killed in action in Belgium. His details are **Private Alfred Percy Plumsted 203511, Oxford and Bucks Light Infantry 2/4th Battalion, Killed in Action 22nd August 1917 aged 33**. He has no known grave and is remembered on the Tyne Cot Memorial. At the time of his death he was living in Stansted with his wife Susannah.

Brief details of the actions **Alfred** died in were thus.

On the 22nd August, shortly before 5.00a.m, the bombardment started. In the advance behind the creeping barrage put down by our guns, of which an enormous concentration was present on the front, 'C', 'D' and 'A' Companies (from right to left) provided the first waves, while 'B' Company followed to support the flanks. Half-an-hour after the advance started 'D', 'B' and 'A' Companies were digging-in 150 yards west of the

Winnipeg-Kansas Cross Road. The losses of these companies in going over had not been heavy, but, as so often happens, casualties occurred directly the objective had been duly reached. Not till the following night was it reduced, and during the whole of August 22nd it remained a troublesome feature in the situation.

Before the line reached could be consolidated or they could act to defeat the enemy's tactics, our men found themselves the victims of sniping and machine-gun fire.

Throughout the 22nd no actual counter-attack or organised bombardment by the enemy took place, but much sniping and machine-gun fire continued, making it almost impossible to move about. The battalion losses in Lewis-gunners were particularly heavy.

Some of the men had to remain in shell-holes unsupported and shot at from several directions for over fifty hours.

Private George Griggs, aged 34, of Burton End was discharged from service this August after having served for sixteen months in India. He was discharged through illness.

Private Herbert Tunbridge 67794, Royal Engineers was discharged this month through illness. He had been on active service overseas from September 1915 to December 1916. Prior to enlisting in February 1915 he had worked as a carpenter/joiner and resided in Recreation Ground. He was 25 years old.

The husband of Adelaide May Banks, of Bentfield End, died during August 1917. His details are, **Private John Banks G/15973, Queen's Own Royal West Kent Regiment 2nd Battalion, died 10th August 1917, aged 34.** His name can be found inscribed the Kirkee 1914-1918 Memorial, India.

He was the son of Mr and Mrs George Banks and was born in nearby Birchanger.

Rifleman Frederick Milton Baker, 200499 Rifle Brigade was listed as wounded this August. He had suffered gun shot wounds to his hip. He was 25 years old at the time and had initially joined the Essex Regiment and then moved to the Cambridgeshire's before his transfer to the Rifle Brigade.

He was living at Bentfield End at the time he joined up and prior to enlisting in the army he was employed as a milkman.

September 1917

He died the noblest death a man can die,
Fighting for God and right and liberty.

On Sunday 30th September **Peter WARWICK** who was the son of Eliza and the late Henry Warwick lost his life on the Western Front. **Lance-Corporal Peter WARWICK, Lewis Gun Section, Essex Regiment, was killed by an enemy sniper at daybreak. Peter** lived with his mother and family at Lower Woodfields and was 24 years of age and single. Prior to the war he was employed by Messrs Mascall Bros. butchers. He joined up in November 1914, enlisting at Saffron Walden, and after serving in Egypt went to France early in 1916, and was wounded in the leg. He had been at home on leave only two months before his sad death.

His Lieutenant wrote to the deceased's mother saying

"The morning before the battalion last came out of the trenches your son was hit by an enemy sniper and died before I could reach him, although at the time I was in the trench but a short distance away. It has been a great loss to the company, as your son was held in great esteem by all and was a steady and capable section leader. It is very difficult to offer you any consolation in such a great loss, but I hope it will relieve your grief a little to know that his death was almost instantaneous, and he was buried in the presence of the whole Platoon. I hope you will accept my sincere sympathy".

A letter has also been received from his Sergeant-Major conveying the sincere sympathy of the N.C.O's and the men of the company, and one from the Chaplain stating that the deceased was buried in a military cemetery and his comrades erected a cross over his grave *"to the memory of a true Britisher and a brave comrade".*

Peter Warwick

Peter's details are as follows.
Lance-Corporal Peter WARWICK 15774
Essex Regiment 13th Battalion
Killed in action 30th September 1917 aged 24

Peter is buried in Gorre British and Indian Cemetery, Pas de Calais, France. Grave Ref IV.E.20. The cemetery is situated in the hamlet of Gorre about a mile north of Beuvry and two miles east of Bethune.

15774 LANCE CPL.
P. WARWICK
ESSEX REGIMENT
30TH SEPTEMBER 1917 AGE 24

GONE BUT NOT FORGOTTEN

Peter was born in Stansted in 1893, he had brothers **Arthur Harry** and **William**, and three sisters Elizabeth, Kate and Mary.

His brothers were also all serving, **Harry**, a corporal, with the Army Veterinary Corps, **Arthur**, like **Peter**, with the Essex Regiment and **William**, a Lance-Corporal with the Royal Garrison Artillery.

Very little information, from either War diaries or Unit histories, is available regarding **Peter's** death except, from the 13th Battalion war diary; we know that his battalion were in the area known as Givenchy Keeps and about 12.30a.m, on the 30th, they were *heavily bombarded with gas shells until the all clear at about 3.00a.m.*

The diary states – 1 other rank killed, sadly this would have been **Peter**.

Lieutenant Austin Theodore Long, of the Royal Scots, was killed in action on the Western Front. He was the third son of the late Rev. Eustace Long, of Stansted, and a scholar at Bishop's Stortford Grammar School from 1893 to 1899. The outbreak of war found him, teaching, at Stramongate School Kendal, as Modern Language Master, and as soon as term ended he joined the Royal Army Medical Corps. In February 1915, however, he was urged to undertake more arduous duties and accepted a commission in the Royal Scots, then stationed in Scotland. After a strenuous time there, during which he held the positions of Grenade Officer to his Brigade, temporary Captain and Adjutant, **Lieutenant Long** was in June last posted to a battalion on active service in France, where on August 22nd, the first occasion on which he was in the firing line, he met his death and was buried on the field of battle. By nature the most pacific of men, he gladly gave his life and labour in the cause of righteousness. The officer commanding his battalion wrote this of him

*"I had only known **Lieutenant A.T. Long** for a very short time, but quite long enough to know his sterling worth. His loss to me and my battalion is great, as in him I saw an exceptionally valuable officer".*

Austin's details are as follows. **Lieutenant Austin Theodore Long, Royal Scots 10th Battalion, Killed in Action 22nd August 1917 aged 34.**

Austin has no known grave, although it was mentioned that he was buried on the field of battle, his grave was more likely lost due to subsequent actions, and his name is on the Tyne Cot Memorial Panel Nos.11 to 14 and 162.

The news of the very sad loss of two of their sons during September 1917 was received by William and Louisa Jordan. Their son's details are. **Private Harry John Jordan 82498, Machine Gun Corps 58th Company, Killed in Action 20th September 1917 aged 19** and **Private Walter Jordan 19299, Essex Regiment 2nd Battalion, Killed in Action 29th September 1917 aged 26.** Both lads have no known grave and are named on the Menin Gate, Ypres.

They are both listed as having been born in Stansted but at the time of their deaths their family were living in Ugley Green which was part of the rural district of Stansted so its possible they were born their as well.

The death of these two brothers was reported in the *Herts and Essex Observer* thus.

The sad news has been received by Mr and Mrs W. Jordan, of Ugley Green, that two of their sons have been killed in action at the Front. Their eldest, **Private Walter**

Jordan, Essex Regiment, was killed by a shell on the night of September 29th-30th whilst on a work party which were digging a cable trench in a forward area. He was 26 years of age and before enlisting in May 1915, was employed by Mr C. Wright, a local farmer. The other is **Private Harry John Jordan** (the youngest) of whose death an officer in his regiment, the Machine Gun Corps, writes: *"I very much regret to inform you of the death of your son in action on the 20th September. He was seen to be wounded on that date by his fellow gunners in the hottest part of the attack. Afterwards the place was searched for him but he was not found. We presumed he had got back to the dressing station, but yesterday (October 7th) his body was found and buried by some infantrymen of his brigade. A cross is now being prepared by his comrades for his grave, in memory of their lost friend. Your son was a good lad and a brave one. He died where the fighting was hardest and did his utmost to get his gun into action under a withering machine gun fire. The section is exceedingly sorry to have lost such a capable gunner from its numbers and joins with me in expressing its deepest sympathy for you in your sad bereavement"*. Deceased was 19 years of age and joined the army in August, 1916, previous to which he was employed as a gardener by Dr Rowell (see below), of Norman House, Stansted.

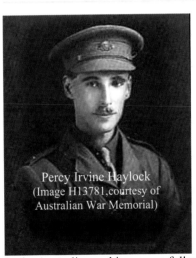

Percy Irvine Haylock
(Image H13781, courtesy of
Australian War Memorial)

Dr Rowell received the sad news this September that his grandson had been killed in action on the Western Front. His grandsons details are, **2nd Lieutenant Percy Irvine Haylock Owen, Australian Infantry, A.I.F. 3rd Battalion, Killed in Action 22nd September 1917 aged 26.** He was the son of Lt Colonel Robert Haylock Owen and Hilda Grace Owen. His grave can be found at Tyne Cot Cemetery Grave Ref. LXI.B.9.

Percy was educated at Felstead College, Essex. From his service records details of his death were as follows. *"This officer was killed in action by a machine gun bullet which penetrated his steel helmet and entered his forehead. He fell unconscious and died a few minutes later"*.

Information about **Percy's** death can be found in the Australian archives – see following page.

151

Mr John Pimblett, a local farmer, was summoned for being drunk whilst in charge of a motor car and driving the car to the danger of the public at the same time. It was alleged that he had been involved in an accident with a local woman. The case was adjourned as the woman was unable to attend due to the death of her husband on the Western Front.

Frederick Palmer, aged 16, was summoned for riding a bike without a light at Stansted. P.C. Pole stated the defendant committed the offence near Stansted House Lodge. Palmer was fined 5 shillings.

Mr Joseph Gibbs, dairyman, of Stansted, was fined 10 shillings for selling deficient milk. The chairman of Stansted Petty Sessions attributed the cause of the deficiency to the selling of the first milk of the cows and not milking the cows out.

A football match was played at Stansted between Stansted Juniors and Bishop's Stortford Juniors, and resulted in a win for the home team by three goals to nil, the goals being notched by Goodey (2) and Dale.

October 1917

I shall not forget him, nor do I intend,
But think of him daily, and will to the end,
When others return, I shall miss him more,
The realisation will make my heart sore.

Mr James Timothy and Mrs Charlotte Bush received an official intimation that their eldest son, **Sergeant James BUSH**, Bedfordshire Regiment, was killed in action on the Western Front on October 8th. The deceased soldier, who was a single man 28 years of age, and had been in the Army thirteen years, was one of the first to go to the front in this war.

Grave of James Bush

His officer, in a letter informing Mrs Bush of her son's death said *"I feel it is my duty to write to let you know how much I and the whole of the Signal Section of the Regiment regret his loss. I was only a few yards from Sergeant Bush when he was killed by a piece of shell which struck him in the head, killing him instantly. I was always struck by his courage and splendid ability as a signaller. I have lost many friends in this war but none whose loss I mourn more than your son. Please allow me to tender my very deepest sympathy in your great loss".*

A comrade wrote *"He died at his post like a true soldier for his King and Country. He was buried by his comrades, and his grave was marked by a cross with his name on. We are all very sorry. He was liked by everybody on the Signal Staff. He was always a very brave fellow, and when duty called him he was there".*

This is the second son Mr and Mrs Bush have lost in the war. **Lance-Corporal Alfred BUSH** was killed in June 1915 (see June 1915).

James's details are as follows.

Private James BUSH 8186
Bedfordshire Regiment 1st Battalion
Killed in Action 8th October 1917 aged 28

James is buried in Hooge Crater Cemetery Grave ref XVII.C.13. The cemetery is situated about 2 miles east of Ypres (Ieper).

Hooge Crater Cemetery

For details of James' family (see June 1915).

The Bedfordshire war diary for the date that **James** was killed has the following information.

A defensive system was made and a continuous front line dug with supports. 'C' & 'B' companies were in front line with 'A' and 'D' in reserve. Communication trenches were dug back from front line to Battalion H.Q. situated in buildings and pillboxes.

The day after the death of **James BUSH** Stansted lost one of its brave officers by the name of **Claude Stewart JACKSON**.

Claude was the fourth son of Sir Thomas Jackson, 1st Baronet and his wife, Amelia Lydia nee Dare, Lady Jackson of Stansted House.

He was born in Chislehurst, Kent, on 30th January 1892, he had three brothers namely, Thomas Dare, George Julius and Walter David Russell, all three later became titled. His sisters were Kathleen, Amy, Beatrice and Dorothy

He was educated at Harrow School from 1906 to 1910 and at Royal Military College, Sandhurst. In February 1912 he was commissioned as Second Lieutenant into the 3rd Battalion of the Coldstream Guards. **Claude** went to France on 12th August 1914, he was severely wounded in the head in September 1914. He married Laura Emily Pearson on 6th May 1916 and after recovering from his wounds he served in several staff positions in France before rejoining his battalion in September 1917.

Claude's details are as follows.
Captain Claude Stewart JACKSON
Coldstream Guards 3rd Battalion
Killed in Action 9th October 1917 aged 25
Claude has no known grave and his name can be found on the Tyne Cot Memorial, Panels 9 to 10, Zonnebeke, West Vlaanderen, Belgium.

Claude Stewart Jackson

Claude's battalion took part in the attack from the Broembeke to Houthulst Forest, Zero hour to be at 5.20a.m. His Colonel wrote the following *"He led his company, as we all knew he would, with the utmost bravery and coolness, under a heavy fire from both artillery and machine guns. Just before reaching the objective he was hit in the thigh by a piece of shell, not at all a dangerous or painful wound, and he was quite cheery when being dressed. Hardly, however, had they finished tying up his wound, when he was hit through the head by a snipers bullet and killed on the spot. I don't think the War had the same horrors for him as it did for some.*
He took it all so quietly and philosophically, and yet he could always be trusted to do his best for his battalion and for his Regiment".

Claude's name can be found in memory on a stained glass window in St Mary's Church. It reads as follows – *'TO THE GLORY OF GOD AND IN PROUD MEMORY OF SIR THOMAS JACKSON BARONET WHO PASSED TO THE HIGHER LIFE ON St THOMAS DAY 1915 AGED 74 YEARS ALSO TO HIS YOUNGEST SON CLAUDE STEWART CAPTAIN COLDSTREAM GUARDS KILLED IN ACTION IN FRANCE ON THE 9TH OCTOBER 1917 AGED 25 YEARS'.*

Official notification was received in October 1917 by Mr George Levey Junior, of Cambridge Road, that his son, **Lance-Corporal George Turner Levey 43573**, Essex Regiment, has been severely wounded by a shell in France. His left leg has been amputated and he is going on satisfactorily in hospital, at Newcastle-on-Tyne. He was previously wounded on the Somme in October of last year. Prior to the War, **Lance-Corporal Levey** belonged to the Saffron Walden Company of Essex Cyclists.

Window at St Mary's

A posthumous announcement was made during October in that **Lieutenant Harry Keppel Chester** (see March 1917), Essex Regiment, son of Mr and Mrs H. Chester, of Pines Hill, Stansted, who died from wounds in Palestine on March 26th, was gazetted Captain, to take precedence as from June 1st 1916, till the time of his death.

A football match was played during this month at Silver Leys Bishop's Stortford between the Bishop's Stortford Juniors and the Stansted Juniors, and resulted in a win for the Stansted team by five goals to nil.

At the Council meeting this month Mr Spencer reported that they had not been able to procure a siren, and they must get an order from the Ministry of Munitions before one could be made. They were not allowed to give air raid warnings after 6.00p.m, so that if they had a siren they would not be able to use it at night, and in case of air raids they did not want people out of doors. He therefore questioned whether it was necessary to go on with it. Mr Prior did not think it was needed and said that guns gave sufficient warning. It was unanimously decided to let the matter drop.

Poor **Private James Haggerwood** was wounded again, this time suffering from shrapnel wounds to his left thigh after intense enemy bombardment of the trenches on the 21st/22nd of this month. He wounds were severe enough for him to be bought back to 'Blighty' where he was treated in a hospital in Brighton.

Private Arthur Snow 290756, aged 31, of Bentfield End was discharged this month through illness. He had served with both the Royal Sussex and East Surrey regiments.

November 1917

Fond thoughts they linger round our hearts,
And tears they often flow,
As to that sad and lonely grave,
Our thoughts they often go.

Captain Leslie Guy Gold, Hertfordshire Regiment, son of Mr and Mrs Charles Gold, Of Gorsefield, Stansted, has been awarded the Military Cross for the following action.

For conspicuous gallantry and devotion on the 4th November, when his company was held up by very heavy machine-gun fire, he himself went out to try and gain touch. He found the left company also held up, with all its officers' casualties. He immediately took command of it, reorganised, and then advanced with the two companies.

His Military Cross award was gazetted on 1st January 1918.

Daryl Leslie Harris

On the 3rd of this month in 1917, the following soldier, who was born in Stansted in 1891 but moved away, died in France. His details are, **Pioneer Daryl Leslie Harris 282404, Royal Engineers, 4th Army Signal Company, died 3rd November 1917 aged 26.**

His grave can be found in Zuydcoote Military Cemetery, Grave Ref II.C.24.

He was the son of Alfred and Evangeline Harris of Grosvenor House, Westgate, Hunstanton, Norfolk and the husband of the late Jannie Dorothea Harris who he had married in 1908, Sadly Jannie died in 1913 of acute meningitis and peritonitis.

The 4th Army Signal Company was co-located with the headquarters of the Fourth Army and thus in a place that was well behind the front lines. So, unless **Pioneer Harris** was killed in a bombing raid (which is possible, but not likely) or by disease (which is also unlikely), he probably suffered a fatal injury in an accident of some sort. In any of these cases, there is a good chance that the cause of the death would be recorded in the company war diary, which is on file at the National Archives. (His death certificate states death by accident).

George Wright, 43, and **William Hutley**, 36, labourers, of Stansted, were both summoned for trespassing, in the search for conies. They both denied the offence. Supt Boyce said there were 15 previous convictions under the Game Laws against Wright, but **Hutley**, who stated he had been away in the Army for the past three years (see below), had not been previously convicted. The Chairman remarked that it was evident that Wright was 'an old hand' at poaching. He was fined £1-4shillings including costs and **Hutley** was ordered to pay 4 shillings cost. The Chairman told Hutley that the Bench hopes they will not see him there again, and **Hutley** replied that he would take good care of that.

Private William Hutley 1247, Royal Fusiliers 8th Battalion, of Thatch Cottage, Grove Hill, had enlisted at the outbreak of war but was discharged, on 16th October 1917, after suffering severe gun shot wounds to his shoulder.

The Battle of Cambrai began on 20th November 1917 when the British Army launched a surprise attack on the enemy using a total of almost 400 tanks. It was the first mass use of tanks in history.

Rifleman Frederick Milton Baker was wounded for the second time in 3 months. This time, on 22nd November 1917 he suffered shrapnel wounds to his lower body.

December 1917

Sleep on dear son, in a far off land,
In a grave we can never see,
But as long as life and memory last,
We will remember thee.

During December 1917 Stansted lost another young soldier at the age of 22, namely, Frederick Charles BUCK who was born in Stansted in 1896. He was the son of Thomas and Emma of New Road Elsenham. The 1901 census shows him as having three brothers Robert, Thomas and Ernest, He also had two sisters Florence and Emily.

Frederick who was living in West London at the time of the war enlisted at Clapham Junction and joined London Regiment.

Frederick's details are as follows.

Private 700493 Frederick Charles BUCK
London Regiment 23rd (County of London Rifles) Battalion
Died of Wounds 15thDecember 1917 aged 22

Frederick's grave can be found in Rocquigny – Equancourt Road British Cemetery, Manancourt, Somme, France. Grave Ref VII.B.9. The cemetery can be found some eight miles north of Peronne and seven south east of Bapaume.

As **Frederick** died of his wounds it is not easy to ascertain when these wounds were inflicted but it is quite likely it would have been in one of the following actions. The likelihood is that it was in an action close to the day he died as he is buried close to the field of battle rather than near a Casualty Clearing Station or Field Hospital.

From the battalion War Diary twenty men were wounded due to heavy enemy shelling on the 6th, 7th and 8th of December. On December 9th the enemy attacked and succeeded in gaining a footing but were then driven out with heavy loss. The attack continued throughout the day with 24 men wounded, then on the 10th the Battalion HQ was bombed by enemy aircraft with 5 wounded.

On December the 11th the battalion was relieved by the 1st Royal Berks. Regiment .A few days later they marched to billets in Bertincourt.

A brief account taken from the 1/23rd London Regimental History was as follows.

Whilst supporting the 140th Brigade on 2nd December 5 men were killed and 13 wounded. The following evening the battalion took over the front line to the left of Bourlon Wood. On the evening of the 4th a decision was taken to withdraw in small parties so as not to alert the enemy, a skeleton force only was to remain in the forward trenches. Their orders were to remain until 4-30a.m. and move from point to point and fire rifles and Verey lights (flare) just as if a normal garrison had been there. The rest of the battalion had moved back to Hughes Switch (a communication trench between the Hindenburg front and support lines just south of the Graincourt Road) which now became the main line. Early on the morning of the 5th the enemy attacked the evacuated positions and halted when finding empty trenches. For the next four days the Germans were feeling their way towards the British line, frequently being fired upon by small parties of Lewis gunners left out to harass them. At 6-30a.m. on the 9th a hurricane bombardment by grenade throwing machines began causing casualties and trench damage. Parties of the enemy began to advance in single file and with the aid of flame throwers it penetrated on both flanks. Captain Durrant ordered a counter attack and after a sharp bombing fight the enemy was ejected and communication with the 21st was restored. Using rifle grenades they caused the enemy to withdraw out of range. At 11-00a.m. the Germans again using flame throwers made another determined attack on the post. By this time Captain Durrant had lost about half his original strength. It was hand *to hand fighting and with very little artillery support therefore at about 1-00p.m. he reluctantly decided to evacuate the position. He then withdrew the remnants of his company (about thirty men of which ten were severely wounded) to old gun pits about 300 yards in the rear. He then occupied these and prepared to defend them.*

The action on the 21st is the most probably the day Frederick succumbed to his wounds.

Intimation came to hand that **Private Harry Green**, Lewis gunner, King's Liverpool Regiment, only son of Mr and Mrs Alfred Green, of 27 Sunnyside, Stansted, has been severely wounded by shrapnel in the side and is now in a military hospital in Birmingham. **Private Green** was formerly clerk in the offices of the Saffron Walden and District Farmers' Association at Saffron Walden and joined the army in February last. On reaching the age of 19 he proceeded to France on September 5th, and was transferred to the King's Liverpool Regiment as a Lewis gunner. Writing home to his mother he says it was on November 20th that he was wounded, and added,

'I got hit during the first half hour of the advance. I managed to crawl into a shell hole, but I found it was too warm to remain there, so I crawled on my hands and knees back to the trenches 1,600 yards away. I laid there for about an hour and was then brought down to a dressing station, where I was operated on, and afterwards put in a Red Cross train and brought down to the base. Apart from the wound in my side I am not affected in any other part of my body, but I am afraid I shall not be able to get up for some time to come'

Mr and Mrs E. Harbridge, of Lower Street, Stansted, have received news that their son, **Private Ernest Harbridge**, East Surrey Regiment, has been awarded the Military Medal for gallantry and coolness on December 10th. When a wounded man was being carried on a stretcher the enemy opened a heavy fire round the party. **Private Harbridge** immediately picked up the wounded man and carried him up a steep bank into a cave. 'By this prompt and gallant act,' says the Major General of the Division, 'you undoubtedly saved his life.'

Prior to joining up, **Private Harbridge** was employed on the Great Eastern Railway as a porter at Dunmow station. His parents have another son serving in France, namely **Private William Harbridge**, 9th Essex Regiment. **Ernest**, later in the war, was taken prisoner on March 25th 1918.

January 1918

Across the world the voice of God hath spoken,
Midst earthly warfare and a deathly strife,
Called our beloved through death into the wonder
Of his eternal life.

Another brother of **Ernest LUCKEY** (See August 1918) died this month in 1918. He was **Gunner Harry Bartrop Luckey** whose details are as follows, **Gunner Harry Bartrop Luckey 3511, Australian Field Artillery, 25th Howitzer Brigade, 113th Howitzer Battery, Died 5th January 1918, Harry's** grave can be found in St Mary's Churchyard in the village of Birchanger and his name is also on the war memorial there.

From Australian service records we find out that **Harry's** time on active service and his subsequent death was a very sad one. Much of his time was spent in different hospitals until his sad death which occurred from diabetes contracted in Egypt.

He was discharged from the A.I.F. on 9th December 1916 and the following statement was made on his records. *He is a man who is incapable of any work whatever and will need hospital treatment for some time yet.*

The following soldiers, Corporal Edward Warner, Private George Shepherd and Private Albert Worley, who were billeted in the village, all of the Royal Bucks Hussars were summoned for consuming intoxicating liquor on licensed premises during prohibited hours at Stansted on January 4th. The incident took place at the Willow beer house, Bentfield End, which was kept by landlord Richard Winder. The three soldiers were all fined 14s and the case against the landlord was dismissed.

February 1918

We cannot tell who next may fall
Beneath our chastening rod,
One must be first, but let us all
Prepare to meet our God.

February 1918 saw the sad death of the youngest soldier to be commemorated on the Stansted Memorial, namely, **Albert John PATMORE.**

Grave of Albert John Patmore

Albert was the son of Herbert Horace, a house painter by trade, and Bessie Patmore, of Vine Cottage, Woodfields, Stansted.

Albert's details are as follows.

Boy Albert John PATMORE 158778
Royal Flying Corps
Died on Sunday February 3rd 1918 aged 16

Albert died of Cerebro Spinal Fever (type of Meningitis) in Lucknow Isolation Hospital in North Tidworth, Wiltshire. He had been at Delhi Barracks in South Tidworth before being admitted to hospital.

Albert's body was bought back to Stansted for burial in St Mary's Churchyard.

Albert had two younger brothers namely Harold Horace and Reginald and also a younger sister named Cissie May. Details about **Albert** from his nephew are as follows, *"Albert, I know, was courting a girl from Braintree. I have no doubt this was why he joined the Braintree Congregational Church. The girls name was Alice Radley, she never married but remained one of the Patmore family staying for holidays at*

Albert John Patmore

Stansted etc. I always knew her as Auntie Alice but I didn't know the background until years later, we used to visit her at Braintree. I also have a small locket with Albert and Alice's photo in it, which belonged to my Grandma. According to the family tree he was born on the 19th December 1901 which would make him seventeen although I do not think Grandma and Grandad would have a headstone with the wrong age on". (A copy of his death certificate clearly states aged 16)

Details of **Albert's** death were recorded in the Braintree Congregational Church Free Magazine thus, **Albert** *Patmore, having reached military age received his call up at the end of last year. With other young people, he was about to take his first Communion, on Sunday evening, December 16th, as a member of the Church, but was commanded to present himself before the authorities at Chelmsford at 6 o'clock the same evening. Again, his reception was deferred in the same way on the first Sunday of this year. He was sent to a Military Camp, and on the first Sunday of February, yielded up his life to God and entered into full communion with Him to whom he had dedicated himself. His parents were unable to reach him before his eyes were closed together on this world. They were however permitted to bring his body home and in his native village of Stansted it lies, a dear and sacred spot to those who nurtured him there. We sent from the Young People's Society, of which he was Treasurer, a letter of sympathy to his parents, whose grief we share; for he was sturdy and true, and would have given yet greater service as a soldier of Jesus Christ, and a citizen of His Kingdom.*

Albert with his Parents Herbert and Bessie and brothers Harold and Reginald and sister Cissie May.

March 1918

Sleep on, our dear one
Sleep on, and take thy rest,
We love you well,
But Jesus loves you best.

The sad news reached the village during March 1918 that three more of the brave soldiers fighting on the Western Front had lost their lives.

The first casualty was **Albert Bertie FLOREY** who lost his life on the 23rd. **Albert** was born in South Lopham, Suffolk, the son of Benjamin and Sarah Florey. He had brothers Harry, Samuel and Jesse, and two sisters named Eliza and Hannah. **Albert** enlisted in 1914 at Bishop's Stortford joining the Bedfordshire Regiment.

Albert's details are as follows
Sergeant Albert Bertie FLOREY 4/6974
Bedfordshire Regiment 6th Battalion
Killed in Action 23rd March 1918 aged 31

Albert, who has no known grave, is commemorated on the Tyne Cot Memorial, Panel 48 to 50 and 162A, at Zonnebeke, West Vlaanderen, Belgium.

From the War Diary the following information can be found. *After moving to support and relieve the 1st Essex Battalion on the 22nd March 1918, they were then on 23rd, in support and three other ranks were killed.* **Albert** would have been one of those killed.

Tyne Cot Cemetery where Albert's name can be found on the panels in the background.

Albert's brother **Private Samuel Florey 105975** was serving with the Army Service Corps having enlisted in June 1915. He was living at 10 Woodfields and had three sons, Samuel, Benjamin, Arthur and a daughter Marjorie. Prior to the war **Samuel** was a steam engine plough driver.

The second casualty for the month of March 1918 was living in Stoneyfield Common. He was **George Herbert HICKLING** who was born in Hethersett, Norfolk before his family moved to Stansted in about 1900. He had four sisters, Florence, Annie, Maude and Nora, as well as two brothers named **Charles** and **Donald**, who both also served King and Country. **George** enlisted in Saffron Walden where he joined the Royal Field Artillery.

George's details are as follows.

Driver George Herbert HICKLING 14781
Royal Field Artillery 235th Brigade 'B' Battery
Killed in Action 27th March 1918 aged 21

George has no known grave and is remembered on the Arras Memorial, Bay 1, Arras, France.

The Chaplain of the Brigade has written to Mr and Mrs Daniel Hickling, of 12 Woodfields, conveying to them the sad news that their second son has been killed in France. **Driver Hickling** was 21 years of age and had been in France for the last three years. Formerly he was employed by Messrs Pamplin Bros., agricultural engineers. Another son, **Private Donald Hickling**, Bedfordshire Regiment, has been twice wounded and is in hospital in France. **Donald** had seen action since November 1914 and later after recovering from his wounds served with the Labour Corps.

From the war diary details there seems to be no mention of any casualties, although as a driver **George** could possibly have been away from his brigade at the time of his death.

"We were formed into a group with 104th and 112th Brigades under command of 104th Brigade. Enemy concentrations were frequent but were dispersed by artillery fire and their attacks completely stopped. It was a splendid day for the guns".

Unfortunately it was not a *splendid* day for **George** or his family. A week before **George's** death his brother **Private Charles Frederick Hickling 44771,** a removal worker in civilian life, was sent to the Western Front with the Bedfordshire/Hertfordshire Regiment where he remained until the end of the war.

Stansted's last soldier to be killed during March 1918 was **William RATCLIFF**, the son of William J. and Priscilla Ratcliff, of 11 Woodfields. **William's** father worked as a bricklayer and before moving to Woodfields the family resided in Lower Street.

William enlisted in Saffron Walden where he joined the Essex Regiment, but at some stage during the war he was transferred to the Royal Irish Rifles.

William's details are as follows

Rifleman William RATCLIFF 41876
Royal Irish Rifles 2nd Battalion
Died of Wounds 28th March 1918 aged 22

William has no known grave and is commemorated on the Pozieres Memorial, Panel 74 to 76, Somme, France. It's not uncommon for a soldier who died of wounds and buried to subsequently have no known grave as many graves were lost in the subsequent fighting.

As **William** died from his wounds we need to look back through the War diary during the week prior to his death to ascertain the actions where he may have received his wounds.

From the War diary of the Royal Irish Rifles 2nd Battalion comes the following information

On the 21st March, at 5.00a.m an enemy bombardment of our front system and battalion area which had been intermittent throughout the night began to intensify and at 6.30a.m orders were received to man 'Battle Stations'. Companies then moved independently to previously arranged points of assembly, with the Headquarters in Quarry east of Grand Seraucourt. At 2.00p.m orders were received to take up position along the Grand Seraucourt, Essigny Road. The battalion was not yet in contact with the enemy, but was being heavily shelled with both gas and high explosive shells. A thick mist then rendered all observation exceedingly difficult. Then at 4.00p.m orders were received to assume former positions in the Quarry. Later at 7.00p.m 'D' Company advanced to Contescourt to attempt to re-capture the Village but the enemy put up a stubborn resistance, and at the same time advanced to the attack, under cover of a very heavy gas shell bombardment. In spite of the utmost gallantry displayed by all ranks of 'D' Company, no ground was gained. Very heavy losses were inflicted on the enemy but all except about forty of 'D' Company became missing. Within a few minutes of the company advancing orders were received to cancel the assault, but these orders were not received in time to halt the advance. That night at 11.00p.m the battalion withdrew, under orders, to the Le Hamel – Happencourt Road. Defensive positions were then taken up, and the night passed quietly.

The following day the 22nd at 11.00a.m the battalion withdrew to an old French trench system, south east of Happencourt. The mist had by this time cleared, and the enemy observing this movement shelled the troops on the move, but without inflicting too many casualties. The battalion remained there until dusk when at 6.00p.m the enemy, who had made some minor attacks during that afternoon, advanced in force and orders were received to withdraw back to Sommette-Eaucourt, and the to Tugny where they billeted .

On the 23rd the battalion paraded and reorganised prior to taking up a defensive position north east of the village. Reports were received that enemy patrols of cavalry

had entered Flavy-Le-Martel and orders were that Cugny was to be held at all costs. With the exception of one or two minor attacks, the afternoon passed quietly. Hostile aeroplanes were however, very much in evidence. Later that day at 6.00p.m the enemy attacked in force, but after a stiff fight was repulsed on our front but later they succeeded in driving back the troops on the right and they occupied positions between the battalion and the village. The next morning of the 24th, at Cugny the enemy machine gun fire was very heavy and that afternoon at 2.00p.m the enemy advanced, preceded by a very heavy artillery bombardment, in overwhelming strength, on our front line and flanks, and although the battalion put up a most stubborn resistance, all, with the exception of about ten other ranks wounded and ten unwounded, were killed or taken prisoner.

On the day of the 25th the battalion moved to Guerbigny. Various officers and men who had returned from leave or fighting with other units were collected and re-organised as a battalion. The diary only lists one other wounded, on the 27th, when a ration party was charged twice by enemy cavalry patrols.

Pozieres Cemetery and Memorial.

Private Herbert Dorrington Thurgood, Middlesex Regiment 19th Battalion, son of Mr J.H. Thurgood, of Bassingbourne Hall, Stansted, has been wounded in the recent heavy fighting in France and is in Netley Hospital. **Private Thurgood** was discharged from service in the following August having enlisted back in December 1915.

Private Cyril Haggerwood, Queens Regiment, son of Mr John Haggerwood, of Lower Street, has also been wounded, in the eye, and is in hospital in France. He later served with the Labour Corps.

The London Gazette, for March 1918, included the following D.C.M. citation.
Sergeant W.J. Peoples, Welsh Regiment, Stansted.

For conspicuous gallantry and devotion to duty when in command of a platoon. The battalion was ordered to advance and retake a position from which another unit had been driven back. During the advance under a heavy enemy barrage he kept his platoon well in hand, and collecting detached men of other units, advanced through a village just in time to meet the advancing enemy. He drove back the advanced parties of the enemy and, under heavy rifle fire which caused many casualties in his platoon, succeeded in establishing a firing line on the far side of the village and held the enemy until reinforcements arrived, when a further advance was made. His courage and good leading were instrumental in saving the village, and his gallantry and coolness were a most inspiring example to his men.

Research has been to no avail in finding out more about his connection with the village of Stansted other than the local *Herts and Essex* newspaper also mentioned the award of the D.C.M. but only mentioned Stansted, nothing more.
The Stansted connection was confirmed on his London Gazette citation, but nothing from census records etc.

His service records which are available at Kew again give no evidence of Stansted. He was a regular soldier having served from 1895 (at the age of 15) to 1906 in India and was part of the British Expeditionary Force at the outbreak of the Great War.

Two other Stansted soldiers were wounded in the heavy fighting in France, namely **Sergeant Evan Bright 5959**, Gordon Highlanders, son of Mr and Mrs A. Bright, of Lower Woodfield, who is now in a Sheffield hospital, and **Private Walter Watts**, son of Mr and Mrs Walter Watts, of Mont House Garden Cottage, formerly in the employ of Mr A. Sanders. (see picture of scouts at the beginning of the book showing **Walter Watts**)

Another Stansted soldier has won the D.C.M.
An intimation has been received that **Regimental Sergeant Major George Chappell**, of 15 Sunnyside, Stansted, has been awarded the Distinguished Conduct Medal, for gallantry while serving with the Forces in France.
For conspicuous gallantry and devotion to duty over a long period. He carried out his duties with great energy and skill, and set a splendid example to his men.
R.S.M. Chappell 4898, who was aged 43, has served for the long period of 23 years in the Royal Horse Artillery and is now attached to the Royal Field Artillery, and has

been with the forces in France nearly three years. He holds the Long Service and South African medals. He was recently home on sick leave, and the D.C.M. was presented to him before his return to France. He was married to Rose Emma and they had two daughters named Violet and Margerite.

An accident occurred in March 1918 at the Stansted level crossing. A schoolboy named Albert William George Ingold, son of soldier **Private George Ingold 3320,** Essex Regiment, had a remarkable escape from being killed at the level crossing just outside the Stansted Railway Station. It appears that the boy was warned by the gate lad not to cross the lines as a goods train was approaching. Notwithstanding the warning it seems the boy attempted to cross, and the result was he was struck by the engine and knocked between the metals where the whole train passed over him. He was removed and medically attended, the doctor finding him suffering from a severe cut upon the head, extensive bruising on the face and legs, and injury to the ribs.

Soldier, **Private Arthur Stock**, who was bought up living in Water Lane, Stansted, lost his life on the Western Front during an intense barrage concentrated not only on the infantry holding the forward posts, but on British artillery and machine-gun positions, headquarters, telephone exchanges, railways and other important centres of communications. This was the first day of the German offensive named 'Operation Michael'. **Arthur's** details are as follows. **Private Arthur Stock 30310, East Lancashire Regiment 2nd/4th Battalion, Killed in Action 21st March 1918 aged 31.** He has no known grave and his name can be found on the Pozieres Memorial. He was the son of Charles and Emma Stock.

April 1918

It may be a soldier's honour
At his country's call to fall
But we cannot think of glory
With the sorrow it caused us all.

Major and Mrs Charles Gold, of Gorsefield, Stansted, have been officially informed, by the War Office early in April 1918, that their second son **Flight-Lieutenant Donald Gold**, has been missing since Saturday last. According to reports received from France a storm came on and some of our airmen failed to return that day. He had only been in France a few weeks. Their eldest son, **Captain Leslie Guy Gold**, Hertfordshire Regiment, was wounded a few weeks ago, and is now in hospital in London.

The only soldier from the Tank Corps on the Stansted Memorial is **Philip Hallings SMITH** who lost his life this month. **Philip** was the son of Harold John and Minnie Maud Smith. His father Harold worked as a Manager and Traveller for a Gravel and Sand Quarry in Saffron Walden. **Philip** was born in Stansted but the 1901 census shows him and his family living in Saffron Walden.

Philips details are as follows.
Private Philip Hallings SMITH 96755
Tank Corps, Battalion unknown
Killed in Action 14th April 1918
aged 19
Philip is Buried at 'Y' Farm Military Cemetery, Bois Grenier. Grave Ref N.8. Bois Grenier is a small village about 4 miles south of Armentieres.

The Tank Corps battalion that **Philip** was fighting with is as yet unknown (The medal rolls, found on a soldiers Medal Index Card, at the National Archives, Kew, quite often list the battalion but on this occasion did not). From the location that **Philip** is buried it is very possible that he was one of the detachments that were sent to fill a breach in the front line, as Lewis Gun units.

173

Our next sad loss was **Henry William CHAPMAN** who was the son of Daniel and Jeanette Chapman. He had two brothers, Alfred and Josiah, and two sisters Elizabeth and Ethel. **Henry** was born in Great Shelford, Cambridgeshire in 1884 and worked as a General Labourer before enlisting in Cambridge joining the Suffolk Regiment.

Henry's details are as follows

Private Henry William CHAPMAN 15965

Suffolk Regiment 11th Battalion

Killed in Action Friday 19th April 1918 aged 34

Henry is buried at Suffolk Cemetery (pictured below), La Rolanderie Farm, Erquinghem-Lys. Grave Ref I.B.8. The Cemetery is situated a few miles south west of Armentieres. The cemetery contains the graves of forty-three soldiers from the United Kingdom, of whom thirty-six belonged to the 11th and 12th Suffolk Regiment, and of whom eight are unidentified. The name, originally La Rolanderie Farm Military Cemetery, was changed in May 1925 at the request of the 11th Battalion, Suffolk Regiment.

Henry had been involved in the fighting near the French Belgian border, from the war diary we find that they had been heavily shelled, with considerable violence, by the enemy. But on the day of **Henry's** death the battalion had been relieved and moved to reserve trenches so it's probable that **Henry** had been killed by enemy shellfire in the reserve trenches or the date of his death may have been a day out.

The next brave Stansted soldier to lose his life was **Edward George CAMP** who died in a War Hospital at Condé, France.

Edward had been taken prisoner and ended up in Minden Prisoner of War camp. Minden was an old Cathedral town lying on both banks of the River Weser 40 miles from Hanover. The camp was three miles from the town and was surrounded by farms. It consisted of a big square with six blocks of huts with a capacity of 18,000. Many NCO's were concentrated here at one time.

Condé was well behind the lines throughout the War, some 25 miles east of Cambrai and the Hindenburg Line.

Edward Camp pictured with his wife Clara and son Philip

We can only speculate as to why **Edward** ended up dying in a Hospital in France, one reason could have been that he was taken back to work behind the front line. But any speculation on **Edward's** death was surrounded by mystery as his wife, Clara, received the following sad news from two Essex men who were also prisoners of war in Germany that her husband had died from tuberculosis in a war hospital in Germany.

Edward's details are as follows

Private Edward George CAMP 203263 (Commonwealth War Graves Commission has his middle initial incorrectly listed as 'C')

Queens Royal West Surrey Regiment 6ᵗʰ Battalion

Died on 28ᵗʰ April 1918 aged 36

Edward's grave can be found at Conde-Sur-L'Escaut Communal Cemetery. Grave Ref A.31. Conde-sur-L'Escaut is a small fortified town in the Department of the Nord, north of Valenciennes towards Belgium.

Edward was the son of William and Jane Camp, he was born in Henham and lived there with his family. He had brothers named William and **Albert** (also serving) and two sisters called Florence and Alice. On the 10th October 1908 he married Clara Brand and they had a son named Philip George who was born in July the following year. During the War they were living in Woodfield Terrace. **Edward** was formerly in the employ of Mr Gerald Gold at the Stansted Remount Depot. He joined the Royal West Surreys in July 1917 and after his training went to France and was taken prisoner in December that year. In a letter received from him by his wife he urgently asked for food, and parcels were sent to him through the Red Cross. Both **Edward** and his wife were natives of Henham and they afterwards lived for a time at White Friars Farm, Duddenhoe End.

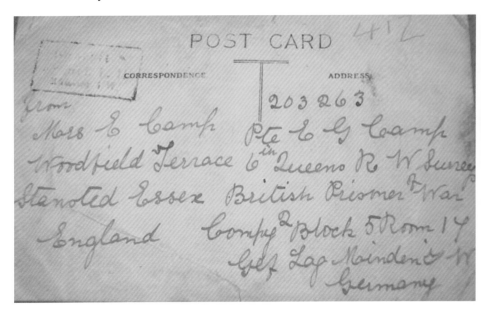

Postcard sent to **Edward** from his wife while he was a POW.

In Affectionate Remembrance
OF
MY DEAR HUSBAND,

✝ Edward George Camp. ✝

Who died in War Hospital, Conde, Germany,

April 28th, 1918.

Aged 35 Years.

Day by day we all shall miss him,
Words would fail our hearts to tell,
But in heaven we hope to meet him,
Never more to say farewell.

Edward was first reported missing in December 1917, having been missing since the 4th of that month. His wife was officially notified that he was a Prisoner of War in Germany during January 1918. Whatever confusion there may have been over **Edward's** place of death it would appear from an official letter his wife received in July 1918 that he had died in a French hospital at Conde.

George Arthur Amey

George Arthur Amey 27779, cousin of **William James Amey** (see June 1918) Northamptonshire Regiment, was listed among the wounded in April 1918 as was **Sergeant W.J. Barnard**, Oxford and Bucks Light Infantry. **Private Amey** was born in Stansted in 1882 the son of Joseph and Susannah Amey of Bentfield End. He later served with the Labour Corps. Prior to enlisting in May 1916, at the age of 34, **George** was employed as a Carman for the local coal merchants. He was married to Dinah and they had a daughter Phyllis. From his service records we find that he still had shrapnel left in his back from a previous wound.

Information has been received that **Flight Lieutenant Donald Gold**, Royal Air Force, who was reported missing earlier in the month, is a prisoner of war in Germany, and unhurt. He was shot down north east of Wartisse in the afternoon of the 6th April by German air ace Hans Kirschstein.

Mr F.R. Armitage, of Bentfield Bower, Stansted, is amongst the list of successful candidates who passed the recent examination for admission to the Royal Military College, Sandhurst.

Old soldier **Private George William Thompson** was sadly killed this month. He was born in Stansted in 1879 the son of Eliza Thompson and later in 1901 was listed as serving with the Royal Dragoon Guards and living with his widowed mother (who had re-married James Herrington) and the Herrington family at 85 Upgrove (Grove Hill), His details are as follows, **Private George William Thompson 400502, Essex Regiment 10th Battalion, Killed in Action 26th April 1918 aged 39**. He is buried at Hangard Communal Cemetery Extension, Somme, France. **George** lost his life during the actions of his battalion in the attack on Hangard Wood, south of the French village of Villers-Brettoneux.

At 5.15a.m. the Essex objective was through the left portion of the wood, but as soon as the enemy had sight of them through the mist they opened up with heavy machine gun fire and the Essex began to fall thick and fast.

The battalion lost over 70 men during the days fighting but hung on to half of the wood enabling the French to complete the victory two days later with the aid of tanks.

On the 29th of this month the following soldier, who was born and lived in Stansted during his early years, was killed. His details are – **Private James Edward Hutley 3130, Australian Infantry, A.I.F. 4TH Battalion, Killed in Action 29th April 1918 aged 26**. He was the son of Eliza and Charles Hutley. The family prior to the war were residing at 140 Cambridge Road, Stansted. Reports of **James's** death, from a comrade, were as follows, *'I had been repairing lines in a big farm and at about 9.00p.m. on April 29th, just as I was coming out of the billets a shell exploded in it killing **Hutley** outright and wounding 2 other men fatally. He was taken down to another farm about 100 yards away and buried in a paddock there'*. This was one of a few similar reports into how **Private Hutley** met his death. His grave can be found at Meteren Military Cemetery, Grave Ref. IV. G. 750. Meteren is a village 12 miles south-west of Ieper (Ypres, Belgium) and 2 miles west of Bailleul. **James's** younger brother, **Richard**, had been killed earlier in the war (see November 1916).

James had enlisted on August 23rd 1915. According to his service records he was a small man only 5 feet 3 inches in height and weighed 8 stone with fair complexion and light brown hair. He had been wounded in August 1916, a severe gunshot wound to his right forearm, and returned to England. Having recovered from his wounds he was back in France in the December of 1916, but a few weeks later he was sent back to England and hospitalised suffering from Trench Foot. (Trench Foot is a medical condition caused by prolonged exposure of the feet to damp and cold. It was a particular problem for soldiers engaged in trench warfare during the winter months of the Great War)

James was fortunate to have a couple of weeks leave in March 1918 before returning to his battalion in the April just weeks before he was killed.

He had originally been buried at Le Roukloshille Military Cemetery, Meteren, a little south of the hamlet of Le Roukloshille, between Meteren and Godewaersvelde. Here, in April to August, 1918, thirty-eight soldiers from Australia, twenty-six soldiers and airmen from the United Kingdom and one French soldier were buried by fighting units. These graves were, in 1919, like others nearby, centralised at Meteren Military Cemetery.

May 1918

If we only could have clasped his hand,
And heard his last farewell,
It would not have been so hard to part,
With the one we loved so well.
(From **James Walter Crockford's** wife Rose.)

The next Stansted soldier to make the supreme sacrifice in the Great War was **Private James Walter CROCKFORD** who was the eldest son of James, a platform porter at Stansted station, and Harriet Crockford of Grove Hill, Stansted.

James Walter Crockford

The sad news reached the village that he had died in a base hospital in Rouen, France on May 17th, from wounds he had received on May 12th/13th after being hit by a gas shell when his company were laying cables at Fonquevillers. Private **James Crockford** had enlisted at Purfleet and joined, under the Derby scheme, the 34th Battalion of the Royal Fusiliers in August 1916. He went to France in November 1916. Before the war he had been in the employ of Mr D. Robinson as a bricklayer. He lived with his wife Rose Anna at Sunnyside, Stansted and was 5'4" tall. He had three sisters Edith, Alice and Constance and a brother named **Albert** who was serving, in the Suffolk Regiment, and who had been wounded twice.

James's details are as follows.
Private James Walter CROCKFORD (54077) 60111 (Royal Fusiliers 34th Battalion)

Transferred to 101st Labour Company
Died of Wounds Friday 17th May 1918 aged 36

He is buried at St. Sever Cemetery Extension, Rouen France. Grave Ref Q.II.K.11. The cemetery is situated a couple of miles south of Rouen Cathedral.

James had arrived in France on 16th November 1916.

After his death, his wife was awarded a pension of 13/9d a week. (less than 70p in today's monies)

The Hospitals at Rouen remained there in almost all cases for practically the whole of the war. They included eight General, five Stationary, one British Red Cross, one

179

Native Labour Hospital and a Convalescent Depot. A number of the dead from these hospitals were buried in other cemeteries, but the great majority were taken to St. Sever and in September 1916 it was found necessary to begin an extension.

Typical surgical ward at Rouen Base Hospital

Ten days after the death of **James Walter CROCKFORD** Stansted lost another son by the name of **William John HAGGERWOOD**.

    William was only reported missing at this time and it was not until after the war in December 1918 that his death in action was actually made official.

    William was attached to the 2nd Battalion of the Devonshire Regiment and this regiment was involved in heavy fighting at Bois-Des-Buttes.

    Shortly before midnight on the 26th May 1918 **William's** battalion was established in underground shelters at the Bois-des-Buttes. These shelters took the shape of a system of tunnels running through a hill, which had been fitted up with electric lights and provided comfortable safe quarters. This was fortunate as at 1.00a.m on the 27th a bombardment suddenly opened in tremendous force, deluging the position with a flood of high explosive and gas shells, which compelled everyone for miles to put on gas masks. The Devonshire Regiment, in their shelters, escaped almost entirely, except a few men who despite their masks were gassed. Orders were received to leave the shelters and occupy the trenches. They were soon taking up their position in the firing line, since when they emerged from the shelters they found themselves, almost immediately, heavily engaged with the enemy. One platoon on reaching its trench found German machine gunners already behind it. *"We obliterated these before they new what was happening"* said one platoon commander *"and that cheered up the troops enormously"'*.

The Devonshire Regiment put up a splendid stand along the northern edge of the Bois des Buttes. One eye witness described the Devonshire's as *"an island in the midst of an innumerable and determined foe, fighting with perfect discipline, and by the steadiness of their fire, mowing down the enemy in large numbers"*.

With the enemy all around them and in a maze of old trenches, it was only natural that companies and platoons soon got split up. Some platoons were greeted by bullets on all sides including above because German aeroplanes were also co-operating in the attack and pouring in heavy fire.

The Devonshire Regiment stood their ground and fought against all the odds. The fighting soon broke down into disorganised and isolated fighting, but Bois de Buttes became an island in the centre of the German advance, and as such disrupted the enemy and bought time for the defences to be organised and reserves committed. The last stand was made by the Commanding Officer, Lt Col Anderson-Moreshead, and a dwindling band of men, along a vital road. The Colonel died along with his men who fought to the last. Of The battalion 23 officers and 528 men were killed, wounded or were taken prisoner. Only 40 succeeded in crossing the canal to rejoin the rearguard.

Soissons Memorial

William, who was killed in the above fighting, had the following details.

Sergeant William John HAGGERWOOD 8611
Devonshire Regiment 8th Battalion, posted to 2nd Battalion
Killed in action 27th May 1918 aged 28

William has no known grave and is commemorated on the Soissons Memorial.

The Memorial, which stands in the town square, commemorates 4000 members of

the UK forces who died during the 1918 battles of the Aisne and the Marne and who have no known grave.

William was the son of John and Fanny Haggerwood of Woodfields, Stansted. He was born in Birchanger and had two brothers namely **Cyril** and Percy. He enlisted in Bishop's Stortford where he joined the Devonshire Regiment and had been in action since the outbreak of war in 1914.

Mr Arthur Levey, of Cambridge Road, Stansted, has received official intimation from the War Office that his youngest son, **Private Robert Levey 27062**, Wiltshire Regiment (previously Essex Regiment), is a prisoner of war at Cassel Germany. Before joining the Army **Private Levey** was in the employ of Messrs Holland and Barrett at Bishop's Stortford.

Mr and Mrs H.H. Bass, of Alsa Lodge Farm, Stansted, have received the gratifying news that their son, **Second Lieutenant Guy Ronald Bass**, Machine Gun Corps, has been awarded the Military Cross. Particulars of the act of gallantry which won for him this decoration have not yet been publicly announced, but it is believed it was awarded him for carrying one of his men, who had had a leg blown off, out of the German lines under heavy machine gun and rifle fire.

His award was gazetted later in the year (July) which read as follows.

For conspicuous gallantry and devotion to duty while in command of one Vickers gun. He kept his gun in action in face of direct enemy machine gun fire, and when compelled to withdraw it 100 yards went back for ammunition to his original position. While there he saw a wounded man lying 200 yards off, and went out and bought him in. He displayed fine courage throughout.

Mr and Mrs R. Winder, of Bentfield End, have been informed that their eldest son, **Private Horace Winder 18774**, Royal Sussex Regiment, has been wounded in the arm. Before joining up **Private Winder** was footman at Stansted House, the residence of Lord and Lady Jackson.

June 1918

There is a link that death cannot sever,
Love and Remembrance last for ever.

The following soldier who was born in Stansted lost his life in June 1918. He was **Private William James Amey**, son of Henry and Rachel Amey and husband of Annie Elizabeth Amey. He was born at 100 Cottage, Bentfield End in 1880. In 1901 he had moved away from the village and was living with his Uncle and Auntie in Camberwell, as were his two younger brothers. The reason for him and his brothers living with their uncle was due to the fact that both his mother and father had died in 1887 and 1895 respectively.

William's details are as follows, **Private William James Amey 485094, Labour Corps 816th Employment Company, formerly 26770 Rifleman Rifle Brigade 15th Battalion, Died 23rd June 1918, aged 37.** He is buried in Pieta Military Cemetery, Malta. The island of Malta was used for hospitals and convalescent depots during the war chiefly dealing with those from the campaigns in Salonika and Gallipoli. **William** had been serving in the Salonika campaign and is not remembered on the Stansted memorial. **William's** cause of death was malaria.

William was the cousin of **George Arthur Amey**. (see April 1918)

184

July 1918

One year has passed since that sad day,
When one we loved was called away,
His cheerful smile, his loving face,
No one on earth can take his place.
Friends may think that we forget him,
When at times we're apt to smile,
They little think that grief is hidden,
Beneath the surface all the while.

William (Lally) HERRINGTON, eldest son of William and Isabel Herrington, of Woodfields, Stansted, died from wounds received on 7th July on the 14th July in Hospital at Wimereux, France, aged 23 years. **William** had gone to France in August 1915 after enlisting at Saffron Walden and joining the Essex Regiment. He had two brothers Cecil and **Henry**, and four sisters Blanch, Ellen, Evelyn (who was married to **Francis Edward Patmore**, the brother of **Alfred William PATMORE,** see May 1915) and Kate. The family had moved to Woodfields after living in Stoneyfield Common.
William's details are as follows.
Private William HERRINGTON 14060
Essex Regiment 2nd Battalion
Died of Wounds 14th July 1918 aged 23
William is buried at Terlincthun British Cemetery, Wimille, France. Grave Ref I.E.50. Terlincthun British Cemetery is situated on the northern outskirts of Boulogne. The first rest camps for Commonwealth forces were established near Terlincthun in August 1914 and during the whole of the First World War, Boulogne and Wimereux housed numerous hospitals and other medical establishments. The cemetery at Terlincthun was begun in June 1918 when the space available for service burials in the civil cemeteries of Boulogne and Wimereux was exhausted. It was used chiefly for burials from the base hospitals. It was one of these hospitals that **William** died in.

    William had been wounded in the Busnettes area which is a few miles north-west of Bethune. The war dairy, for the 7th July, states that, the enemy artillery was more active than usual during the day and Battalion Headquarters received a direct hit. His brother **Henry** had also served with both the Essex and Yorkshire regiments having enlisted in late 1915.

    William was the cousin of the **Patmore** brothers who figure quite prominently throughout the book and his sad death is mentioned in the personal war diary written by **Sidney Patmore** which can be found later in the book

Grave of **Private William 'Lally' HERRINGTON**

Another soldier died on the same day as **Private HERRINGTON**, he was **Private Arthur James Smith**, son of Elijah and Edith Smith of Building Yard, Elsenham. He had grown up living on the Elsenham Road which was classed as part of the Civil Parish of Stansted Mountfitchet, with his mother and father and elder brothers Ernest and Bertie.

His details are as follows, **Private Arthur James Smith 23097, Bedfordshire Regiment 7th Battalion, died 14th July 1918 aged 20**. Arthur had died as a prisoner of war and is buried in Cologne Southern Cemetery, Grave Ref. XVIII. B. 24. He is remembered on the Elsenham War Memorial. (pictured below)

August 1918

In the prime of early manhood,
Like the dawn of a beautiful day,
He fought with the bravest of the brave
In the thickest of the fray;
What could we have more glorious,
Who paid a greater toll,
Than he who fought through the Western Front
Gave life and soul for all.

The sad news was received by his mother on 15thAugust, that Bombardier **William Albert SAPSFORD**, Royal Horse Artillery, attached to the Royal Field Artillery, younger son of Mrs Caroline Sapsford, of Station Road, Stansted, was dangerously wounded and gassed on Wednesday 7th and died in a casualty clearing station in France on Saturday morning the 10th August, at the age of 24 years.

Bombardier Sapsford was in the Regulars and went to France with the British Expeditionary Force at the beginning of the War. He went through the Mons battle and retreat and was awarded the Mons star. In 1915 he sustained severe shell shock and was rendered deaf and dumb for eight months, but eventually made a good recovery in hospital at Liverpool and returned to duty. He was then attached to the Mesopotamia Expeditionary Force for eighteen months before returning to France early in 1918.

Before joining the army **William** was groom to the late **Captain William Fuller-MAITLAND** (see September 1914) at Stansted Hall. **William's** elder brother **Thomas** was also serving King and Country as a Driver in the Royal Horse Artillery.

William was born in the village of Takeley, in 1894, and also had a sister named Winifred. In 1901 his family were living in Takeley but some years later moved to Stansted.

William's details are as follows.
Bombardier (Gunner) William Albert SAPSFORD 77773
Royal Field Artillery, 28th Battery, 9th Brigade
Died of Wounds 10thAugust 1918 aged 24

William's grave can be found at Ligny-St. Flochel British Cemetery, Grave Ref II.B.3. The cemetery is situated about four miles east of St. Pol off the main road to Arras.

The action **William** sustained his wounds in, as mentioned above, was in an area north of Arras. **William**, unlike most other ranks, is actually named in the war diary for the 9th Brigade as, *along with two other men from the 28th Battery, being gassed on 7th August and taken to hospital during the night.*

A week later it was reported that Private **Frederick (Herbert) CAVILL**, son of James and Fanny Cavill, of Bentfield End, had been killed in France by a shell.

Frederick was born in Stansted in 1882. He had a brother Arthur and a sister Alice. His father, James, worked as a horse keeper on a farm and **Frederick**, prior to enlisting at Saffron Walden, was in the employ of Mr H.E Dudley.

Frederick's details are as follows
Private Herbert Frederick CAVILL 53522

Labour Corps 90th Company, Formerly 78616 King's Liverpool Regiment
Killed in Action 18th August 1918 aged 37
Frederick has no known grave and his name is commemorated on the Vis-En-Artois

Memorial. This Memorial bears the names of over 9,000 men. It is for those who fell between the Somme and Loos, in the period from 8th August 1918 to the date of the Armistice, and who have no known grave. The memorial, situated in the village of Vis-en-Artois, is approximately 6 miles south east of Arras. At the time of his death **Frederick's** company were at Guillacourt in the Anzac Corps area probably working on the railway.

Mrs Rhoda Jane Luckey, of 24 Sunnyside, Stansted, received the sad news that her husband, **Private Ernest LUCKEY**, had been killed in action by a machine gun bullet in an early morning attack on an enemy position on Wednesday 21st August 1918. **Private Luckey** was the son of Mr William Luckey, of Birchanger, and was 34 years of age.

    Ernest had joined up on November 8th 1915, enlisting at Marylebone, London, and joined the Coldstream Guards. Prior to joining the army he had been the butler to Dr. R. Russell, of Wimpole Street, London. He left a widow and three young children.

    This was the third son Mr William Luckey had lost during the war, having lost **Private Arthur Luckey** and **Gunner Harry Barltrop Luckey** (see January 1918 and February 1916), and a fourth, **Thomas Luckey** was so severely wounded that he was discharged as unfit for military service.

Ernest's details are as follows
Private Ernest LUCKEY 17183
Coldstream Guards 1st Battalion
Killed in Action 21st August 1918 aged 34
Ernest is buried in Bac-du-Sud British Cemetery, Bailleulval, France. Grave Ref. III.A.21. The cemetery can be found on the Arras to Doullens road about eight miles south west of Arras.

From the battalion war diary we learn the following about the actions that **Ernest** was involved in on the day he was killed.

The battalion was in position by 3.00a.m. Zero hour was 4.55 am. It was a very quiet night as regards shelling, but unfortunately a thick mist developed, which caused the tanks great difficulty in finding their assembly positions in a country they did not know.

The tanks helping Number 1 Company arrived in time, but those for Companies 3 and 5 did not put in an appearance. At Zero hour 1, 2, and 4 companies got off the mark with their tanks. By this time the fog was impenetrable and this was increased by the smoke barrage put down by the artillery. It was impossible to see three yards to one's front.

Number 3 Company waited ten minutes in the hopes that their tanks would arrive, but this not being the case Captain Gamble started without them. By 6.30a.m the battalion had gained all their objectives. Taking everything into consideration this was a fine achievement and gives great credit to all company officers and N.C.O's who led their men through an impenetrable mist for some 1,000 yards without losing their way.

The tanks owing to the fog were of little or no assistance, and as matters turned out were not needed.

Battalion causalities up to reaching their objectives were approximately ten and over sixty prisoners were captured. Lieutenant J.V.T Roderick was killed by a chance bullet on reaching the final objective. The battalion then consolidated the position they had won.

At 7.30a.m the 3rd Battalion Grenadier Guards had passed through the 1st Battalion Scots Guards and crossed the railway gaining the high ground beyond it. Number 2 Company swung their right flank forward and gained touch with them on this railway. About this time the hostile artillery came down on Moyenneville pretty heavily, and casualties mounted up. Throughout the afternoon and the following day the battalion had to sit still under heavy hostile shelling, and their casualties accordingly increased. On the night of the 21st Number 2 and 3 companies advanced their line some 500 yards across the railway into the outskirts of Hamelincourt and established and maintained strong posts there. Strong opposition was encountered but was overcome and the posts were firmly established.

The fourth soldier to make the supreme sacrifice during August 1918 was **Herbert Thomas WRIGHT** who was born in the nearby village of Ugley. He was the son of Thomas and Harriet Wright and had an elder brother William and a sister Gertrude.

Herbert had enlisted in Saffron Walden where he joined the Essex Regiment but later during the campaign was posted to the London Regiment, Artists Rifles.

In October 1914, the Artists' Rifles was established as an Officers Training Corps. Over fifteen thousand men passed through the battalion during the war, ten thousand of them becoming officers. The battalion eventually saw battle in France in 1917 and 1918, suffering thousands of casualties and earning hundreds of honours.

Herbert's details are as follows

Rifleman Herbert Thomas WRIGHT 52144
London Regiment 1/28th Battalion Artists Rifles, Formerly Essex Regiment
Killed in Action 27th August 1918 aged 26

Herbert, like so many others, has no known grave and his name is commemorated on the Vis-En-Artois Memorial.

From the War diary of the Artists Rifles we can find out about the action in which **Herbert** lost his life.

The battalion moved into position with artillery formation behind and the Royal Fusiliers on the left and Bedford's on the right. Heavy shelling by the enemy was taking place. The Brigade was then held up by machine gun and sniping fire which was extremely heavy. At 5.15p.m a barrage of shelling took place on the village of Thilloy. The Bedfords and Fusiliers were set to attack at 6.00p.m. Information was then received that only elements of the Royal Fusiliers were in front of the Artists so 'B' company on the left and 'C' company on the right were ordered to attack. The battalion attacked, under heavy machine gun fire from the left of the village and also some from the right. 'C' company (right front company) reached the eastern side of Thilloy capturing an enemy machine gun on route, and attempted to consolidate their position but in finding no support on either flank and being machine gunned from both flanks they were forced to withdraw. 'B' company (left front company) had advanced to about 200 yards west of the village but were held up by enemy machine guns. 'D' company (in support) of 'B', were heavily enfiladed by machine guns as they attempted to outflank machine guns but were unable to get round.

'A' company in support of 'C' advanced to within 200 yards of the village of Thilloy but were held up. On ascertaining their position a message was sent asking for support on their left to outflank the enemy situated on the brickfield, but support was not forthcoming. Finding it impossible, without support from their left flank, to carry on to their objective, a line was established.

August 1918 was the worst month of the war for the village of Stansted, as it lost a total of five brave soldiers and that figure is only those that are commemorated on its Memorial. The last soldier, from the village, to lose his life during this month of August was **Arthur TURNER.**

Arthur's details are as follows.

Rifleman Arthur TURNER 48805
1/8th Battalion (City of London Regiment) Post Office Rifles
Killed in Action 28th August 1918 aged 21
Arthur is buried at Hem Farm Military Cemetery, Hem-Monacu. Grave Ref II.D.18.

Monacu and Hem-Monacu are two villages about eight miles south-east of Albert, a little south of the road from Albert to Peronne and north of the River Somme.

Arthur was born in Stansted in 1898, the son of Alfred and Emma and a brother to John and Clara. He had enlisted at Saffron Walden where he joined the Rifle Brigade and was subsequently posted to the Post Office Rifles. At the time of his death he was living at Limehouse.

Information from the War Diary relating to the action in which **Arthur** lost his life is as follows.

Zero Hour was set for 4.55a.m. on the 28th August. The attack will be carried out by 'A' Company on the left and 'B' Company on the right with 'D' and 'C' Companies in close support. Prior to zero hour considerable difficulties were experienced in getting Companies into their assembly positions. The attack took place at 5.05a.m and was covered by artillery barrage at a rate of 100 yards in six minutes. The objectives were carried out without difficulty but our new line was shelled all day and some casualties occurred. One of these casualties would have been **Arthur TURNER**.

From the 11th Essex war diary we learn of how **Private James Haggerwood** was wounded again, having already sustained many wounds during his overseas service.

On August 1st the day passed fairly quietly but during the evening a ration party carrying to the front line were hit by an enemy shell with three killed and four wounded.

Private Harold George Harvey 21767, aged 19, of Millfields Stansted, was wounded in action on the 27th August 1918. He was serving with the 1st Battalion Coldstream Guards and had enlisted back in September 1916. He was the son of James and Mary Ann and before living in Millfields his family were resident at Bentfield End. **Private Harvey**, during his war service, became a 1st Class Signaller.

Two soldiers from the village were this month gazetted as receiving the Military Medal. They were **Sergeant C. Gowers**, Royal Field Artillery, 71st Brigade and **Sapper William Wiffen 181150/WR257060**, (both pictures below) Royal Engineers, Railways Operations Company.

Sapper William Wiffen was born on 11th March 1897 and had one sister Eva. He entered the war in 1916 serving with the Royal Engineers. His Military Medal was mentioned in the London Gazette on 29th August 1918. He would have been awarded this decoration sometime prior to this date. No actual citation can be found but family members have been told that his act of bravery was that *"He had saved a colleague on the field of Battle"*.

Prior to joining up he had first worked at the local quarry and then moved onto employment with the railways. He returned to working on the railways in 1919 and in 1924 he married his sweetheart Francis (nee Higgins). They had one daughter, Doris, born on 5th June 1924. **William** died in 1953 aged 56.

September 1918

Weep not dear mother, be content,
For I was only to you lent,
The Lord has only had His due,
And very soon may call for you:
Farewell dear father, brothers and sisters,
I am not dead but sleeping here
Somewhere in France as you can tell,
I have done my duty and done it well.

(From the sorrowing family of **Victor Valentine POOLE**)

Twenty two year old **Isaac Joseph FELSTEAD**, son of Isaac and Eliza Felstead, of Sheppard's Cottages, Bentfield End, Stansted, was the next Stansted soldier to lose his life. **Isaac** was born in Stansted in 1897 and from census records we learn he had a younger sister, Jesse. He enlisted in Saffron Walden where he joined the Royal Fusiliers. **Isaac's** details are as follows.

Private Isaac Joseph FELSTEAD G/48119
Royal Fusiliers (City of London Regiment) 4th Battalion
Killed in Action 18th September 1918 aged 22

Isaac has no known grave and is commemorated on the Vis-en-Artois Memorial. Panel 3.

From the battalion war diary we learn the following about the actions of his battalion on the day he was killed.

At 3.30p.m the enemy began heavy shelling of our battery area using a large proportion of gas. At 4.15p.m an intense barrage was put down on our front and support lines. At 5.00p.m the Germans attacked and succeeded in penetrating our line in three places, pushing vigorously along the sunken road and Havrincourt. A counter attack on the right and left fronts then drove out the enemy and completely re-established the original front line. Seventy prisoners and five machine guns were captured during the counter attack.

The battalion had suffered 73 casualties including the death of one officer, Second Lieutenant Twigg, and 19 other ranks who were killed in this action.

The day after the death of **Isaac Joseph FELSTEAD**, Stansted lost another of its very young sons with the death of **Victor Valentine POOLE**. His parents, George and Mary, of Woodfields, Stansted, received the sad news that their youngest son had been killed in action after serving only six weeks in France, at the age of 18. Previous to his enlistment at Saffron Walden, **Victor** was working for Mr Gold at the Remount Depot.

The bereaved parents had another son **Percy Frederick POOLE** (see chapter October 1918) who was also serving.

Victor was born in Takeley in 1900 and was the youngest child of seven, four brothers **Percy**, Horace, Harry and George, and two sisters named Gertrude and Kathleen.

Victor's details are as follows.

Private Victor Valentine POOLE G/66851
Queen's (Royal West Surrey Regiment) 6ᵗʰ Battalion
Killed in Action 19ᵗʰ September 1918 aged 18

Victor's grave can be found at Epehy Wood Farm Cemetery (below). Grave Ref. VI.A.17

Epehy is a village, in the Somme region of France, between Cambrai and Peronne about twelve miles north east of Peronne.

An attack on Epehy took place on 18ᵗʰ September. Enemy strongholds at Malassise Farm and Fisher's Keep held on stubbornly and caused heavy casualties but gradually resistance was overcome. Over the next few days further attacks were made against heavily defended posts and trenches; fighting was intense and progress slow.

At 11.00a.m on the 19ᵗʰ Victor's battalion attacked Molasses (Malassise) Farm in conjunction with the 6ᵗʰ Buffs (East Kent Regiment) on the right and 35ᵗʰ Infantry Brigade to the left. Much opposition was met with, the enemy machine gun fire being very intense. Molasses Farm was captured and the battalion consolidated 500 yards from it. Casualties from **Victor's** battalion during the attack included six officers wounded and twenty-one other ranks killed.

196

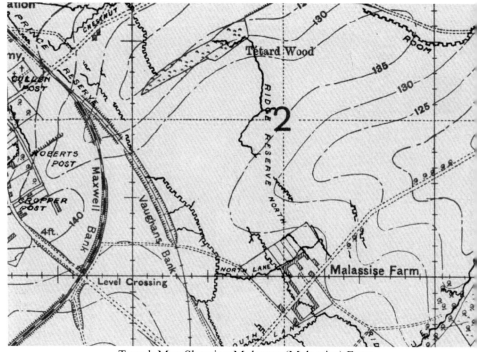

Trench Map Showing Molasses (Malassise) Farm

Lance-Corporal Arthur Clarke, Queen's Royal West Surrey Regiment, formerly employed at the Stansted Remount Depot, has been severely wounded in the left leg. **Lance-Corporal Clarke** is the son of the late Mr Clarke and son-in-law of Mr J. Crockford of Stansted.

Mrs A.E. Johnson, of Grove Hill, Stansted, has received an intimation that her husband, **Sergeant Albert Edward Johnson 8212**, 1st Battalion, Bedfordshire Regiment, is in hospital suffering from gas poisoning, and progressing satisfactorily. **Sergeant Johnson** was called up as a reservist on the outbreak of war and went to France with the first Expeditionary Force. He went through the battle and retreat of Mons and wore the Mons Star (1914 Star) and the Military Medal which he was awarded in 1916. On one occasion he and four others were buried for three days by a shell and when dug out three of the five men were dead. He is the son of the late Mr Albert Edwin Johnson, of Bentfield End.

October 1918

Now the soldier's task is o'er;
Now his battles' day is past;
Now upon the farther shore
Lands the voyager at last,
Father, in Thy gracious keeping
Leave we know Thy servant sleeping.

Early in October 1918 Stansted lost a brave soldier during the Battle of St Quentin Canal. He was **Charles ROBINSON**, the son of Alice Maria Robinson who was, in 1901, the innkeeper of the *Robin Hood* public house in Elsenham.

Charles was born in Elsenham in 1885 and had a brother Ernest and two sisters named Dora and Florence. He enlisted in 1915 at Saffron Walden where he joined the Essex Regiment but was later transferred to the Cameronians (Scottish Rifles).

Charles's details are as follows

Private Charles ROBINSON 203399
Cameronians (Scottish Rifles) 5th/6th Battalion, formerly 15636 Essex Regiment
Killed in Action 3rd October 1918 aged 32

Charles is buried at Villers Hill British Cemetery, Villers-Guislain. Grave Ref. IV.E.1

Villers-Guislain is a village ten miles south-south-west of Cambrai and three miles east of Gouzeaucourt, on the main road from Cambrai to Peronne. Villers Hill British Cemetery is about half a mile south-east of the village.

Details of any action **Charles** was involved in on the day he died are scarce other than the following.

Forward posts were established commanding the canal crossings. Enemy machine gun fire opposed all attempts by patrols to reach the eastern bank of the St Quentin Canal.

It can only be assumed that **Charles** was killed during one of these patrols.

Charles name is also listed on the Elsenham Memorial.

Less than two months after the death of there youngest son, Mr and Mrs G. Poole were mourning the loss of another son namely **Percy Frederick POOLE**. He had died in the V.A.D. (Voluntary Aid Detachment) Hospital at Whittlesford, from pneumonia following influenza. He was 22 years of age, and had recently been on service in France. He was invalided home, being unfit for military service, and had been working on a farm at Duxford. **Private POOLE** was bought home to Stansted and laid to rest in the St Mary's Parish Churchyard, the funeral being attended by seven comrades from the V.A.D. hospital. Since his death Mr and Mrs Poole sustained a further loss of a married daughter, leaving four young children.

Grave of Percy Frederick Poole

Percy's details are as follows.
Private Percy Frederick POOLE 496577
Labour Corps 431st Agricultural Company, formerly 1/5th Essex Regiment 24048
Died 27th October 1918 aged 22
Percy is buried in St Mary's Churchyard, Stansted, Essex. He had been born in Takeley and enlisted, joining the Essex Regiment, in Saffron Walden.

Percy was the last soldier with a Stansted connection to be both killed and named on the Memorial prior to the armistice on November 11th 1918. The Agricultural Company that **Percy** was in was based at Bury St Edmunds and men serving in these companies either lived at home or on the farms they were working on.

Another Stansted soldier has been awarded the Military Medal with a gilt card of commendation from his Brigadier-General. He was **Private Leonard Powell**, Essex Regiment, fourth son of Mrs Mary Powell, of 65 Lower Street.

"Your gallant conduct in the field on October 17th, 1918, in carrying messages under heavy fire and through thick mist has been reported to me, and I have much pleasure in reading the record of your gallantry".(signed) Brigadier General, November 1st, 1918.

Leonard was born in the village in 1894 and had brothers named, Edward, Arthur, **Frederick** and **Walter**, he was also a brother to Ada, Katie and Mabel. **Leonard** had been awarded his Military Medal whilst serving with the 11th Battalion of the Essex Regiment. Details of the actions **Leonard** was involved in on that day (October 17th) are as follows.

Vaux-Andigny was shelled with gas (Phosgene) heavily during the morning but the battalion was eventually in its jumping off position two hours before zero hour, with only three casualties, all wounded.

The morning was very misty, so misty it was almost impossible to see a man five yards away, making communication and direction very difficult. The enemies reply to our barrage was weak on our assaulting companies but heavy on the approaches to the railway embankment south of Vaux Andigny. There was considerable hostile machine gun fire from all directions. The assaulting companies captured the trench, Bellevue, by cutting their way through the wire and assaulting. 10 Machine Guns and over 50 prisoners were taken.

After this companies lost some direction owing to the heavy mist. They heard a tank but did not locate themselves until they reached and captured Regnicourt, taking over 100 prisoners. All the time hostile machine gun fire, from enemy guns in cunningly made and skilfully hidden emplacements, was experienced. The whole of the company headquarters of the left front company was wiped out by a big shell in the vicinity of Bellevue Trench.

During these actions it was without doubt that the mist prevented far heavier casualties being incurred.

Records show that at least two of **Leonard's** brothers also served, **Frederick** and **Walter**. **Walter** was discharged early in 1915 with illness.

November 1918

It may be a soldier's honour,
At his country's call to fall;
But we cannot think of glory,
With the sorrow it caused us all.

Captain Loftus J. Gibbs M.C. was officially reported as being wounded during November 1918. He was the fourth son of Mr and Mrs Joseph Gibbs of Chapel Hill, and had recently been awarded the Military Cross.

Mrs Harbridge, of Lower Street, had a postcard from her son, **Private Ernest Harbridge 204366**, East Surrey Regiment, who had been a prisoner of war in Germany since March 1918, stating that he has arrived safely in England. Her third son, **Private William Harbridge**, Signal Section, who was wounded for the third time on August 22nd 1918, is now making satisfactory progress towards recovery.

Rifleman James Gray 11576, of 3 Water Lane, was severely wounded on the 7th of this month at Cambrai. He was serving with the 4th Battalion of the King's Royal Rifle Corps when he suffered gun shot wounds to the arm and chest. Since joining in 1915 he had seen active service in both France and Salonika. He was twenty two years of age.

A re-visit to the memoirs of **Sidney Patmore** in his own words –
Just before the war finished we were in a town, we were able to stop and listen to President Poincare who was making a speech in the town square telling the people the war was nearly over. It finished on November 11th 1918. I stayed on until June 30th 1919 in the Army of occupation. I had seen three Christmases in France and three years altogether there. Our pay after the armistice was raised to 25 shillings per week and I felt quite rich and on time off was able to get about. I really enjoyed that bit of army life until I demobilised on June 30th. We had to go to Purfleet in Essex to get our final papers then it was back to civvy life again.

On the 7th day of this month in 1918 saw the sad death, from Spanish Flu, of **Captain Bentfield Charles Hucks.**
   The 1918 flu pandemic, commonly referred to as the Spanish flu, was an influenza pandemic caused by an unusually severe and deadly influenza virus. Many of its victims were healthy young adults, in contrast to most influenza outbreaks which predominantly affect juvenile, elderly, or otherwise weakened patients.
   The Spanish flu pandemic lasted from 1918 to 1919 and estimates are that 50 million to 100 million people worldwide died, possibly more than that taken by the Black Death.

Bentfield 'Benny' Hucks details are as follows. **Captain Bentfield Charles Hucks, Royal Air Force, Aircraft Manufacturing Company, died 7th November 1918, aged 35.** He was the son of William and Kate and was born in Bentfield End, Stansted, Hence the Christian name of Bentfield. **'Benny'** is buried in Highgate Cemetery, London.

Captain B.C. Hucks, a test pilot, was the inventor of the Hucks Starter a mechanical device, driven by a car engine and first introduced in 1917, which swung the prop. It was used on airfields and by air forces around the world up into the 1930s. It was normal practice for commissioned officers in the Royal Flying Corps to be released back to the aviation industry whilst retaining their rank. Their company was deemed to be their unit. It is also said that **'Benny'** was the first man to receive a wireless message whilst airborne and also the first English airman to fly upside down. **Captain Hucks** name is not found on the local memorial.

December 1918

Darling we will not forget you,
You gave your all that we might live.
(From the wife of William John Haggerwood)

On the 23rd December the following soldier died, he was **Albert Edward Freeman**.

Grave of Albert Edward Freeman

His details are as follows, **Gunner Albert Edward Freeman 176838, Royal Garrison Artillery, 69th Siege Battery. Died on 23rd December 1918 aged 39. Albert's** connection to Stansted was bought to my attention by Bob Pike (a Great War researcher from Saffron Walden) who noticed his headstone on a trip to Solesmes British Cemetery which is situated in the town of Solesmes about twelve miles east of Cambrai, or six miles north-west of Le Cateau, France.

At the base of his headstone was inscribed the following – *'Born at Tollerton Yorks. Late of Stansted Essex. He was a good sport and game till the end'.*

Further research shows that **Albert** was the son of Joseph and Ann Freeman of 148 Woodfields Stansted. He had five brothers named Ernest, Joseph, Lewis, Percy and Wallace and two sisters Constance and Sarah. Albert is not named on the Stansted Memorial.

Lance-Corporal A. Leech, Essex Regiment, son of Mr and Mrs Charles Leech, of Walpole Farm, Stansted, who had been a prisoner of war since the German offensive in March 1918, returned home to his family this month. He stated that he was working behind the German lines under heavy shell fire the whole time.

Private Cyril Sampford, Essex Regiment, (see October 1916) son of Mrs Sampford, of Grove Hill, who had been a prisoner-of-war in Germany, also arrived home this month. He was the first to volunteer for service from Messrs Green's Stores.

News was received this December through the Red Cross by Mrs Haggerwood, now of Aberdeen Place, St Johns Wood, of the death in action on the Western Front, of her husband, **Sergeant William John HAGGERWOOD** (see May 1918), of the Devonshire Regiment, at the age of 28. He had been reported missing since May 27th last and now it appears that he was killed by a shell explosion. The deceased who had been in the army for seven years when war broke out and at the front ever since, was the second son of Mr and Mrs John Haggerwood, of Lower Street, Stansted and his wife was the third daughter of Mrs Blake, of 131 London Road, Bishop's Stortford.

Mr and Mrs Daniel Robinson recently received the gratifying news that their fifth son, **Private Cyril W. Robinson 861115**, London Regiment, was decorated with the Military Medal ribbon on December 1st. The distinction was gained for conspicuous bravery and devotion to duty whilst carrying messages under heavy enemy shell and machine gun fire at Comines, on the river Lys, also for good work on the River Scheldt. **Private Cyril Walter Robinson** joined the Army in February, 1917, was wounded at Cambrai, November 1917, also suffered from trench fever, and went back to France in June of the present year. **Cyril's** family were from Lower Street, Stansted.

January 1919

He has no fear, he only prays
That someday he'll return,
Back to that dear old home
Whose heart for him does yearn.

It has been my intention throughout this book not only to remember those who gave their lives but also those that fought and were fortunate enough to come home to their loved ones. During my research I have been fortunate enough to have been given photographs of some Stansted lads that served.

Tom Johnson

Sidney Louis Dixon

Both of the lads pictured above were bought up in the Stansted area and also served with the Royal Artillery during the Great War. Both would have joined up and entered the war in their teenage years as they were born in the late 1890's. Their names are remembered on the 'Roll of Honour' in St Johns Church as are all those from the village who served King and Country.

Gunner Thomas (Tom) Johnson 179099, Royal Garrison Artillery (pictured in scout photo at the beginning of the book) was the son of Thomas and Annie and had a brother Charles (Known as 'Skipper') and a sister named Annie Elizabeth.. He later in

1923 married Stella Boswell and they had seven children namely, **William** (see WW2), Richard, Angela, Thomas, Constance, Molly and Hilary.

The photo on the following page is of **Gunner Tom Johnson** and his Artillery group.

Bombardier Sidney Louis Dixon 41961, Royal Garrison Artillery, was born in Elsenham. The 1901 census has his family listed as living at Gall End. He heralded from a large family consisting of four brothers, James, Thomas, Herbert and Redvers and four sisters namely Annie, Elsie, Olive and Alice.

Tom Johnson with his Artillery group

February 1919

Freely, willingly, cheerfully, he gave all that he had,
Even his life,
For the Great Cause,
Faithful unto Death.

Mrs Eleanor Staines, of Mill Field, Stansted, received official notification of the death of her eldest son, **Stephen Stanley STAINES**, at the 42nd Casualty Clearing Station, in the town of Douai, France.

Before joining up **Stephen** had spent many years in South Africa, and at the outbreak of hostilities rendered yeoman service in that country as a motor cycle dispatch rider, injuring himself to such an extent that an operation was necessary. Returning to England to recuperate, he could have secured exemption, but desirous of joining up and serving his country he entered the Suffolk Regiment and saw much service during critical times and was wounded. After a period in a Sheffield Hospital he was marked fit and returned to France before the great push. He contracted Flanders fever (influenza) and never fully regained his former A1 condition. He was home on leave in December 1918, but very unwell. He returned to France, but after a few weeks his condition necessitated hospital treatment, where after a period of three weeks he finally succumbed to the illness and passed away.

Stephen, named after his father, was born in Stansted, in 1878, living with his family firstly at Woodfields and lastly at Mill Road. He had two brothers Albert and Percy and a sister Kate.

Stephen's details are as follows
Private Stephen Stanley STAINES 166291
Machine Gun Corps 49th Battalion, formerly Suffolk Regiment 27961
Died 16th February 1919 aged 41

Stephen's grave can be found at Douai British Cemetery, Cuincy, France. Grave Ref D.27. Douai is a large town about fifteen miles north-east of Arras and the cemetery lies on the outskirts near the main road to Lens. The 42nd Casualty Clearing Station was posted in the town from the 28th October 1918.

Grave of Alfred Sanders

93667 GUNNER
ALFRED SANDERS
ROYAL GARRISON ARTILLERY
21ST FEBRUARY 1919 AGE 26

GONE BUT NOT FORGOTTEN

Five days later **Alfred SANDERS**, the husband of Mrs E. Sanders of 14 Woodfields, died. He was serving with the Royal Garrison Artillery, the R.G.A was responsible for the heavy, large-calibre guns and the howitzers that usually were positioned some way behind the front line, and from his Medal Index Card we find that he was awarded the Silver War Badge - (SWB), sometimes erroneously called the Silver Wound Badge, which was authorised in September 1916 and takes the form of a circular badge with the legend *For King and Empire-Services Rendered* surrounding the George V cypher. The badge was awarded to all of those military personnel who were discharged as a result of sickness or wounds contracted or received during the war, either at home or overseas.

Alfred was born in Stansted, in 1885, and spent some of his childhood growing up in number 13 Lower Street with his father, a carpenter named Charles, his mother Emma and a brother Walter. He had five children, four sons named William, Reginald, Leonard and Frederick, and a daughter May.

Alfred's details are as follows

Gunner Alfred SANDERS 93667
Royal Garrison Artillery
Died 21st February 1919 aged 36

Alfred is buried at the local St Mary's Churchyard.

In civilian life **Alfred** was a bricklayer by trade before he enlisted in the army in December 1915. He was discharged from service in March 1918 due to being 'no longer physically fit for service' after spending almost all of 1917 overseas where he had served with the 203rd Heavy Battery and later posted to 124th Heavy Battery. The ill health that **Alfred** had suffered with and which was the reason for his discharge continued and he finally succumbed to it in February 1919.

Corporal Alfred Lewis Laird 16173, Bedfordshire Regiment, received his discharge papers this month after serving throughout the whole campaign. He was the son of Mrs Laird of Water Lane, Stansted. Sometime shortly before the outbreak of war he had moved to Wales where he enlisted, at the age of 19, on 4th September 1914. During his time on the Western Front he was wounded on two occasions, the first was when he was with the 7th Bedfordshire Regiment on 30th September 1916 when he received shrapnel wounds to the thigh and arm. He was transferred to a hospital in Manchester where he spent six weeks recovering.

He returned to France in January 1917 and in March 1918 he was wounded for the second time. This time he was with the 4th Bedfordshire Regiment and suffered gun shot wounds of the face and chin and was also gassed. Again he was bought home for treatment and spent two months recovering in Clyne House Hospital Stretford, Manchester. He never did return to France and saw out the rest of the war at home. He had certainly *done his bit*. Prior to the war **Alfred** was employed as a railway porter.

April 1919

Yet again we hope to meet him,
When the day of life is fled;
Then in Heaven we hope to greet him,
Where no farewell tears are shed.

Our last Great War soldier, from the names on the Memorial, to lose his life was **William Henry HARVEY**. **William** was the son of William and Edith Harvey, of 23, Sunnyside, Stansted. He was born in the tiny village of Berden, near Manuden, in 1885 and later lived with his family at Woodfields, Stansted. He had three brothers, Sydney, George and Ernest, and a sister Edith. Prior to his enlisting, **William** was working with has father who was an agricultural Engineer.

William's details are as follows.

Private William Henry HARVEY M/428149
Royal Army Service Corps, formerly Essex Regiment 18th Battalion 26956.
Died 8th April 1919 aged 35

Grave of William Henry Harvey

William is buried in the St Mary's Churchyard, Stansted.

From the *Herts and Essex Observer* archive newspapers the following article, titled "A Stansted Soldier's Death", relating to **William** was found.

The death has occurred in Coats Hutten Hospital, Colchester, of Private W.H. Harvey, Essex Regiment, eldest son of Mr and Mrs W. Harvey, of 23 Sunnyside. ***Private Harvey*** *was wounded and severely gassed in France a year ago and died from the injury to his lungs from the gas poisoning. He was 35 years of age and a single man, and prior to joining up was a driver of the electric engine of Mr Thurston's roundabouts.* ***Private Harvey*** *had enlisted in 1915 and had seen overseas service in France with the 9th Battalion of the Essex Regiment. He was wounded in May 1917; suffering gun shot wounds to his arm and spent five months back in England recovering before returning to the front in October 1917. In January 1918 he suffered with 'Trench Foot', again he was bought back home where he remained until his sad death caused through tuberculosis.*

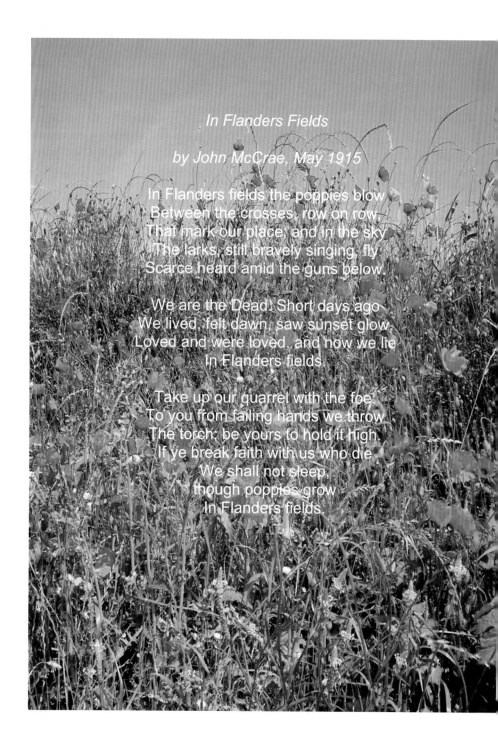

In Flanders Fields

by John McCrae, May 1915

In Flanders fields the poppies blow
Between the crosses, row on row,
That mark our place; and in the sky
The larks, still bravely singing, fly
Scarce heard amid the guns below.

We are the Dead. Short days ago
We lived, felt dawn, saw sunset glow,
Loved and were loved, and now we lie
In Flanders fields.

Take up our quarrel with the foe:
To you from failing hands we throw
The torch; be yours to hold it high.
If ye break faith with us who die
We shall not sleep,
though poppies grow
In Flanders fields.

Tommy's Letters from the Western Front

These are the letters sent home by a Yorkshire lad, born, in 1883 and bought up in Garforth near Leeds. His name is **Thomas (Tommy) Alfred Brownridge**, he was my Step-father's Uncle. I have in my possession the originals that the following has been transcribed from.

Tommy, who, prior to enlisting at Garforth, where he joined the Royal Engineers, was a bricklayer by trade. He was the son of John William and Annie Elizabeth (nee Cockram) and had two younger brothers, Albert and Ernest and a younger sister Gladys.

I have left the letters as they were written by **Tommy**. Any small additions, to aid the reader, are in brackets. The reader should understand that **Tommy** left school at the tender age of twelve years, as did most children in the late 19th Century. In the small close knit community of Garforth, it is probable that he never needed to write a letter to anyone until he volunteered for the army in 1915. He was not married. He was a skilled bricklayer and he played football for the local team.

Tommy's details are as follows,

2nd Corporal Thomas Alfred Brownridge 153934, Royal Engineers 126th Field Company, Killed in Action 22nd March 1918, aged 35. Tommy has no known grave and his name is commemorated on the Pozieres Memorial, Panel 10 to 13.

The Pozieres Memorial relates to the period of crisis in March and April 1918 when the Allied Fifth Army was driven back by overwhelming numbers across the former Somme battlefields,

Letter dated (early) 1916 (before Tommy went to France later in the year).

Dear Brother and Sister

In answer to your letter I have not had time to write (as) we have so much to go through just now. I shall be glad when this week is over it is our last week in the square & we have a rough time till Friday when if we are alright and pass the officers we shall be going to Gravesend for a week (for) firing etc & it will be a bit easier. It is the worst week of the lot but we shall manage it I think. We had an easy day on Friday, we finished with the gymnasium & bayonet fighting & had a competition before the gentry and captain etc. I was one of the selected 8 of our section & managed to get 2nd prize but it was not much they don't give much away here. We had a rather rough time on Wed night, we had been hard at it till nearly 9 at night & then we went for something to eat. We were dead tired and was only away about half hour & when we came back there was an alarm that is all have to get ready for off & there is something going on I can tell you. We have to get a blanket & our small kit together & parade, then they marched us away & we go about a mile & get rifles & equipment on. Everything had been a whirl for about 3 hours, then it is all over (and) back again we come. It is just to see how long it will take to mobilise. We landed back at half past 12 at night, dead beat, then we had marching orders for morning, first thing, that is our rifles and equipment all ready for inspection so you will see we have not much time for letter writing at present but shall be alright after this week.

I am pleased to hear that Father and Mother are keeping alright & Gladys, in fact all of you, but you don't surprise me about our Ernest at all, for it is like I always said, getting married is like a * Bran Tub (*A large tub is decorated with crepe paper, filled with bran or sawdust, then wrapped gifts were hidden in the bran. Everyone at the party had a chance to pull out a prize from the tub) some gets prizes and some gets nothing. He should not be so soft (as) he is old enough to have more sense. You say I should try to do without some beer well I don't get much now there is not time, but you want something as you don't get much to eat, nothing after 5 at night till next morning at 7 o'clock, it's a long time but I don't go without, we manage to buy some, but I can say this about the troops here, I have not seen above one or two worse for beer, here it is so weak & does not affect them as much.

I have not enquired about the allowance yet, but will do in a day or two, there is a lot in the same (position as me) getting nothing but 3/6d & the bother will come no doubt. I have seen the Sergeant Major today as Sunday I lost a lot of kit at the alarm but forgot to about the allowance at the time, but will be seeing him again & I will mention it. I don't know whether I will have to pay for it (kit) myself or not, he is going to se the Captain (about it). If I have to (pay for lost kit) it will not be much as they are only small things, my razor & towel & a few more items. I don't see much prospect of the war finishing yet. One of our officers told me we should be about ready for a big advance which he says will be sometime in the summer, so lets hope so and get it over, but we have a lot to learn yet. We have to learn to swim & I made a good show first time I tried. I was soon at the bottom but not by myself as I pulled another bloke (down) with me. Of course it was only in the baths but we shall have to (learn to swim) owing to bridge building etc which we will start doing soon. It will take us about 3 months or nearly so you need not trouble about me going to the front just yet. I want to apologise for (to) sags missus but I just forgot with being in a hurry so ask Maggie to forgive me & I won't do it again. I think to much about her for to try & insult her. Well Albert you must let them all see this letter at home as it will save me writing for a day or two. I have to start cleaning my rifle & kit ready for morning, that is 3 hours work on a Sunday at that. I am writing this about teatime, there'll be no going out tonight but never mind we keep smiling as long as possible, we shall get over it with a struggle. I think by what the sailors tell us here they are getting a strangle hold of the Germans, it is beginning to tell., letting them do their work right & not half as they have been doing.

I hear you had the * Zepps (*After the outbreak of the war, the German military made extensive use of Zeppelins as bombers and scouts), well it is nothing fresh here to have to get up but there is a warm corner for them if they come. I can tell you & I wish one would drop near here, I have a good service rifle at my bedside & plenty of ammunition.

With best to you all & all enquiring friends

Tommy

Excuse writing I am in a hurry
I will write home in a day or so.

Letter dated Sunday 4pm on the 23rd (April or July 1916).
Written on Headed Stationery YMCA on Active Service with The British Expeditionary Force.

Dear Albert

In answer to your letter which I received all intact and correct I may say that I am alright at present and still at the same place. I expect going any time up the line, but some stay a week or two but all my party have gone or very near and I am lucky to have so long, and as regards grub we are a bit better than we were, we are out working all day and today Sunday I have had an hour or two to spare this afternoon so I have just finished my washing, the only time we have a chance and having to do our own we have to make the best of it. I am writing this while they get dry in the sun and watch nobody takes them so you can understand how we are accommodated but we get used to it and make the best of it.

Well now to the money matters in the first place the extra allowance is wrong, my pay is 17/6d a week (skilled 2/0 per day). I made 6d per day in the first case and when I came out, I made it up to 1/9d per days so you will see that there should be 8/9d more every week so you had better write and tell them that there is a mistake and ask them to see to it, as for the money that I left well mother had best put it into the bank into her own name so that if she is in want of anything she can draw when she likes it will no doubt be better and as for a will we are all suppose to make one if we want to leave anything to other then our nearest relatives so I have not troubled about it, if anything should happen to me father has the first claim and I don't see that I could make it any better at the present time, we have a will in our pay books out here but what good are they if you are missing or buried etc., they are of no use so I left things as they were but I am coming back I hope I don't get downhearted so soon, we are not here although everybody wishes the job was over and they seem to think it will as reports from the front are good but a heavy price we are paying for the advance.

I am pleased to hear that you are alright at present for the married men out here would like to be back they have no heart left when they think of home and kids etc some have been here since the beginning and no leave so you can understand them being sick of it, so just tell mother not to trouble herself about me. I shall look after myself best I can and do my bit when the time comes. I think you will get some good news in a day or two so you just keep smiling and hope for the best, if there is anything more you want to know write but as soon as possible and I will give you the answer as soon as I can, so excuse more. I cannot say much more, or I would, so give my respects to Mr and Mrs James and with best love to Maggie and Baby.   *Yours truly*   **Tommy**.

Letter dated on 31st October 1916.
Dear Brother & Sister

Just a line or two to let you know how I am going on in this land of scientific murder, for it is nothing else! But first of all about the letters - I have received no letters from you since I last wrote, till the 29th, the letter with the cigs in, which were alright & smoked very well & I thank you for them. Gladys told me in a letter a while back that you were writing me, but I never received it, no doubt a lot goes astray, but we cannot help that, so I am replying to your last one.

217

I have not told them all about my experiences at home which would not do, but just to let you know how we have had to go on since I left the base, I will try. First of all we went up country in (a) railway train, crammed to the utmost & spent two days nearly, in the carriages, with Bully Beef & Biscuits to eat & a drop of water. Then we got to a town, or what is left of it, a few miles from the firing line, & in the big advance, as they call it in England, & the sights we saw, I shall never forget!

At last I landed to my company which was in the thick of the fighting at the time, having been in from the beginning. Well, we looked round for our place to sleep, but we (were) informed that we should have to do the best we could, but we managed to get in with some of the boys. And our bedroom for 4 of us was a shell hole, with a bit of a roof, as best as we could make it. Of course it rained in a bit, but that was actually nothing compared with what we had to go through!

We got no sleep for a time till we got used to the conditions, for Fritz was shelling us all night & day & with our big guns going, you can understand we was not so comfortable, but we was lucky to have no one hurt. The company that relieved us took our places & had 7 killed the next night.

The next morning I turned out with the rest of the section & had to go up to the fighting line, or nearly, clearing the communication trench out & making things passable, as all was blown to pieces, every thing has to go down, all buildings & woods are level.

Well, all day Fritz shelled us & we had one killed in our lot, but a lot of other fellows were knocked out & horses. Well, it is nothing to see one or two blown to pieces, they cannot get into shell holes for cover, you can't help but pity them, let alone the men.

I could not describe to you what the scene was like& I don't think you would care to see it. I was there where young Asquith* was killed and the sight would make anybody

sick! Nearby there were dead all over the show, our own men & Germans together, just as they had died & not been able to bury them, they were left & with the wet weather & dead horses intermixed & broken guns etc, the smell was awful as so (you) will understand & a sight I don't wish to see again! Although since then I have got a bit more used to it, for it is nothing now to see them bringing dead men out & sometimes falling over them in the dark.

*Raymond Asquith - son of the Rt Hon Herbert Asquith (Prime Minister from 1908 to 1916)., served with 3rd Bn Grenadier Guards, on the Somme and died of his wounds (he had been shot in the chest) on 15th September 1916 aged 37: he is buried in Guillemont Road Cemetery.

At last we got relieved & a bombardment shelling just before we came away, we being in between our guns & the German lines, I was glad when we got clear! And then we had a look around, for we could see Fritz line about a mile away & our side is bad enough when they start, but I should not have cared to have been at there's. You could see there trenches & other things in the air, then over the top our boys went & were soon back with a good many prisoners, who looked frightened to death & seemed glad to have been taken.

Well we were all glad when we were out of it. After that we had a week on the march to another part of the line which is all trench warfare & not quite so bad, but bad enough. I have been on night work, for as you know our work is mostly making trenches & repairing at present, & it is not so pleasant at dark in the middle of the night & only 50 yards from Fritz. You have to be very quiet, but he treated us gently till last Friday our boys went & raided his trench, but he replied with trench mortars all along the line. Of course we got out as soon as possible but were very lucky again. I missed by inches only, but 9 or 10 of our Yorkshire lads were killed by one shell bursting right in trench on top of them.

We are at days this week which is a little better, as you have a chance to get out of the way. You can understand what it is like at dark, up to the knees in water & mud & trying to dodge shells. I hope you* are lucky enough to miss it (*reference to his brother), but someone has to do it. They keep saying in the papers it will soon be over, well I hope so, but don't think so, it can last as long again this sort of fighting where I am.

Well, Albert I have considered again what I wrote in my last letter to you & I think it is only right that if any thing should happen to me that our Gladys should have something of mine, as she has had no chance her self, so I leave it to you to carry it out. That is give her £20-0-0 of my money & dad & mother the rest between them, but I am hoping it does not come to that. We shall have to hope for the best, everybody is tired of it here & we shall all be glad when we get back home again.

I am not surprised to hear about Jim Thompson, but it is hard to see the boys here in the trenches for days together wet through & others at home in comfort. They say we have plenty of men, well send them here, there is plenty of room for tryers, but shirkers are not wanted!

So I must now close with best love to all & Mr & Mrs James (surname Barber). I have just received a letter from Gladys, tell her I will write in a day or two, so good luck, hoping it finds you in the best of health, as I am under the present conditions

Yours **Tommy**.

Do not tell them anymore than you think best at home, but say I am alright & the other business don't mention it at present.

Letter dated 27[th]December 1916. (France)

Dear Albert

I have received (the) watch etc alright safe & sound & it is just what I wanted. I have not received any letters from home lately so just tell them I shall be writing as soon as I get back to my Com. (Company) which will no doubt be anytime. I should have gone back today Thursday but our Division is coming out for a rest, & of course don't know where they are, so I have to wait orders, I am about alright again as well as I can expect to be, I have enjoyed my Xmas fairly well, but of course not as well as if we all had been back in Blighty. I hope you have enjoyed yours, there seems to be a lot of talk about peace, well all out here does not care how soon, I reckon they will soon have to send the women out if it goes on much longer, as there will be no men left, it is alright for the heads to keep on talking, they want to come out here & have a go at it, they would soon be glad to be out of it.

Well there is not much news that I dare say so excuse now this time just tell them at home I will write in a day or two & answer all letters etc that is if I get them, remember me to Mr & Mrs James.

With best love to Maggie and Baby

Hoping that you all keep well & it will soon be over then I can talk about it which I cannot now. **Tommy**

Thanking you very much for sending the watch.

I hope you get your Xmas card.

Letter dated 19thFebruary 1917. (France)

Dear Albert & Maggie

I have just received your letter dated 8/1/17 it has been on the road a long time. I received the other parcels etc alright & have wrote home to that effect no doubt you will have seen the letter by now, but I thought you would like to know how we are going on out here, you say you were pleased to hear that we was well, but since then we have had a rough time of it, we have been on the march for a week or two & you can quite understand by the weather you have had at home. I have not known it so here before & to make things worse we had to travel at night nearly frozen to death sleeping in old barns etc, many a time snow on our blankets when we woke up in the morning & if not snow plenty of frost, everything frozen up, we had to wash & shave best way we could. We could hardly tell whether our hands & feet were on at all, it has just about knocked us up, I have been in worse conditions that at anytime since I came out, in fact all of us (have), some keep going sick but there is no consolation in that, they are horse doctors out here, no sympathy for anyone, you have to stick it, & to make things worse we have been on short rations, if it had not been for having some money in my pocket it would have been a bad lookout. I could buy a bit of bread etc now & again, but that has stopped now, you cannot buy bread from the French, it is forbidden by our Army Authority, so now when you have no rations hardly you have to go without. I have had some infantry working in the trenches with me & they have hardly (the) strength to lift the pick & shovel, what with the cold & no grub, fancy 4 or 5 men to a small loaf for a day & not much else, (we) have to make up with bully & biscuits which is no good to work on. They say we are winning, well if we are I pity the losses if the people at home knew what, & could see what, the men have to go through, they would go mad, I have seen men cry like kids that are fairly beat & hungry, I have given them mine many a time, as I knew I could get some having some money & now the thaw has set in the trenches is up to the knees in water & mud, the Infantry that have to stop in the trenches, it is a marvel how they stand it, you can reckon on being some invalids after this job, it is alright for the big heads at home sitting at ease, but they want to come out here I wish I had some of them with me tonight in the trenches I bet peace would soon be declared, but I cannot see any hope myself out here of it ending, I am in some trenches which we have occupied since the war started nearly & looks like stopping, I expect there will be a big advance as they call it before long, but no doubt we shall break there lines but the cost will be dear & the men we have, some of them are frightened to death before they get in the trenches, let alone go over the top, but we shall have to hope for the best. Fritz must be getting in a bad condition the shells we send over, I am sleeping in an old cellar among a battery of guns & they are booming day & night you bet we don't get much sleep, but never mind it wont last for ever, we shall have to keep smiling. I am pleased to hear that you have not had to come up yet, there is a chance of you missing it & I hope that Gladys gets that job you mention it will be a help for mother & she would be able to do a bit at home as well & by what I hear that food stuffs are getting very dear, well out here it is like buying money, we put so much a piece together & buy extras now we are more settled, but you cant hardly see 5 or 6 shilling worth of potatoes they are nearly a luxury.

Well Albert I don't think there is much more that will interest you, I could write all night if I had to relate all my experiences but I will leave that for the present, thanking Maggie for the Ginger cake it was alright, hoping to find you all in the best of health as I am a lot better at any rate as well as the others & not beat yet, so I will now close with best love to all & best respects to Mr & Mrs James, of course not forgetting the youngsters. **Tommy**

The cigs were alright the ticket enclosed was inside, * those fowls have had a good trip they ought to lay well.

(*Authors Note: Not sure what Tommy was saying here but it's exactly as written)

Letter dated 19th April 1917. (France)

Dear Brother & Sister,

I received your letter etc alright, but it had been opened, I expect somebody thought there was some money in it, but would be a bit surprised.

I wrote to Gladys when the parcel came & no doubt you will have seen the letter by now, so I shall not have much to say here, I have escaped out of the last scrap alright with a bit of luck I am well at present, you ask me about the fags, they are alright & I should be pleased for a parcel anytime just now, as we cannot get much at present. It does not matter how rough only that I get it, I don't know how I should have gone on if it had not been for the last & my mates parcel which of cause we generally share till it is done, all the stuff I have received up to now has been alright. I am pleased to hear that you are alright & still at home & hope you still continue, we have had as you say some very bad weather lately & (it) makes things bad. I was up to the knees in water in the trenches & starved to death but we have done very well up to now as you will have seen by the papers & I hope it goes on the same for it is time this job finished, but they seem to stick it does the Germans, it is amazing how much bombardment they can stand but time will tell no doubt, sooner the better you would think so if you saw the trenches after our artillery has had a go at them, but he has been well prepared but cannot stand against our guns, I think you will have seen plenty in Gladys's letter for the time. I will write you a more vivid account when I have time so excuse now for the present hoping you

221

are all in the best of health with best love to baby & all at home & Mr & Mrs James &
Family. **Tommy**

Letter dated 24th September 1917. (France)

Dear Brother& Sister,

I take the pleasure of writing a few lines to you & yours, I am pleased to hear that you are still at home & in the same employment, things out here are a bit busy where I am at present we have gone up the country since I saw Quigley but I hear he has come on leave & no doubt will have told you, we are in reserve on this new push, waiting for an infantry coming up. I don't know when we shall be going into action but I dare say it depends how we go on. We have done well this last week as you will have seen in the papers, I do not think Fritz can stand the guns that we have now, so long at a time, we can advance a 1,000 yards when we like. It is a rough job as there's not much cover up here like in the south owing to water, but by accounts they have got a good shock this time & you can expect more by the time you get this letter, we are all wishing it was over, but as you say I don't think it will end by fighting, if it has to well there will be a lot more to go under, for it is on a big scale & the guns employed are more powerful than ever. I wish you could see the amount we have you would not think that Fritz could hold out at all, it is a marvel how he stands the bombardment, the prisoners we have seen seem glad to be out of it & no wonder by what I hear we are not far from the line, I have been up to the front once just to get our bearing for when we go & he has lost heavily for there is dead everywhere, our artillery is killing them by hundreds.

We are having some fair decent weather here at the present & not much to grumble about only air raids, he visits us nearly every night but we have been lucky up to now & had no casualty, it is a poor way of fighting for us down below have no chance & the anti-aircraft it is bad for them at night, you must watch the papers & I feel confident that you will have better news in the next few weeks at least I hope so & get it over it has lasted long enough. I expect you will have seen Quigley & he will give you a better account than I can on paper for we dare not say too much.

You ask me when I shall be coming on leave, I was in good hopes to be home in a few weeks time, but with this job on I expect leave will be cancelled for a time but I am not sure & as there is not many before me now with a bit of luck I shall not be long & then I can give you a better account they don't treat us as we ought to be treated as regards leave, for officers & staff men & bosses get leave more often than those like me who have all the work to do, it has not troubled me up till now about coming home, when I know you (are) all well, but I can tell you it is getting a bit exciting now I am getting near for I have earned my leave & could manage a week at home very well, so I shall have to hope for the best in the next few weeks.

You mention about the money well the reason I was in debt it was a mistake in the book & as you know I don't allow myself much at this end & everything is so dear, it does not go far; but I have not drawn much lately & now stand £2 in credit at this end so I don't use much & with my 4s a day extra for my stripe it makes things better, I knew pretty nearly what I have had from home & also know that I was well in hand at home, but you spend more sometimes out here than you would but the conditions you are under & as we have been for 2 months & not seen civilisation you are apt to let yourselves out

222

a bit, to get the sights & your nerves back to something like order. I have lost my mate he has got to Birmingham Hospital he used to suffer from fits but is expected to be alright in a day or two but has done well to get to Blighty, he will miss a lot now, good luck to him for a man is lucky that gets a nice Blighty & gets out of it.

*I was sorry to hear about **B. Breed** * & the other Garforth boys going under but they will have consolation they have done there best.*

Well I don't think I have any more news at present, just congratulate Mrs James & tell her I wish I was as young as the baby, I should be a lot safer, so I will close with best respects to all including Mr & Mrs James & not forgetting Jess tell him is lucky to be a collier.

With best love to all I remain yours **Tommy**

(* **B. Breed** – Second Lieutenant J. B. Breed, Royal Garrison Artillery 236th Siege Battery Killed In Action on 31[st]July 1917 – From Garforth, Leeds, Yorkshire.)

Letter dated 26 February 1918 France – written less than two months before **Tommy** was killed in Action.

Dear Brother and Sister.

In answer to yours which I was pleased to receive to hear that you are all fairly well, I must apologise for not writing before, but really there is nothing to add to my few lines (sent) to Gladys. I am nicely as regards health, but I had a little accident yesterday, we were pulling some old rusting wire up round some huts that Fritz had bombed and I tore my hand a bit and of course had to be inoculated again and got excused duty, so that accounts for me writing for to tell you the truth, we have not much time, we have not had a half day off since we came back from leave. Sundays and all days are alike, in fact we cannot tell what day it is hardly. We did used to have Church Parade when actively in the line but now it does not seem to matter about the men at all and their comfort, things are pretty much the same, as you say at home, its still going on by guess and trusting to luck. I sometimes think about what we hear about the conditions at home and by what we see out here, which is the real thing, that somebody yet will have to answer for a lot after this job is over, for we are all fed up and get galled up, that (they say) it will be soon over and still there is no sign by what I can see. Everybody at home, and here, seems to be getting the wind up about a big attack by Fritz. Well what he could not do in the past I don't think he can do now, for he will not do as he did a few months back where he could do as he liked he will catch a cold if he tries, by my opinion is that he will not attack on a big scale.

I don't think either side can afford to throw men away as they have done in the past, but no doubt things are getting in a rough state and a big attack might decide the issue, if so the sooner the better and get it over. We have not had bad time lately, in fact, I have not seen the front line for some time, there is that much work just behind for us you know.

He leaves nothing standing and we have to fix our camp to the best way we can, he gives us a good reception with his bombing raids all night, especially this last moon.

I am sorry to say we had a good many casualties but he got something to go on with, some planes bombed him for hours, followed him back and we have had not much trouble since, that is the only way to stop him, they want to build as many as possible and have a right go at them in Germany, never mind women and kids they are all Huns and it would soon punish them.

I don't think they would stand much and I believe yet that is the only way it will finish not with fighting in the trenches, that has gone on too long a scale to come to anything to advance for a time, I am waiting to see what the Yanks have go to say about it, no doubt they will have a good air service and that added to ours will make a difference for we hold our own easily now, we are having poor weather here so if there is going to be something doing we expect (it) soon, it might be Italy not here, I have seen some Italians, Portuguese and all other soldiers out here but there is none that will face what we have to, so we shall have to wait and see, it might finish this year with a bit of luck and some better management and less red tape.

I should have been pleased to hear that you had got that property, I think it would have turned out alright and a good speculation in a few years time, you say I want to start for myself when this is over, we will get out of this and then well see what we can do, it is no use counting chickens before there are hatched for anything might happen but you can depend on me doing my best in all courses as I have done up till now but it is telling a tale on a lot out here, I guess they will not be much good for work after, knocked up and others won't have it so there will be plenty of chance for anybody earning a living especially in the building trade for I scarcely come across any bricklayers out here they must have all gone west, the Government will realize when it is too late that they cannot make a good tradesman in a day or two and will be in the cart when the time comes for beating the Hun in the markets again, I have known too many good tradesmen knocked out that was practically no good here, broken in health to start with, but would no doubt have earned his and family living at home, where here he is eating a good soldiers rations especially Labour Batts (battalions) they don't earn there grub let alone anything else. We have them sometimes when we are out for camp buildings and they make us that wild, the way they dodge the work, if we had them in the trenches some of them would not come back, we would lose them somehow or other and we are throwing more money away out here in useless men and staff.

Well I don't think I have any more to say, I had nothing interesting but as you reminded me about not writing but I happened to have the time I have tried and that has shown willing.

Ernest and Ethel are the next but I was waiting to see if I could see their Harold, I am near him but cannot get into touch with him. I might in the next few days so I will close with the best love to all, Mr and Mrs James and family and all friends, you and Maggie.

Tommy.

XXXXXX - these are for your little girl, what she did not get when on leave and she told you about it.

On the 22nd March 1918 **Tommy** was killed in action, his Royal Engineers' unit, the 126th Field Company, were moved into front line trenches alongside the 6th Battalion Leicestershire Regiment in the Guyencourt area south of Cambrai. From the diary we learn the following about events on the day **Tommy** died.

During an early morning heavy mist, the enemy were heavy shelling the trench at 5.00a.m. Both the 97th and 126th Field Company's were manning the trench at this time. The 6th Leicesters were holding the slope of the Sunken Road. Boche got round our flank and cut us off. Orders were received to withdraw to Saulcourt-Epehy Road. Position taken up at 10-30 as the mist began to lift encouraging strong forces of enemy to advance. Two tanks moved north to south and with great execution forced the Boche to 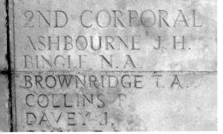 *run back. More orders were then received at midday to withdraw to Longavesnes Aerodrome to reform.*

Tommy, as mentioned, has no known grave and is remembered on the Pozieres Memorial.

The Pozieres Memorial relates to the period of crisis in March and April 1918 when the Allied Fifth Army was driven back by overwhelming numbers across the former Somme battlefields, and the months that followed before the *Advance to Victory*, which began on 8th August 1918.

The following letter was received by **Tommy's** brother Albert Brownridge who had asked after **Tommy's** disappearance. It was written by Corporal G. Henry Royal Engineers and was addressed 106 Queens Terrace, Rishton, near Blackburn, Lancashire. It was dated 2nd December 1918 (Tommy had been killed in action on Friday 22nd March 1918)

Mr. Brownridge,
Dear Sir,

"I received your letter this morning after crossing from France where I have been a prisoner over eight months. I am very grieved to hear that you have not heard from your brother for it makes me think that the worst must have happened on that never to be forgotten day.

Tom was near to me all the time till the enemy swept down upon us, and after that everything was like 'hell' I could only think there was about twenty of us left out of the whole Company, and most of us were wounded. Your brother was not amongst us then. We were taken to various collecting stations but I never saw any more of our lads. During the whole time I have been a prisoner I have had no letters or mail. I could not get in touch with our old Company. I hope and trust that Tommy is safe and will soon return to you. We returned to France together from leave and he was one of my best friends, for both of us had much in common being both northern lads. I am sorry I cannot give you any definite news, but will be pleased to answer anything you ask or require".

I remain yours sincerely
Lance-Corporal G Henry Royal Engineers

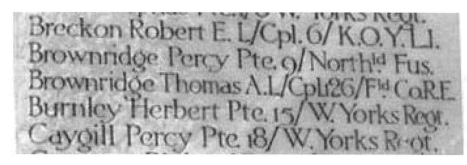

Breckon Robert E. L/Cpl. 6/ K.O.Y.L.I.
Brownridge Percy Pte. 9/ North'd Fus.
Brownridge Thomas A. L/Cpl. 26/F'd CoRE
Burnley Herbert Pte. 15/ W. Yorks Regt.
Caygill Percy Pte. 18/ W. Yorks Regt.

As we know **Tommy** was one of the many who never returned.

Welcome Home

In early July 1919 the village of Stansted gave its gallant men who had served in the war a particularly hearty welcome home. At a recent Parish meeting it was decided to entertain all the discharged and demobilised men of the parish to dinner. Nine officers and over 150 men accepted the invitation to attend and were present. The dinner took place in the Assembly Room at the Working Men's Club. The toast of 'The King' proposed from the chair, was loyally honoured and the first verse of the National Anthem was sung. Packets of cigarettes were then distributed.

The Chairman said it was his happy duty on behalf of the Parish Council and all the inhabitants of Stansted to bid a very hearty welcome home to all officers and men who had gone forth from this parish to do their bit in the Great War.

Lieutenant Norman P. Gold (Hertfordshire Regiment) said that on behalf of his colleagues and service men he thanked them very much.

A copy of the following, appropriately written for the occasion by Miss M Bretherton-Macallan, was given to each guest:-

You left us with a laughing jest, "Just a little trip we'll take";
T'was but a scrap of paper, but our honour was at stake.
We little thought that years would pass before the strife was o'er,
And we smiled as we parted, though our hearts were stricken sore.

The news was wafted homewards, of the valiant deeds you'd done
On the battlefields of Flanders; 'neath the desert's scorching sun.
There was scarce a house we'd enter but a vacant chair we'd find;
God only knew the anguish of those you left behind!

And now at last 'tis over, and we welcome you again,
Our hopes are for your welfare! Great things may you attain!
And though the flesh seems weakly, yet the spirit sure is there;
We thank you! And we bless you! God keep you in His care.

Tribute to the Fallen
The Unveiling of the Stansted War Memorial

On a Wednesday afternoon, in early July 1920, at Stansted, General Sir William Pulteney, K.C.B, unveiled two War Memorials which parishioners have erected to their late heroes and the occasion was one when relatives, friends and parishioners paid touching and impressive tribute to their memory. At 2.12p.m a company of 150 ex-service men and members of the local Friendly Societies assembled outside the Working Men's Club, where they were marshalled by ex- Regimental **Sergeant Major Chappell**, D.C.M., and, accompanied by the 1st Stansted Troop of Boy Scouts, under assistant Scoutmaster V. Watts, they marched to the Parish Church. Seats were here reserved in the centre aisle for the relatives of the fallen, who had personally been invited to be present, and for the ex-Service men in the north aisle, and the church was filled to its utmost capacity, the seating arrangements being made by Mr G. Little and ex-Lieutenant L.C. Pierce, R.AF. A half muffled peal on the bells was rung before the service, the Boy Scouts formed a guard of honour on either side of the Church path, and on the approach of General Pulteney the general salute was sounded at the west gate by buglers of the Essex Regiment from Warley Barracks. The Vicar (the Rev. A.C. Turberville) and the Rev. L.W. Wright (ex-Army Chaplain) officiated. The service which opened with the hymn *'O God our help in ages past,'* consisted of the Memorial Service for the Fallen in the War, sanctioned by the Bishop of Norwich. It included the 23rd and the 121st Psalms, a lesson read by the Rev. L.W. Wright, and the hymn *'Through the night of doubt and sorrow,'* and following the hymn the congregation remained standing while General Pulteney unveiled a beautiful memorial tablet which has been place on the south wall of the church. The tablet is of brass upon alabaster surrounding surmounted with oak leaf engraving and a central cross and bears the inscription:

In proud and grateful memory of the gallant men of Stansted who fell in the Great War 1914-1919, and then follow the names of the 54 officers and men of the parish who fell in the war. (This statement is not true because, for whatever reason the names of **Joe DEBMAN, Frederick Alfred MUMFORD** and **Francis GREYGOOSE** are not on the Tablet. The tablet only has 51 names inscribed on it.)

General Pulteney, in a few well-chosen words, referred to the noble and unselfish sacrifice these gallant men had made for their country and their God, and exhorted the congregation to preserve their loving memory and to teach the children to follow their great example.

The Vicar then dedicated the tablet and read the names of those to whose memory it was erected.

Prayers (including one from the bereaved relatives) were followed by the hymn *'Lo, round Thy throne a glorious band,'* and after a concluding prayer, the buglers sounded the *'Last Post'* and the *'Reveille'*.

The rest of the congregation remained standing whilst the relatives left the church, followed by the clergy and choir, General Sir William Pulteney, members of the Stansted War Memorial Committee, the Boy Scouts, ex-Service men, and members of the Parish Council, Foresters, Shepherds and the general public. The ex-Service men and

Boy Scouts were marshalled outside the church, the former carrying at their head a wreath of Laurels, and marched to St. Johns Church.

Unveiling of Memorial Cross

On reaching St. Johns Church the relatives, clergy, choir, ex-Service men, Boy Scouts, Parish Council members, school children, and the general public, took up their respective positions allotted to them, around a Memorial Cross which has been erected in the garden approach which was given by Lord Blyth some years ago to St. Johns Church, the officials in charge here being Messrs H.H. Bass, T. Gawlthrop, A. Bright and D. Godefroy. The Memorial is a Celtic Cross of Portland stone and stands 13 feet 6 inches high upon a three plinth base, and it could not possibly have a more suitable position than that which it occupies as the centrepiece of the pretty garden approach to the church. The memorial bears the inscription:

'In proud and grateful memory of the gallant men of Stansted who fell in the Great War 1914-1919'

The base of the cross was covered with beautiful floral tributes (fully a hundred in number), from relatives, friends and parishioners, and they included one, which was hung upon the cross, inscribed 'To our fallen comrades, from the Discharged and Demobilised Sailors and Soldiers of Stansted' and one from the Parish Council. The service in the garden around the cross was marked by fitting solemnity and impressiveness. It opened with a prayer, led by the Vicar, and the hymn 'For all the Saints' was sung. The Vicar asked General Pulteney to unveil the cross.

General Pulteney, in withdrawing the Union Jack, said *"I unveil this cross to the Glory of God and in memory of those from this parish who have fallen in the war."* The General saluted the memorial and then gave a short address. He said he must express the great satisfaction it was to him to come to Stansted, where in his early youth he was bought up, to unveil the two memorials which they had erected to those gallant men of that parish who had died in the war. He must congratulate them from the bottom of his heart for the great part they had taken in the European War. He was astonished to see the number of men, in proportion to the population, who had fallen in that great cause; and he asked them all to keep their memory in their hearts and to follow the great lead which they had given them in giving up all selfish ideas and thinking only of their country and their King. They who lived in the country districts scarcely realised what a difference there was between the countryman and the man who lived in the big cities, as a soldier. They found that the town man was not balanced to the degree as the countryman, and although the countrymen might not know it, they had sterling qualities built up in them by the soil they lived on, the pure air they breathed, and their healthy surroundings, which were denied to those men who lived in the big cities. He could not help expressing his extreme regret at the loss this parish had incurred, but he hoped that they all realised the great cause for which it was given. It was not only for the present generation that this nation had fought, but to retain the great possessions our ancestors had secured for the generations that were to come. They must think not only of themselves, but of their children. He must also say that he congratulated them from the bottom of his heart on the excellent taste they had shown in the memorial tablet and cross they had erected. Both were worthy emblems and he hoped they would remain emblems in years to come of the true spirit in all their hearts today. The General then concluded with the remark *"God bless you all"*.

The Vicar said he was sure that any formal vote of thanks would be out of keeping with the solemnity of the occasion, but he knew he could, on behalf of the parishioners, express their heart-felt thanks to General Pulteney for coming, and for the kind, helpful and sympathetic words he had spoken.

General Pulteney suitably replied.

The proceedings closed with prayer and the 'Last Post' and Reveille' were sounded on the bugles.

Before leaving, General Pulteney complimented all on the excellent arrangements made for the ceremony and the way everything had been carried out.

The arrangements for the erection of the memorials and the opening ceremony were made by the War Memorial Committee, of which Mr W. Fuller Maitland was chairman, Mr E.R. Riches secretary and Mr G. Foster treasurer.

The flag was hoisted at half-mast at the Parish Council, at St. John's Church, and at the Council School, until after the services.

IN PROUD AND GRATEFUL MEMORY OF THE GALLANT MEN OF STANSTED WHO FELL IN THE GREAT WAR 1914–1919

CAPTAINS		PRIVATES	
FULLER-MAITLAND W.A.	COLDSTREAM G^	CROCKFORD J.W.	ROYAL FUSILIERS
JACKSON C.S.		FELSTEAD I.J.	
SERGEANTS	BEDFORDSHIRE REG^	GRAY A.	AUST. IMP. FORCE
BUSH J.T.		GRAY W.	ESSEX REG^
FLOREY A.B.	DEVONSHIRE	HARVEY W.H.	" "
HAGGERWOOD W.J.		HERRINGTON W.	
CORPORALS	SUFFOLK	HICKLING G.H.	ROYAL FIELD ART^
BROWN R.G.	ESSEX	LAW H.J.	ESSEX REG^
LAW R.		LEVEY A.	AUST. IMP. FORCE
LANCE CORPORALS		MONK W.T.	ROYAL BERKSHIRE REG^
BUSH A.R.	BEDFORDSHIRE	MORETON A.	ESSEX REG^
CHAPMAN H.W.	ROYAL ENGINEERS	PATMORE A.J.	ROYAL FLYING CORPS
HAGGERWOOD J.	ESSEX REG^	PATMORE A.W.	ROYAL IRISH RIFLES
WARWICK P.	"	PATMORE C.	DUKE of CORNWALLS L.I.
BOMBADIER		PHILLIPS H.	ROYAL FUSILIERS
SAPSFORD W.A.	ROYAL FIELD ART^	POOLE P.F.	ESSEX REG^
GUARDSMEN		POOLE V.V.	R.W. SURREY REG^
LUCKEY E.	COLDSTREAM G^	RATCLIFF W.T.	ROYAL IRISH RIFLES
WARNER E.		REEVE E.J.	QUEENS WESTMINSTERS
PRIVATES		ROBINSON C.J.	SCOTTISH RIFLES
BANKS E.	BEDFORDSHIRE REG^	SAGGERS E.W.	ESSEX REG^
BONNEY A.E.	" "	SANDERS A.	ROYAL GARRISON ART^
BROWN C.W.	SUFFOLK	SMITH P.H.	TANK CORPS
BUCK F.C.	LONDON	STAINES S.S.	MACHINE GUN CORPS
CAMP E.G.	R.W.SURREY	TURNER A.	LONDON RIFLE B^gde
CARRUTHERS D.	OX. & BUCKS.L.I.	TURNER F.C.	NORTHANTS REG^
CARTER G.H.	ESSEX REG^	WARWICK C.W.	ESSEX REG^
CAVILL H.F.	LABOUR BATT.	WRIGHT H.T.	LONDON "
CHILDS A.H.	ESSEX REG^		

229

War Diary of: **Gunner 61175 Sidney Lewis Patmore**

Note: From Sidney's Grand-daughter Valerie.
I am Sidney's Grand-daughter Valerie. I have been handed the diary by my father Patrick William Patmore, as I am tracing our family tree. The diary an original document and some memoirs, were amongst items that have been saved from Sidney's life.

It's with great pleasure that I have included this personal war diary in my book and sincere thanks to Val and Patrick for giving permission to do so. It has been left exactly as Sid had written it. Any annotations are (bracketed in italics).

Sidney joined up as a volunteer (Kitchener's Army) on 2nd November 1915 in the Guild Hall, Colchester. He was enlisted into the Royal Artillery and became a Signaller for the 112th Siege Battery.

His training started firstly in barracks at Great Yarmouth, drilling, and from there to Ireland to Fernard Head Fort which his company shared with the Iniskilling Fusiliers spent Christmas there and moved onto Ebrington Barracks, Londonderry. From Londonderry he crossed back over to *Blighty* via Dublin to Holyhead to Clarence Barracks, Southsea. From Southsea his Company were moved to No Man's Land Fort situated in the middle of the Solent between the Isle of Wight and the mainland.

After two weeks with 179 other men on the fort, he was given marching orders for Cooden Camp, Bexhill on Sea, undergoing route marches in and around Hastings and Battle. It was finally time for gun practice for which the company was moved to Lydd Camp in Kent. As a result of Sidney's accent (or lack of it) he was chosen for a phone test and was promptly taken on as a signaller. He learned phone techniques and Morse Code. Before embarking to France he had one more move, to Stockcross near Newberry where he was kitted out and rigged up with equipment for the front.
He spent a few days' leave at home, 15, Woodfields, Stansted, Essex, before sailing over the Channel.

HAPPENINGS AT THE FRONT.

June 12th 1916. - Embarked at Southampton on board the Ceaserea, passed up the river Seine fine weather, disembarked at Rouen.
June 13th - Stayed at rest camp 3 days.
June 16th - Started for the line in Motor Lorries.
June 17th - Passed through Amiens on the way to Corbie got in a train there and travelled all night.
June 18th - Arrived at Sailly-Au-Bois spent the night digging Battery position.
June 23rd - Went into action D Gun fired first round.
June 25th - Opening of a big bombardment. (Battle of Somme)
June 30th - Bombardment continues.
July 1st 1916 - Early morning a 5.9 (shell) dropped on a bivouac the following men were killed.

Gnr Kemp R.I.P *(Gunner Kemp, James Jubilee 58275 aged 29)*
Gnr Boyne R.I.P *(Gunner Boyne, Bertie Charles 67894 aged 23)*
Gnr Wills R.I.P. *(Gunner Wills, Lionel Reginald 68157 aged 16)*
(Kemp, Boyne and Wills are buried in adjacent graves in Bertrancourt Military Cemetery.)
6.00a.m. intense Gunfire followed by infantry attack. Went to Duollens the same da
July 23rd - Bivouacs were shelled the following were made casualties,
Gnr Crosthwaite killed *(Gunner Crosthwaite, Frederick 66872 aged 32, buried at Bertrancourt Military Cemetery)*
Gnr Wilde and Gnr Easton died of wounds R.I.P.
(Gunner Wilde, William Herbert 66042 aged 36, Gunner Easton, Henry Herbert 67419 aged 21. Both these men are buried in Couin British Cemetery.)
Lt Borthwick, Sergt Elkins, Bdr Burnham and A.S.C. driver were wounded.
August 1916

I saw Cpt Basil (*Hallam*) Radford (Gilbert the Filber pictured left) fall from balloon on the 20th.
(Captain Radford, Basil Hallam, Royal Flying Corps, h is also buried in Couin Britsh Cemetery.

On a windy Sunday evening at Couin, in the vall north of Bus-les-Artois, men saw an observation-balloo tethered near their bivouacs, break loose while bein hauled down. It drifted towards the enemy line. First th watched maps and books being heaved overboard, then man in a parachute jumping for his life, who land safely. Soon after, something black, which had bee hanging below the basket, detached itself and fell son three thousand feet. We heard later that it was Capta Radford (Basil Hallam). His parachute apparent caught in the rigging and in some way he slipped out the belt which attached him to it. He fell near Briga Headquarters. Of those who watched, there was not on that had not seen him at the "Halls" in the immense remote days of "Gilbert the Filbert, the Colonel of th Nuts.")

Sept 1st 1916 - Went to O.P. at Mesnil

(O.P = Observation Post)
Sept 3rd - Intense gun fire, battery shelled with tear and gas shells. (BATTLE OF THE ANCRE)
Sept 26th - Intense gun fire infantry attack Theipval was captured. (The TANKS first appearance)
Oct 19th - Heavy firing continuing for 5 days.
Nov 8th - Fired our 20,000th Round.
Nov 11th - Battery shelled with gas for 3 hours Gnr Towell died of gass R.I.P.
(Gunner Towell Joseph 67857, aged 25, buried at Bertrancourt Military Cemetery)

Nov 13th - Heavy firing by us BEAUMONT-HAMEL was captured.
Nov 15th - Lt Mackay badly gassed.
~~Nov 23rd - Intense bombardment for half an hour to get relief to a patrol, who had for~~
5 days held an advanced position.
Dec 13th - Went to MESNIL
Dec 15th - Went to THEIPVAL to dig a cable trench lots of dead strewn about.
Dec 24th- Returned to SAILLY-AU-BOIS
Dec 25th - Xmas Day at guns telephone.
Dec 26th - Spent Boxing Day on Telephone.

1917

Jan 1st - Spent New Years day on telephone.
Feb 19th - Went to new position at BEAUMONT-HAMEL.
Feb 21st - Gnr C Martain was wounded.
Mar 3rd - Gnr Hawkins was wounded by a bomb exploding.
Mar 16th- BAPAUME was captured by the Anzacs. *(Australian and New Zealand Army Corps)*
Mar 17th - Birthday on duty at control post CP. *(Control Post)*

EVACUATION OF THE SOMME

Mar 23rd - Went to new position at ARRAS. (living in Cellars)
Mar 25th - Gnr Head and Gnr Smith were wounded just relieved me.
Mar 31st - Gnr Robinson and Gnr Meyers were wounded.
April 1st - Gnr Robinson died of wounds R.I.P. (BATTLE OF ARRAS) *(Gunner Robinson, Alfred Norman 64299, buried at Duisans British Cemetery)*
April 4th - Heavy firing until 8th
April 9th - Easter Monday intense fire followed by attack the 6th Corps Captured 100 guns, 6,000 prisoners and a General and his staff many Batteries were destroyed completely.
April 14th - Went to new position at TILLOY.
April 21st - Gnr Jarvis was wounded.
April 23rd - Heavy firing Bdr Knight and Gnr Winship were wounded.
April 26th - New position at WANCOURT.
May 3rd - Heavy firing.
May 14th - C P blown in by 5.9 Lt Muggridge, Gnr Nunn and Gnr Gower were killed. R.I.P. Gnr. Daniels killed R.I.P.
(2nd Lieutenant Muggridge, William, aged 40, buried at Tilloy British Cemetery)
(Gunner Nunn, Arthur 92038 aged 36, buried at Tilloy British Cemetery)
(Gunner Gower, Arthur Ernest 101034, aged 25, buried at Duisans British Cemetery)
(Gunner Daniels, James Eli 87970, buried at Tilloy British Cemetery)
Moved out of line billet in WANQUENTIN.
May 16th - Dump at WANQUENTIN caught fire our huts were knocked flat, Village in flames completely destroyed Gnr Howe was wounded.
May 18th - Stayed at ST VENANT.
May 19th - Arrived at NEUVE – EGLISE.

May 22nd - Went to new position at WULVERGHEM *(Belgium)* 900yds from Fritz.
May 30th - Major ORIEL was wounded.
June 3rd - Bdr Wicks Gnr Rose and Gnr Hartwell were wounded.
June 6th - Bdr Sims was wounded and blinded Gnr Chrisby was wounded badly.
June 7th - 3.10 A.M. Watched the MINES go up at MESSINES also the barrage and battle from KEMMEL HILL O.P.
June 12th - At O.P. near MESSINES many narrow escapes.
June 16th - Sergt Hardy was wounded.
June 19th - Gnr Macgrath, Gnr Alford and 2 reinforcements were wounded.
June 22nd - Majors Motor Car blown up.
June 28th - Gnr Foster wounded.
June 30th - Gnr Alford and Gnr Slessor were wounded.
July 1st - Gnr Slessor died R.I.P, Battery shelled C P blown in Capt Lubbock Gnr Armfield Gnr Daniels and Gnr Clare were wounded.
(Gunner Slessor William Thomson 168253, aged 30, buried at Kandahar Farm Cemetery)
July 8th - Gnr Coalsworth wounded.
July 8th - Went to position at MESSINES.
July 23rd - Gnr Williams died of concussion and Gnr Golder was wounded.
(Gunner Williams, Ernest 55068, aged 27, buried at Trois-Arbres Cemetery)
July 25th - Gnr Spencer Wounded.
July 26th - Gnr Baldwin wounded.
July 29th - Billeted at WULVERGHEM.
July 30th - Passed through CALAIS on way to rest camp at AMBLETEUSE near BOULONGE.
July 31st - First day of battle of FLANDERS.
August 4th - Pouring with rain.
August 5th - Spent day at BOULONGE beautiful weather.
August 13th - Returned from R Camp.
August 15th - Going Home on leave spent night at BOULONGE.
August 16th - Arrived Home!!
August 26th - Back in France.
August 27th - On rest at BAILLUEL.
August 29th - Went to HAZEBROUCK.
August 31st - Bdr Tayler Gnr Crane wounded by Bomb. *(Bdr = Bombardier)*
Sept 9th - Returned to WULVERGHEM.
Sept 22nd - Reinforced by half of 427th Siege Battery.
Sept 27th - Moved out of line.
Sept 28th - Billeted at VLAMERTINGHE position at LANCER FARM near YPRES.
Oct 4th - Intense firing attack all objectives gained.
Oct 5th - Billeted in YPRES, went to O P at Hill 35 lots of dead about. Bty moved forward to BAVARIAHOUSE.
Oct 11th - Heavy firing continues.
Oct 12th - Heavy firing and attack very wet weather.
Oct 14th - Position shelled 2 guns knocked out of action Sergt Smith died of wounds R.I.P. Gnr Howorth and Gnr Fairburn wounded.

(Corporal Smith, Daniel 45559, aged 33, listed as Corporal not Sergeant, died of wounds on 15th, buried at Nine Elms British Cemetery)

Oct 17th - Major Oriel, Gnr Macphial and Gnr Guiness were gassed.

(Gunner Guinness Davud Herbert 121392 died from the gas, buried at Wimereux Communal Cemetery)

(GunnerMacphail Robert 95984, aged 20, died ten days later in hospital and is buried in Etaples Military Cemetery)

Oct 21st - Moved from YPRES passed through POPERINGHE camped at WATTOW.

Oct 22nd - Passed ST VENANT, LILLERS stayed at BRUAY.

Oct 23rd - Arrived at position at ANGRES. (good position) *(north of Arras)*

Nov 10th - Stayed at BARLIN. *(south of Bethune)*

Nov 11th - Stayed at Cavalry Barrack ARRAS.

Nov 12th - Stayed at BAPAUME.

Nov 13th - Stayed at YTRES. *(east of Bapaume)*

Nov 14th - Billeted at RULAULCOURT position about 2 miles front.

Nov 20th - Intense bombardment attack all objectives taken.

Nov 21st - Advance continues.

Nov 23rd - New position DEMICOURT billets at HERMIES.

Nov 30th - Big counter attack could see Hun coming over the top.

Nov 30th - Shelled with gass 20 men and NCO gassed.

Dec 2nd - Gnr Cane wounded.

Dec 11th - New position near DOIGNIES.

Dec 24th - On duty at the O.P.

Dec 25th - Spent Xmas at bivouacs.

Dec 30th - 2 guns moved to SLAGHEAP.

1918

Jan 2nd - Gnr Kane wounded.

Jan 6th - Went to Signal School at VAUCHELLES billeted in barns.

Jan 31st - Went to Hospital in DOULLENS.

Feb 10th - Returned to Bty.

March 12/13th - Big Bombardment Hun ready to attack heavy casualties inflicted on him.

March 17th - Spent my birthday at O.P. POPPY.

Mar 21st - Heavy bombardment big Hun attack, nearly a break through we suffered the following casualties Gnr Speck killed R.I.P. and Gnr Bond, Sgl *(Signaller)* Sims were wounded and Sergt Smith and Bdr Sylvester gassed I was on duty at Battery.

(Gunner Speck, Albert 55793, aged 20, buried at Beaumetz Cross Roads Cemetery)

(Gunner William Walter Bond 67836 later died of his wounds and is buried at Rocquigny-Equancourt Road British Cemetery)

THE RETIREMENT

Mar 22nd - Hun driving us back the following are casualties Gnr Leith Gnr Atchesion R.I.P. Gnr Maclenan were killed Gnr Milne Gnr Herbert and Bdr Wier were wounded, we've got to pull out tonight.
(Gunner Leith George Rae 126001, Pozieres Memorial)
(Gunner Aitchison Philip Theodore 90906, Arras Memorial)
(Gunner Maclennan John Alexander 158676, Arras Memorial)

Mar 23rd - Go to position at VELU WOOD but are soon chased out We take a position at BANCOURT I went to O P, Hun still coming on Cpl Young was wounded and Gnr Monk was badly injured by a gun running over him.

Mar 23rd - Pulled into position at BEAULINCOURT.

Mar 24th - Still retiring passed through ALBERT.

Mar 25th - Pulled into position behind BOUZINCOURT Hun is in ALBERT.

Mar 27th - Seem to be holding the Hun up a bit.

Mar 29th - Good Friday still holding up the Hun (pouring with rain). Went to O.P.

April 5th - Hun attack 3 places but gains very little

April 7th - On duty at forward section. C.P. is in a family Vault Mausoleum on outskirts of MAILLY MAILLET.

April 7/8th - Went out on line shelled very heavily with HE *(high explosive shells)* and gas for over 4 hours.

April 8th - Temp attached to 278 SB5 they have had lots of men gassed.

April 9th - Slow bombardment of gas by the Hun. Had to leave the position too hot all got a touch of gas 13 gone to Hospital.

April 10th - Isolated under observation for gas.

April 12th - Went to O.P. pretty warm time.

April 19th – Spr *(Sapper)* Wright was wounded at O.P. Gnr Bond and Gnr Milne reported died of wounds.

April 21/22nd - 11.58PM went to OP returned 3a.m.

May 25th - Shell dropped in Battery and wounded Sergt Norris Gnr Barnet and Gnr Seabourne.

May 26th - Went to Minnow OP 300yds from the Hun at 4.10PM intense hostile bombardment on the support line finished 5.10PM very rough time.

June 12th - Battery pulled out on rest, go to ROSEL.

June 16th - Went for a joy ride to ST.VALERY *(St Valery-sur-Somme)* small town at mouth of Somme.

June 18th - Returned to position near HEDAUVILLE on guard.

Rest Camp at Saint Valery sur Somme with French Countess and her daughters in the grounds of her mansion.

June 25th - Returned to Rest Camp.

July 1st - Went into action lively activity got S.O.S call 9.41p.m.

July 4th - On rest Bde sports Battery took most honours.

July 7th - Rest is over back again on the ANCRE.

July 7th - Cousin Will wounded 14th died.

(Private HERRINGTON, William (see July 1918)

July 24th - Spent day at SPRAT Observation Post visited by Gen Sir Julian Byng Commander of 3rd Army Battery position is on the field of AGINCOURT.

Aug 6th - Went to Rest Camp at ST VALERY a town on the mouth of the SOMME The effigy of the Virgin Mary was damaged (of ALBERT) Cathedral by an 8 inch shell fired by 57 SEIGE BATTERY, rendered unsafe.

Aug 10th - Having good weather, also a good time at ST.VALERY.

Aug 12th - Went to the Abbey at ST VALERY very old and historical place SAINT VALERY died there.

Aug 20th - Returned to Battery who have moved to FONCQUE VILLERS a village about 8 miles N of ALBERT.

Aug 21st - Terrific bombardment by us all objectives gained.

Aug 23rd - Still advancing BAPAUME said to have been taken.

Aug 24th - Shifted billets to PIDGEON WOOD billeted in dugouts. Battery turn a captured gun round and fired on the enemy I went into GOMMECOURT WOOD.

Aug 25th - Shifted billets near BUCUOY.

Aug 26th - Moved billets to ACHIET_LE_GRAND Battery at BIEFVILLERS *(Biefvillers les Bapaume)* still advancing.

Sept 3rd - Moved in front of FRAMECOURT.

Sept 4th - H.V. *(high velocity)* gun shell seriously wounded 2nd Lt Pearson, hun seems to be retiring, Battery pulls into position at VELU WOOD hun shelling with gass and H.E. Gnr Ellis was wounded (in the same vicinity as we were in before the retirement in March we were chased out of VELU WOOD on March 23rd) Lt Pearson died of wounds R.I.P.

(2nd Lieutenant Pearson, David Easson aged 24, buried at Vaulx Hill Cemetery)

Sept 5th - Gnr Ketley was gassed Gnr Fleming and a new fellow were wounded.

Night Sept 6/7th - A few bombs were dropped by the enemy near our bivouac and wounded Capt Berling and 2nd Lt Godin. (LE BUEQUIERE)

Sept 7th - Bty takes the exact position which we were forced to evacuate on March 22nd (SLAG HEAP)

Sept 10th - Gun put out of action by shell fire Gnr Saunders wounded.

Sept 11/12th - On duty at the same B.C.post which previousl we were forced to evacuate on March 22nd.

Sept 12th - Heavy bombardment local attacks by us all objectives gained.

Sept 18th - Battery pulls out spend night at FAVEREUILLE. *(also spelt Favreuil)*

Sept 20th - Take up position at PRONVILLE billets temp MORCHIES.

Sept 27th - Big attack I watched the battle for BOURLON WOOD from an O.P. called HAWKE.

Sept 27/28th - Battery moves forward takes up position on conquered ground near QUARRY WOOD.

Sept 28th - Pulled into position in front of BOURLON WOOD advance continues.
Sept 29th - Big attack seems to be successful, billeted in BOURLON VILLAGE. *(5 miles west of Cambrai)*
Oct 1st - 5.20a.m heavy Barrage.
Oct 2nd - Left Bty for Leave stayed night at Rest Camp BOISLEUX-AU-MONT.
Oct 3rd - Stayed Rest Camp Brewery BOULOGNE.
Oct 4th - Arrived Home 11.30p.m.
Oct 18th - Back in France spent night at Rest Camp.
Oct 19th - Spent night at Rest Camp BOISLEUX-AU-MONT.
Oct 20th - Spent night in CAMBRAI.
Oct 21st - Spent night in train.
Oct 22nd - Spent night in CAMBRAI. (can't find Battery)
Oct 23rd - Arrived at Battery at NOYELLS.
Oct 24th - Moved to position at HAULCHIN were gassed during the night.
Oct 25th - Bombardment and attack.
Oct 26th - Went to Jerusalem O.Post.
Oct 28th - Battery moves to MAING.
Nov 1st - Very heavy bombardment infantry attack all objectives gained moved to new position in front of MAING Took message Turks and Austrians have accepted our terms.
Nov 2nd - Moved position just over the RHONELLES RIVER, AULNOY every where we have been to lately civilians have been there.
Nov 3rd - Some civilians are badly gassed some have died from the effects.
Nov 4th - Moved to position at SAULTAIN.
Nov 5th - Battery out on rest at SAULTAIN line is rapidly advancing through MONS.
Nov 10th - Went to VALENCIENNES heard an address given by the French president M.POINCARE great talk of peace.
Nov 11th - Armistice signed hostilities ceased 11.00a.m.
Nov 19th - Today it has been read out on parade that we are going to Germany with the Army of occupation. Later cancelled.
Nov 25th - Since the start of armistice our daily routine has been route marches or squad and Physical drill.
Nov 26th - Battery moves to BOUSSU, billeted in a school room.

Boussu

Dec 20th - Moved to new billets at MONS.

Night 20th/21st - All Btrys in Brigade rebel against the rotten conditions and riot 12 midnight. The Colonel speaks to Btys, Btys refuse to parade Colonel address crowd promises fresh and better billets, riot seems to be over.

Dec 22nd - Moved to much more comfortable billets.

Dec 28th - Went to the City of Brussels visited the main buildings.

Dec 29th - Visited the interior of the Hotel-de Ville beautiful place climbed to the of the tower 418 steps had ripping time.

Dec 30th - Visited the interior of the Cathedral very fine and ancient building.

Dec 30th - Returned to MONS very satisfied with trip.

1919

New Years day on parade.

Jan 17th - Moved from MONS, new billets at a village called SOIGNIES very de billets very nice people.

March 15th - On guard at MONS station our guns parked here.

March 17th - Spent my birthday on guard at MONS Station.

March 22nd - Battery moved to new billets at HYON.

March 24th - Returned to BTY at HYON billet.

April 20th - EASTER SUNDAY went to church service in CAFÉ COLUMBIA.

April 21st - EASTER MONDAY. On duty at BUE telephone office.

April 24th - 561 men have passed through 112 SIEGE. BTY

April 28th - Snow and hail storms.

May 27th - Went on leave, beautiful weather.

June 10th - Returned from leave spent night at rest Camp Calis.

June 11th - Entrain for MONS.

June 12th - Arrive at MONS 02.00 hours; the completion of my 3rd year in France and Belgium.

June 23rd - Received the news in CAFÉ METROPOLE that peace had been accepted by the Germans.

June 25th - Warned for demobilisation spent night at concentration camp at MONS.

June 26th - Arrive at demob camp at BOULOGNE.

June 27th - Spent night at Rest Camp.

June 28th - At 3.12p.m the Chief of German delegate attached his signature to the peace treaty unconditionally Spent night at Rest Camp.

June 29th - Arrived back in England went to PURFLEET demobilised.

June 30th - Arrived back Home.

Sidney Patmore in 1922

112th Siege Battery, 'D' Section, Royal Garrison Artillery. After the 11th November 1918 armistice.

112th Siege Battery Signal Section, Royal Garrison Artillery. In Mons, Belgium. Sidney Patmore 4th from left centre row

World War 2

Stansted Mountfitchet, Essex (Between the Wars)

The following is a brief insight into the village of Stansted Mountfitchet prior to the outbreak of World War 2, kindly penned by **William (Bill) Johnson** the son of Great War Veteran **Tom Johnson**.

I was born on the 8ᵗʰ April 1924 at "Garth Cottage", Chapel Hill, Stansted, the eldest of a family of six children.

Chapel Hill afforded a wonderful view towards the Stansted Hall estate lands, much the same as it does today.

"Garth Cottage" was a neat two up and two down brick built house with a slate roof, looking across the road to St. John's Church gardens with its impressive World War 1 memorial dedicated to those who didn't return after the war ended in 1918.

Built on to the rear of the house was an outbuilding with a toilet and next door to it a scullery containing a brown earthenware sink with a cold water tap (next to the door) and against the far wall was a brick enclosed copper for heating water for the weekly wash and baths. The family had a weekly bath in a traditional metal bath in front of the kitchen stove in winter and in the outhouse in summer. A hooped wooden barrel took the rainwater off the outhouse roof; this was used for washing hair and watering the useful-sized vegetable garden at the rear of the house.

The family expanded at "Garth Cottage"! In fact it became a bit of a squeeze! My parents had a daughter sleeping in their room whilst the three boys slept together in the back bedroom. Then a heart-breaking event occurred when in 1929 my fifth sibling, a baby girl, was born (at home) and sadly died the same day. In those days, she was what was known as a 'blue' baby – without hospital care and a blood transfusion she didn't have a chance! The sadness of this family loss was the beginning of the end for our home at 'Garth Cottage'. By the time we moved across the road to "St. John's Villa" it was 1930. Our new home was a large house occupying three floors (four if you count the cellar!), a large garden for a growing family and a future full of hope! In the November of that year, my sixth sibling was born, a girl, and seven years later my seventh and final sibling arrived, another girl! Our family was complete and "St. John's Villa became the family home to which the post-war, far flung families of Tom and Stella Johnson returned to celebrate birthdays, Easter and Christmas until age, distance and family size brought these pleasures to an end.

*In the years before my birth in 1924, grandfather Thomas Richard Johnson started up an engineering and electrical business, covering plumbing, water pumps for agricultural use, installing home electricity generation plants for the 'big houses' in the locality, until national electricity generation became the norm. The firm, T. Johnson and Sons was a partnership of grandfather, my father, **Thomas William Johnson** and my uncle, Charles George Johnson known locally as 'Skipper' – (a talented local artist). The business was located in an old wooden, mill-type building at the end of a drive opposite the old Fire Station, marked at the Chapel Hill entrance by two imposing large*

244

concrete (?) balls sitting on brick pillars. The old building was destroyed by fire sometime after I left Stansted in 1942 on war service. The firm occupied all four floors of the building. The ground floor was a garage for the van, known as the '(tin) Lizzie' and a car which was changed every few years for a new one. I believe the first one was a 'bull-nosed' Morris and one of the later ones was a Standard.

The first floor housed the general office which also served as a drawing office. Outside the office was an area where grandfather charged 'low tension' glass accumulators (wet batteries) for members of the public. The wireless set was becoming more and more popular. The charge was two-pence (old money) for the smaller 'batteries' and three-pence or four-pence for the larger ones. I used to earn six-pence a week as his battery-boy on a Saturday morning for identifying customer's 'batteries', checking they were fully charged, and putting a dab of Vaseline on the terminals before handing them back to their owner in exchange for the requisite fee! The rest of the second floor housed a large strong workbench and a storage area.

The second floor was entirely given over to storing electric light bulbs, piping, metal trunking, conduit, belting, miscellaneous nuts, bolts, screws, fittings of all descriptions, cables, flexes and a host of other impedimenta connected with electrical and general engineering.

The third floor housed more stores and was a general dumping area. Originally it looked as if stores were hauled up by way of the overhanging gantry – but not in the lifetime of T Johnson and Sons!

One of the difficulties the firm had to live with was the problem of securing payment from the gentry for services rendered. Everybody wanted their own petrol driven dynamo and storage battery system (30v. DC, I believe). Grandad was among the first in Stansted to have his own 'Petter' 2-stroke petrol engine and belt-driven 'dynamo' at his home in Woodfield Terrace. This installation was housed in a glass-roofed extension to the house, which linked the main building to the scullery and copper room, bathroom and battery room. When the engine was running the bank of batteries sizzled away like witches brews! The petrol was stored in metal cans in a locked steel container in the garden – conforming to the safety regulations of the time!

Sunday was a quiet day. There was no rampaging around the garden let alone going out on the street. We children went to Sunday school at the Central Hall prior to 'crocodiling' down to 'St. John's Church' for morning service at 11am. Lunch was served immediately after dad had tuned in the one o'clock news on his home-constructed wireless. We had to be very quiet while that was on! When I was old enough I joined the church choir and attended the evening service as well as the morning one. Choir practice for both men and boys was held on Friday evenings in the church. The choir master and organist, Mr. Torey, kept a register of our attendances every week and periodically we received a little envelope containing our 'choir money'.

My Sunday school teacher was **Charlie Johns** (**R. C. Johns** see December 1943) – a wonderful, gentle, Christian man who grounded me in the Christian faith, which I will ever remember him for. Charlie was a Burma veteran who never returned from World War II.

At the age of eleven (1935), I won a Scholarship to Newport Grammar School where I stayed until 1942 when I joined HM forces. Apart from my studies at Newport I had an early morning job with the W H Smith bookstall at Stansted Station, delivering newspapers and magazines to customers at Burton End and points east. I used to report for work at 6.20 pm, sorted the papers for my round into house order and was away on my bright red 'trade' bike by soon after 6.30am. My furthest point out on the round was Bassingbourne Hall farm which now, alas, is no more having been replaced by Stansted Airport! I finished my round and caught the train for my six mile journey to Newport at 7.40am. I received half a crown (30 pence, old money) for my labours.

Leisure time in my early adolescent years was spent as a member of the Stansted Art and Craft Society. The brain child of one Sammy Sanders and his friend Dennis Bass (Newportonians like myself), the club met weekly in the converted garage of Dr. Bluitt with an entrance on the Recreation Ground road. We wrote and produced sketches for our own amusement and enjoyment and on one or two occasions put shows on for public consumption at the Central Hall on Chapel Hill. They were happy days! We had no television and only few had gramophones to entertain themselves at home. We had to make our own own entertainment. One wonders whether young people have the same incentive today.

In my teens, I used to work at Elms Farm (by the railway line) treading silage. This was one of the most boring jobs a young person could have! Grasses from the hayfield were pitch-forked into a round container, some fifteen feet in diameter, and I had to tread this down and periodically add molasses to the 'mix' followed my more tramping down. My boots became sticky and heavy, not to mention smelly. Eventually, the container was full and the 'mix' was left to ferment and mature as a winter feed for cattle. I received sixpence (old money) an hour for this work and glad to get it!

My wife Doris was a Stansted girl from the age of eleven. She was a Sunday school teacher at the old Congregational church (now URC) on Chapel Hill for many years, working with Miss Tunbridge. Her father, William Brett, was a sawyer working for Daniel Robinson in Lower Street. Doris was an enthusiastic member of Audrey Bickerstiff's Stansted Girl Guide Company. Doris was her lieutenant. When the Second World War broke out Doris' company was camping in the south of England. They were ordered home. Doris had the responsibility of organising the girls' journey home, with their personal equipment. Across London in a fleet of Taxis! Mission successfully accomplished.

In November 1945, I flew home on a month's leave from the Far East to marry Doris at the Stansted Congregational church, but that's another story!

© **W. B. Johnson**

Skipper's sketch of the 'Works' where T. Johnson & Sons ran their business – Interpretation by Bill Johnson

1939

He heard the call and he was there,
To do his bit and take his share;
His heart was good, his spirit brave,
His resting place a soldier's grave.

The following soldier lost his life on 23rd November 1939 but he is not named on the Stansted memorial. He was **Sub-Lieutenant Redvers Henry Taylor, Royal Naval Reserve** on board HMS Rawalpindi. His connection to Stansted is that he was the son of Thomas and Elizabeth Taylor and the husband of Georgina, of Stansted Essex. HMS Rawalpindi was a British Armed Merchant Cruiser (a converted passenger ship) that was sunk on the 23rd.

1940

We think of you in silence
And oft repeat your name
(From Mum Dad and Sisters)
(Roll of Honour from Herts and Essex Observer Archives)

December 1940's roll of honour was from the parents and sisters of the first casualty of World War 2 to be remembered on the Stansted Memorial, who is **Private Patrick Allen SNOW** whose details are as follows.

Private Patrick Allen SNOW 6016202
Essex Regiment 1/5th Battalion
Died on 28th December 1940, aged 32

He is buried in the churchyard of St Mary's, Stansted.

Pat was the son of Charles and Lucy Snow. Addresses at which **Patrick** resided were Forester's Cottages, Stoney Common and Millfields. His sisters were named Hilda, Dora and Daphne.

The only details about **Patrick's** death are that he was possibly killed when he unfortunately trod on a mine on the beach.

On the 21st November 1940 **Driver Sidney John Wren, Royal Army Service Corps**, died aged 23. He was the son George and Annie of Stansted.

1941

He died for the cause of freedom
And for the country that he loved
May he now rest in perfect peace.

Leading Seaman Herbert William PATMORE was a Stansted boy before moving away to Highams Park. This was the reason that on every Remembrance Sunday his name was read out but for some unknown reason his name was not to be found on the local Stansted Memorial or at Highams Park. This was to be rectified when the local Royal British Legion looked at all the factual information and decided to approach the Parish Council and a decision was made, as it was thought to be right and proper, to add his name to the Memorial. His son and daughter attended the next Remembrance Sunday and were moved to see his name inscribed on his home village memorial.

His details are as follows.

Leading Seaman Herbert William PATMORE
Royal Navy 'H.M.S. Fearless'
Killed in Action 23rd July 1941 aged 38

Herbert is commemorated on the Plymouth Naval Memorial, Panel 46 Column 1, along with the names of over twenty three thousand from both wars. The Memorial is situated centrally on The Hoe which looks directly towards Plymouth Sound.

Leading Seaman Patmore was the nephew of **Alfred William PATMORE** (see May 1915).

HMS.Fearless was an "F Class" destroyer of 1,375 tons. Launched in May 1934 at the Cammell-Laird

Herbert William Patmore

shipyard in Birkenhead, she had four 4.7 inch guns and eight 21-inch torpedo tubes. She was involved in the Spanish Civil War in 1937 before teaming up with HMS Brazen to sink U.49 off Harstadt in 1940. In June 1941, again with other ships, she helped sink U.38 west of Cape Trafalgar, only to suffer torpedo damage one month later from Italian aircraft whilst screening HMS Ark Royal. Fearless caught fire, lost all power, and when judged too damaged to tow, she was sunk north of Bone by HMS Forester on 23 July 1941.

She was scuttled by

torpedos from the "Forester" another destroyer of our flotilla. Fortunately there were only four or five casualties in the HMS "Fearless". Unfortunately one of these would have been **Herbert**.

'Fearless' on fire

1942

At the rising of the sun,
At noontide and in the evening,
We will remember them.

Noorddijk General Cemetery

On the 20th January 1942 49 Squadron sent five Hampden's to attack Emden (known as the 'seaport of the Ruhr area). Two aircraft failed to attack any target owing to icing and failure of heating and two aircraft bombed the primary target. Of the fifth aircraft, no signals were received and the aircraft was reported missing. Flight Officer Alex Harvey (AT148) and crew were shot down over Groningen by Obfw Paul Gildner of II/NJG.2.

Hampden Bomber

Sadly, all the crew perished when S-Sugar fell to earth near the farm of Mr Ritsema at Roodehaan, Noorddijk in Holland. The crew rest together in Noorddijk General Cemetery. They are the only war graves in this cemetery.

One of the crew on that day was **Sergeant William Arthur Bill GRAY.** He was born on 23rd July 1917 and was from Stansted, Essex, living at Silver Street with his parents William Brant Gray and Miriam Gray, and his two sisters Elizabeth and Ellen. He was an observer on a Hampden bomber with 49 Squadron. The crew consisted of pilot, Flight Officer Alexander Muir Harvey, wireless operator/air gunner Sergeant John William Hallam and air gunner Sergeant Richard Mannering Knapman.

William had been educated at Newport Grammar school and after worked in a Statistical office at Liverpool Street Station. His parents owned a cycle shop in Silver Street.

William's details are as follows,
Sergeant (Observer) William Arthur Bill GRAY 963946
Royal Air Force Volunteer Reserve 49 Squadron
Killed in Action 20th January 1942 aged 24
His grave can be found at Noorddijk General Cemetery. Grave Ref – Plot B. Row O. Grave 23. Noorddijk is three miles north-east of Groningen and about a mile north of the road from Groningen to Delfzijl. The cemetery is south of the village, on the western side of the road from Groningen.

The husband of Cynthia Elizabeth Bentley, from Stansted, Essex, was killed in March 1942. He was **Sergeant Samuel Frederick Bentley 408 Squadron R.C.A.F**, aged 21, who lost his life on 27th March 1942. **Sergeant Bentley** was a member of the crew of Hampden L4140, EQ-B Bar that was lost without trace whilst mine laying in the Estuaries of the Jade and Weser rivers. 408 Squadron lost three aircraft that night on the same task. He was the son of Joseph and Mary Bentley.

News that Stansted lad **Frederick James BRAND** had been killed whilst training in Canada reached the village during July 1942. His details are as follows,
Leading Aircraftman Frederick James BRAND 1337274
Royal Air Force Volunteer Reserve
Died 29th July 1942 aged 20
His Grave can be found at Lethbridge (Mountain View) Cemetery, Alberta, Canada. Grave Ref. Lot 12. Block B. Grave 4E.
His plane a Stearman (a training aircraft), FD980, collided with another Stearman, FD990, whilst training with No.36 Elementary Training School. His co-pilot A.G. Clark was also killed.
He was the son of **Christopher** and Emily Brand from Millside, (Mill Field in *Herts and Essex Observer*) Stansted. He had two brothers Edward and Alfred.
His father **Christopher** had served during the Great War in the Kings Liverpool Regiment. **Acting-Corporal Christopher Brand** was at the Western Front from July 1917 till the end of the conflict.

On the 12th August 1942 HMS Cairo was sunk by an Italian submarine. On board at the time, and sadly lost, was **Able Seaman William Arthur Halsey, Royal Navy,** who was the son of Ernest and Hetty and the husband of Susan from Stansted, Essex. **William** was aged 42 and was listed as having been 'Mentioned in Dispatches'.

September 1942 saw the loss of two Stansted soldiers. The first of these was **Driver Harold George GUNN**, the son of Charles and Mary Gunn and husband of Eileen Frances whom he married in the August of 1941. At the time of his death **Harold** was living in Great Hallingbury with his wife, and his parents were at Sunnyside, Stansted.

Harold's details are as follows,
Driver Harry George GUNN T/254647
~~Royal Army Service Corps~~
**Died as Prisoner of War 3rd September 1942
aged 38**
He is buried at Caserta War Cemetery in Italy.
Grave Ref – II, E, 7.

The sad news reached the village of Stansted that
Gunner Leslie John Carter of the Royal
Artillery had died. He was the son of Thomas
and Edith Carter and aged 23. He had died as a
prisoner of war after the capture of Hong Kong.

The second Stansted son to lose his life during
September was **Lance-Corporal George
Bertram ECCLESTONE**.

George Bertram Ecclestone

He was the son of George and Edith
Ecclestone and had a brother named
Thomas Stanley (see May 1944) and a
sister Edith Mary.
Edith Mary, who lives at 'St Stephens',
Silver Street, (Top of Chapel Hill)
Stansted had the following recollections.
*"George joined the British Expeditionary
Force and left Dunkirk on the last boat
back to England. He was uninjured. At
home he slept solidly for days from
extreme exhaustion. In 1942 he went to
El Alamein and soon into battle. He was
missing for several days, and was found
in a German prisoner of war camp. His
right knee had been shot away and he
could not survive. He is buried out there
in a grave looked after by the Imperial
Graves Commission* (Commonwealth
War Graves Commission C.W.G.C.). *He
had refused to become a corporal"*.

George's details are as follows,
Lance-Corporal George Bertram
ECCLESTONE 6346144
Queen's Own, Royal West Kent
Regiment 5th Battalion
Died from Wounds as a Prisoner of War
7th September 1942 aged 23
He is buried in El Alamein War
Cemetery, Egypt. Grave Ref – XIX. G. 20.

1943

At our fireside
sad and lonely
the children I do tell
how their noble father fell.

The seven crew of Lancaster III ED783 KM-F were lost whilst heading off, from their base at Waddington, on a night bombing raid on Essen. They were shot down by a German night fighter and crashed at 03.20a.m. All seven crew members now sleep side by side in their heroes' graves at Dalfsen General Cemetery, Holland. This was the first Lancaster Mk III lost from the Squadron.

The seven crew members included **Herbert Charles ELLIS** who was born in Kensington but grew up in Ugley Green where he lived with his parents in one of the White Cottages. His father was a chauffeur at Orford House.

Herbert was married to Marjorie and had a son named Michael who at the time of his father's death was only six weeks old. Marjorie was the sister of **Albert 'Sonny' BONNEY** (see August 1944). It is probable that **Herbert** then lived with his wife Marjorie at her parent's home in Sunnyside, Stansted, as it was in Sunnyside that son Michael was born.

Herbert Charles Ellis

His details are as follows,

Sergeant (W/Op./Air Gunner.)
Herbert Charles ELLIS
Royal Air Force Volunteer Reserve
1270431
Killed in Action 1st May 1943

Herbert's grave can be found at Dalfsen General Cemetery, Overijssel, Holland. Dalfsen is a small town seven Miles east of Zwolle. The cemetery is about 800 metres west of the town, on the north side of the road to Zwolle.

It is only fitting that we also remember the other six crew members who lost their lives with **Herbert** that night. They were, Sergeant Robert Williams, Flying Officer William Arnold Rollings, Sergeant Stanley Stuart McClellan, Sergeant Rex Lake Le Page, Pilot Officer Leslie James Ellis and Sergeant John Bonser Brown.

Details of operations from Bomber Command were as follows.
30th April/1st May 1943

305 aircraft including 190 Lancasters, 105 Halifaxes, and 10 Mosquitos flew to Essen. Cloud was expected over the target so a Pathfinder technique based solely on Oboe Mosquito skymarkers was planned. This was not expected to give such good results as ground-marking but the plan worked well and 238 crews reported that they had bombed Essen. Because of the cloud, no bombing photographs were produced. The Krupps factory was hit again. The losses were 6 Halifaxes and 6 Lancasters which was 3.9 per cent of the force that night.

On the 14th June 1943 the following soldier connected to the village lost his life. He was **Private George Harry Clark**, 1st Battalion Duke of Wellingtons West Riding Regiment. George was the son of Kate from Stansted and was 27 years old.

Private Stanley Albert Gray, the son of Albert and Gertrude from Stansted, was listed as being killed during November 1943. He lost his life on the 2nd of November and is buried at Sangro River War Cemetery, Italy. He was serving with the Essex Regiment 5th Battalion.

Having been a Prisoner of War in Thailand since 1942, official news reached the parents of **Private Robert Charles JOHNS** that he had died on the 12th of this month. His details are as follows,

Private Robert Charles (Charlie) JOHNS 5779228
Royal Norfolk Regiment 5th Battalion
Died as a P.O.W. 19TH December 1943 aged 32
Robert is buried in Chungkai War Cemetery, Thailand. Grave Ref. 3.K.2.
He was the son of Percy James and Ada Elizabeth Johns from Lower Street, Stansted, and prior to joining up *'Charlie'* **Johns** worked at Barnard Brothers, Corn and Coal Merchants at High Street, Newport and he was also the local Stansted Sunday school teacher. **Charlie's** parents managed Thomas Hicks, (associated with Barnard Brothers) situated in Lower Street, Stansted.

1944

If we could have seen his loving face,
And bade him a last farewell,
The blow would not have been so hard,
For the one we loved so well.

This month's roll of honour was from the wife of **Private Charles William (Bill) CARTER** who was killed in action on the 10th of January in Italy.
His details are as follows,
Private Charles William CARTER 751178
Essex Regiment 5th Battalion
Killed in Action 10th January 1944 aged 37
Charles's grave can be found at Sangro River War Cemetery. Grave Ref. XVII.B.37.

He was the son of Alfred William and Alice Carter and the husband of Isabel whom he lived with in Silver Street, Stansted. They had one daughter.

One of Stansted's young soldier sons died in April 1944. At the age of only nineteen, **Gunner Frederick George DARBY** died on the 3rd of this month.

He was the son of Edward Joseph and Amelia Elizabeth Darby. Very few details have been found about how **Frederick** died. His details are as follows,
Gunner Frederick George DARBY 14576982
Royal Field Artillery, 195th Field Regiment
Died 3rd April 1944 aged 19
Frederick is buried in St Mary's Churchyard, Stansted.

258

May 1944 saw the sad loss of **Thomas Stanley ECCLESTONE** whose elder brother **George** had also been killed earlier in the war. (see September 1942)

Details about **Thomas** from his sister Mary, in her own words, are –

"He joined the Royal Air Force and was partly trained in Montreal. He was a fighter pilot. He was congratulated during training for bringing his aircraft down safely when there was a power cable in the way. His last duty was to keep flying alone non-stop over the English Channel at night. He had to control the plane, and fight of any aggressor; circling between England and the continent. His fate is not really known but he was probably shot down by ackack guns. He died just before Whitsun 1944. His last leave was given him so that he could spend the whole of it studying a new, super plane which he was to have on his return. It was a very complex machine and the dashboard was absolutely full of gauges, buttons and printed information. I am certain he was not given enough time to really master these controls. There was a fat booklet of details to study in addition to the illustrated dashboard. He was dreading the great responsibility and ordeal of flying this plane on his own".

Details from research tell us that on the day **Thomas** died he was not alone in his aircraft.

Pilot Officer Thomas Stanley ECCLESTONE and Sergeant John Harold Shimmin (from the Isle of Man) took off in Mosquito NS932 at 23.42p.m. from their base at Little

Snoring and were hit by flak and came down near Wemeldinge, Holland. Both are laid to rest in Bergen-op-Zoom War Cemetery.

Other details of this loss were slightly different. From the crash sheet of the late Hans de Haan, a well known Dutch Air War historian, details were that the Mosquito hit a searchlight and crashed close by on a flak battery. It is more than likely that **Thomas's** aircraft had already been hit by flak prior to hitting the searchlight.

Thomas's details are as follows,

Pilot Officer Thomas Stanley ECCLESTONE 176416
Royal Air force Volunteer Reserve 515 Squadron
Killed in Action 11th May 1944 aged 23

His grave can be found in Bergen-Op-Zoom War Cemetery, Holland. Grave Ref. 18.B.9. Bergen-op-Zoom is a town in the Dutch province of Noord-Brabant, thirty miles north-west of Antwerp (Belgium). 515 Squadron was formed at Northolt in October 1942 part of Fighter Command. Later, in December 1943 it became part of Bomber Command based at Little Snoring, Norfolk.

Sonny

An extract from the book 'The Men who went to Warsaw' by Lawrence Isemonger reads as follows.

"Of the eighteen planes that took off for Warsaw on the night of August 16th eight succeeded in reaching the dropping area and another eight failed to return to base. The returning crews reported intense air opposition over the entire area north of the Carpathians. Searchlights probing about the sky co-operated with night fighters, using magnesium flares to flush out the Liberators".

One of the unfortunate Liberator's crew was **Flying Officer Albert (Sonny) Milvein BONNEY** (spelt Milvron on some documents) who lived with his parents Charles Harold and Daisy Ellen in Sunnyside, Stansted. **Sonny** and the rest of the crew of Liberator EW161/M of 31 South African Air Force Squadron were on Special duties that night, but were shot down by Luftwaffe night fighters over Lysagora while en route to drop supplies to Polish Partisan forces in Warsaw.

Sonny's details are as follows.

Flying Officer (Air Gunner) Albert (Sonny) Milvein BONNEY 53201
Royal Air Force 31st Squadron
Killed in Action 17th August 1944 aged 22

Sonny

Sonny, along with his fellow crew, are all buried together at Kracow. **Sonny's** grave is at Ref: Coll. grave 1. D. 3.

The other crew members also killed and buried at Krakow are as follows -
Captain G. Lawrie, South African Air Force, 102792V, aged 27.
Lieutenant A.J. McInnes, South African Air Force, 157105V, aged 22.
Lieutenant O. Coleman , South African Air Force, 328600V, aged 20.
Sergeant George Swift, Royal Air Force, 1454102, aged 20.
Lieutenant H.H. Lewis, South African Air Force, 136470V,aged 24.
Flight Sergeant Ronald Zambra, Royal Air Force, 1322578, aged 22.

Sonny was the Brother in Law of **Herbert Charles ELLIS** (see May 1943) who had married his sister Marjorie.

Sonny during his youthful days was a much-liked *'Jack the Lad'* and he had once been thrown out of the school choir for smoking.

Sonny Booney **(centre)**

The son of Arthur and Olive Brown, of Stansted Essex, received the sad news that their 21 year old son had been killed on active service. He was **Flight Sergeant Brian Arthur Keith Brown**, Royal Air Force Volunteer Reserve. He was listed as missing on the 23rd September 1944 and his name is remembered on the memorial at Runnymede. The Air Forces Memorial at Runnymede commemorates by name over 20,000 airmen who were lost in the Second World War during operations from bases in the United Kingdom and North and Western Europe, and who have no known graves.

Flight Sergeant Brown was stationed at RAF East Fortune in East Lothian, Scotland. Actual details of his death are that on this date Beaufighter JL423 of 132 Operational Training Unit failed to return after take off for a night training exercise.

On 21st November 1944 the son of Alfred and Florence Beatrice Salmon, of Stansted, Essex was killed. His details are **Corporal Alfred Charles Salmon**, Dorsetshire Regiment, 4th Battalion, killed on 21st November 1944, aged 31.

His grave can be found at Reichswald Forest War Cemetery. The cemetery was created after the Second World War when burials were brought in from all over western Germany and is the largest Commonwealth cemetery in that country.

Winnie Johnson

.On the 19th December 1944 the Hoffman ball bearing factory in Chelmsford was bombed when the 367th V2 to hit England fell on a residential area close to the works and not far from the Marconi electronics factory which may also have been the target. Thirty-nine people were killed and 138 injured, 47 of them seriously, while several dwellings were destroyed and hundreds more damaged. The bombing happened at 1.00a.m. in the morning. A monument to the dead, recently restored, is in the cemetery in Writtle Road.

One of the unfortunate civilians to lose their life in this tragedy was **Winifred Joan JOHNSON**, who was the eldest daughter of Mr. and Mrs. Albert. E. Johnson of 12 Sunnyside, Stansted. Her father Albert served in the Police War Reserve at Stansted. Her details are as follows **Winifred Joan JOHNSON, Killed 19th December 1944 aged 21.**

1945

He sleeps not in his native land,
But under foreign skies,
Far from those who loved him,
In a hero's grave he lies.

The only son of the late Mr. F. Rous Mallory of Toronto and Mrs. Mallory of The Golf House, Stansted was killed on active service this month. His details are as follows.
Sergeant William Rous MALLORY 1808885
Royal Air Force Volunteer Reserve
Killed on Active Service 16th January 1945 aged 20
William's grave can be found in the nearby village of Birchanger and as well as being remembered on the Stansted Memorial his name can also be found on the memorial at Birchanger.

    William was killed, along with his fellow crew, when their Lancaster Bomber III, DV161, flew into the ground at Morcott, Uppingham, Rutland on the night of the 16th after taking off at 23.03 from North Luffenham to practice circuit flying but crashed two minutes later while turning onto the crosswind leg, coming down at Morcott. The two survivors (Maycock & Longman) were taken to the RAF hospital at Ely.
His fellow crew members on that dreadful night were,
Flight Sergeant Pattinson, Norman David Royal Australian Air Force 419969 aged 20.
Flying Officer Goodman, Stanley William Royal Air Force Volunteer Reserve 156058 aged 22.
Sergeant / W/Op Pasquill, Norman Royal Air Force Volunteer Reserve 1038029 aged 23.
Sergeant Nav./ Bomber King, John Paynter Royal Air Force Volunteer Reserve 1335881 aged 23.
Pilot Officer Marritt, William Arthur DFM Royal Air Force Volunteer Reserve 182843 aged 23.
Sergeant Porter, William Frank Royal Air Force Volunteer Reserve 3006161 aged 19.
Maycock G.L. – Survived.
Longman G.L. – Survived.

The following sad letter was received by Mrs J. F. Kitchener a month after her husband was killed. *"Dear Mrs Kitchener. Brigadier Leech – Porter has asked me if I will write to you and tell you how your husband was killed. This is the reason for this letter.*

    During the early hours of the morning the billet received a direct hit from a flying bomb. I am perfectly certain that your husband was killed instantly and that he did not even wake up. I saw his body and he looked very peaceful. He was buried alongside his comrades, and I can assure you that everything was done that could be done. Any belongings that were found have been returned to the U.K. and you will also receive them through official channels. You will also receive notification of the place of burial.

263

Please allow me to express my sincere sympathy for you in your great loss and assur
that if there is anything further you wish to know or anything I can do to help, you hav
only to write and ask me". Yours Sincerely, W.L.M. Swan Major R.M.

His details are as follows,

Lance-Corporal James Frederick KITCHENER, PO/X 106532
H.Q. 5th R.M. A.A Brigade, Royal Marines
Killed on Active Service 23rd February 1945 aged 22

His grave can be found at Schoonselhof Cemetery, Antwerp, Belgium, Grave Re
IV.A.3.

James Frederick Kitchener

James Frederick Kitchener

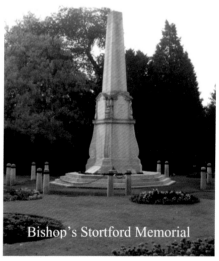

Bishop's Stortford Memorial

He was the son of Mr and Mrs F.E. Kitchener and the husband of Evelyn Kitchener (nee Prior) (See July 1917)

James's name can also be found on the nearby Memorial in the town of Bishop's Stortford.

Phillip James Brett

Having spent over two years as a Japanese Prisoner of War **Sergeant Phillip James BRETT** lost his life. His details are as follows.

Sergeant Phillip James BRETT 565691
Royal Air Force 205 Squadron
Died 19ᵗʰ March 1945 aged 31

Phillip has no known grave today and his name is commemorated on the Kranji Singapore Memorial.

Phillip was the son of James, a local blacksmith, and Maud Brett. They lived on the western side of Cambridge Road and it is also believed that he had a sister who was killed whilst working in a munitions factory

After capture he was held at Java, Singapore, Borneo (Jesselton, Sandakan) From research his service number tells us (565691) he was probably a Halton Apprentice Entry 24 enlisting in September, 1931. Further information found leads us to believe that **Phillip** was buried at Pagintan Cemetery which contained 95 unidentified Prisoners of War (Australian and British) after losing his life to Malaria.

Here is an extract taken from the book *'Sandakan - A Conspiracy of Silence'* by Lynette Ramsay Silver.

The POWs captured in Java had been on the move ever since being captured. After spending six months in various compounds in Batavia they were transshipped to Singapore only to be uprooted three weeks later and sent to Borneo leaving Singapore on 9ᵗʰ October 1942 and arriving at Jesselton on 19ᵗʰ. They remained there until April 1943 until it was ordered that the camp be shut down. The first party was transferred to Sandakan on 8ᵗʰ April 1943 and the second on the 10th. On 28ᵗʰ January 1945 the first of 455 POWs in nine groups set out for Ranua. In mid February the first five groups arrived (70 died on the way) and groups six to nine (40 died on the way) arrived at Pagintan. The survivors, 50 to 60, of the second group left Pagintan for Ranua on 26ᵗʰ March 1945. On 1ˢᵗ April 1945 of the numbers that had left Sandakan at least 302 were dead. The main march had accounted for 123,the Pagintan camp for 69, Ranua for 89 and the just completed Pagintan - Ranua march for 21. By the end of April there were less than 60 left alive.

Of the 2434 prisoners - 1787 Australia 641 British - incarcerated by the Japanese at Sandakan POW Camp, only six survived. Many died of malnutrition, maltreatment and disease. In 1945, in response to an order from the Japanese High Command that no prisoners were to survive the war, those still able to walk were sent on a series of death

marches into the interior. Anyone unable to keep up was ruthlessly murdered. Those left behind were systematically starved to death or massacred.
This was a great but little known tragedy.

On the 31st March 1945 **Lieutenant Maurice Hammond,** Royal Engineers lost his life. He was the son of Arthur and Lois Hammond from Stansted, Essex.

Finally one name on the Stansted War Memorial has proved very difficult to find out any information on and interestingly it would be the last entry into my books timeline as his death occurred on July 14th 1945. **His name is Donald Douglas Arthur FROST.** There is no record of him with the Commonwealth War Graves Commission. A record of his birth which was registered in April – June 1921 has been found and I have also obtained his death certificate which states.
Douglas Donald Arthur FROST
Where and when died – 14th July 1945, 6 Grey Friars Place, Stafford. Aged 24.
General Labourer. Cause of Death – Pulmonary Tuberculosis.
W.A. Frost widow of deceased was present at death.

So far I have not been able to pin down **Donald's** military service but a local villager did tell me that he seems to remember the name and added that he was fairly certain that **Donald** had lost a leg during the fighting in France.

No doubt, a few days after this book goes to print and is available someone will come forward with the necessary information and most likely a lovely photograph.

My World War 2 experience by Patrick Patmore (son of Sidney Patmore)

My name is **Patrick William Patmore**, *born July 1926 and I lived as a child at No 15 (now No 43) Woodfields, Stansted. I was educated at the Council School on Chapel Hill until the age of 14. The only two highlights of that period were the visit of Queen Mary to open Hargrave House as the Mary Macarthur Home for Working Women in 1936, it rained and my little flag got all wet! The other occasion was the open day of the newly built Debden aerodrome in 1938, this was a very exciting outing for us children. As far as I can remember the aircraft there were Gloster Gladiator biplane fighters and also one of the early Hawker Hurricanes, they also did a parachute drop from a Bristol Bombay bomber. Great stuff for us kids.*

In spring 1940 we moved to Burton End, and as I had then left school I started work at Mayhew Bros Cambridge Road garage as a trainee mechanic. At 15 I joined the AFS (Auxiliary Fire Service) at the sub station in a stable at Major Cawkell's house, Burton Bower. This was also shared with the ARP (Air Raid Precaution) wardens, our equipment was a mid 30's Vauxhall 14 saloon car fitted with a roof rack for the ladder and a tow bar for a Coventry Climax trailer pump, the Leading Fireman was Fred Banks.

I received my calling up papers on 3-8-44 and went to Mary Hill Barracks, Glasgow (HLI) Did 6 weeks primary training in the General Service Corps, and di some ability tests one of them consisted of a tray with several disassembled items only two I can remember was an old fashioned door lock and a small metal smoothing plane, there were several other items as well. Having managed this Ok it was deemed that I did not need a trade course so was posted to Mill Hill, London. This lasted about two weeks and consisted of a bit of metal bashing and written papers on motor vehicles. The food at this outfit was absolutely diabolical, but I managed to survive and pass and then mustered in the REME (Royal Electrical and Mechanical Engineers) in the rank of Craftsman. First posted to Salt Hill Camp at Slough, Bucks and went to 602 B Vehicle workshops on the trading estate near the Mars chocolate factory. I was almost immediately sent out on attachment to other regiments such as RAOC, RASC and even the Welsh Guards. These postings were wherever I was needed to do mods or maintenance to trucks and motorcycles for periods of a few weeks to several months. I never ever actually served in a REME unit. This was a nice little number as I was largely my own boss, and as I did not belong to the outfits I was working at I did not get lumbered with guard duties or fire pickets. The only snags were as I was not on their payroll my pay was always in arrears catching me up. The other was to put my laundry in to them and then get moved on somewhere else before it returned, so to sum up I was always skint and with grubby underwear!

The units I went to were places like Burnham Beeches, Aynho,Dorchester, Great Missenden and Chilwell. The jobs were fairly run of the mill but I will mention a few of the more interesting.

At Aynho ,Oxon was 46 VRD (Vehicle Reserve Depot) and I did work preparing Norton 16H motorcycle combinations for shipping to the continent, these were a bit unusual as they had drive to the sidecar wheel, only to be engaged on soft going also all three wheels were interchangeable. Another was preparing Excelsior Welbikes, these were packed in containers and dropped with the paras; these appeared after the war a bit redesigned as the Corgi scooter for the civvy market.

Another was 45 VRD at Dorchester on Thames, the unit was on the opposite side of the road to a airfield at Culham and strangely enough it was a Fleet Air Arm base with a ships name which I have now forgotten. It was about this time that I was made up to Lance-Corporal. There were a number of odd vehicles at this site, unadopted experimental machines. And some old Mann Egerton.trucks with no cabs and solid tyres dating from the early 20's, they were petrol electric, the engine driving a dynamo to an electric motor on the rear axle. The current could be switched to power a searchlight mounted on board. One machine that intrigued me was a Bombardier Snowmobile made in Canada rubber tracks at the rear and steerable skis in front, a body a bit like a section of aircraft fuselage with a Ford V8 engine amidships. Possibly got for evaluation if we needed to return to Norway? My last UK post was to Easton Lodge near Dunmow on to the airfield vacated by the Americans. We had several thousand trucks and jeeps parked there. This was summer of 1946 and I had the job of preparing some Commer radio vans, these had been de-kitted and were to be loaned to the Post Office for the Christmas period, so it was just a matter of fitting batteries, refilling radiators etc and road testing. Being so near home was too good to last so they posted me to Germany.

I sailed from George V dock at Hull on a Liberty ship HMS Halberd to Cuxhaven, and from there to Bramsche about ten miles from Osnabrucke. This was to 155 TVP situated on an ex Luftwaffe airfield which had been the base for the jet fighters that they were just starting to use in the final stages of the war. We had around 50,000 vehicles parked there as this was the result of clearing up from all over Europe. They were of every make, age and nationality. My main job here was removing generating sets from radio command trucks and with a small crew of civilian workers installing them in houses commandeered for officers and NAAFI people, this was because the mains electricity supply was somewhat erratic.

I got my demobilisation orders on 7-12-47 and went to No 1 Cavalry Barracks at York to get my civvy suit and be discharged, so ends my army career.

In 1955 I joined the Royal Observer Corps at the Much Hadham post and served for 26 years, after ten years I became L/Obs and was post instructor until the Corps was disbanded. I received the Long Service Medal with Bar.

303539 Captain William Bill Johnson
(son of WW1 veteran Tom Johnson)
One man's war service (1942 – 1947)

During my research I have been in touch with a few relations of those that served in the Great War. The following was kindly produced by **William (Bill) Johnson** the son of Great War soldier **Tom Johnson.** (see January 1919)

I left Newport Grammar School, Newport, Essex, in July 1942, having gained my Cambridge Higher School Certificate in four science subjects to main standard. I was 18¼ years old at the time.

In September of that year, I was accepted for a War Office post a six month Short Course in Engineering subjects at Manchester University, with a view, ultimately, of getting an emergency commission in the Royal Engineers. After completing my university course, from March 1943 to the end of the year, I went through the ranks, then a pre-O.C.T.U course at Wrotham, Kent, and finally was given my commission in the Royal Engineers after completing my O.C.T.U course at Newark.

At the turn of the year, I had to escort a draft of sixty men out to Bombay India on 'SS Otranto'. It was a long journey round the Cape (about three months, I recall) and to while away the time I did a concentrated course on Urdu. I passed the oral and written test on board and on arrival at our destination having handed over my 'draft' and was posted to the Bombay Sappers and Miners at Poona.

After recovering from Sand Fly fever which I had contracted on arrival, I was sent to No. 6 Mechanical Equipment Group at Lahore (now in Pakistan). There I was trained in the handling, maintenance and deployment of heavy mechanical equipment in the construction of roads and airfields.

At this time, 1944, the British Army's retreat from Burma back into India was complete. Plans were afoot to get the Army moving forward again to push the Japanese back to where they had come from. Not an easy task as the top priority for vital supplies was to enable the Second Front to be opened in Europe. We could be forgiven for thinking we were the forgotten army! Nevertheless, progress was made. It was decided that an all-weather road was required to join Tamu, on the Indian/Burmese border, to Kalewa on the Chindwin, some one hundred miles plus long, to take men, supplies and heavy transport including 70-ton tank transporters to support the advance parties which were already engaging the enemy and pushing them back to the Chindwin river.

I was second in command of 721 Mechanical Equipment Platoon I.E. We were one of three such units entrusted to push this 'all-weather' road through the jungle from Tamu to Kalewa within six months to complete the project before the monsoon rains came.

The road was a miracle of ingenuity! There was no road 'metal' or special road-making equipment as such. Magnificent Teak trees were bulldozed down, the terrain levelled by 'cut and fill' where necessary by 'dozers, 'scrapers' and 'graders' after which the heavy 'sheep's foot' rollers compacted the soil to make it like concrete. To finish the sector, deep ditches ('nullas') were dug along each side and the road surface was covered with 'bithesse' (overlapping strips of Hessian cloth, dipped in bitumen). That one hundred miles of road proved able to take a thousand vehicles a day when the monsoon came! The successful outcome of the 14th Army's campaign to get back into the heart of Burma, depended on our road holding up under these tremendous volumes of traffic. Typical of the man, General Slim dropped by and thanked us all personally on completing our job on time – in six months!

Immediately after the completion of this project, all our personnel who had been in the field long before I arrived on the scene were moved back to base in Lahore. After debriefing everyone was sent on leave. I went up to Srinagar, in the Kashmir, for three weeks where I had a whale of a time with three members of the Chindit force.

On my return from the Kashmir I learnt that I had been given a further month's leave – in the UK!! I flew home in a Lancaster by courtesy of the RAF and back again six weeks later in the bomb-bays of a Liberator.

I arrived home at the end of the first week in November 1945 and was married to my wife Doris on the 10th March 1945. The hard part was returning to India again over the New Year 1946 to serve another fifteen months before returning to the UK for good.

Back in India, my unit was posted to the Sind desert, north of Karachi (now Pakistan) to clear scrub land for the resettlement of Indian servicemen following their demobilisation. Every returning serviceman, who wanted it, was to receive a parcel of land acknowledging their loyalty and service to the State during the war.

When that project was successfully completed, I was transferred to the Madras Sappers and Miners and spent the rest of my time in training men in the duties involved providing "Aid to the Civil Power" in preparation for the Partition of India into two new countries – India and Pakistan – and the departure of the British from India.. A very difficult time for all!

I returned home in March 1947 and was "demobbed" some months later after assisting in running special courses for the War Office to train new army recruits to become mechanical equipment operators for "Operation Woodpecker" which was part of a scheme to help Germany recover from her post war devastation.

---

look forward to writing a revised edition in the not too distant future with all the extra pictures and information I hope to receive once this book has been read by a few family members.

In the meantime I will sign off with the following.

"They shall grow not old, as we that are left grow old.
Age shall not weary them, nor the years condemn.
At the going down of the sun and in the morning
We will remember them".

(Taken from, For the Fallen, Laurence Binyon)

Selective Index.

275

The following is a list of all the names found on the Memorial Scroll in St John's Church of those who served in the Great War 1914-1919

Your Prayers are asked for the following Men who have gone from STANSTED to serve their King and Country.

ADAMS W.E
ALDER SIDNEY
AMEY REGINALD.W.
AMEY GEORGE
AMEY
ANDREWS ARTHUR
ARCHER FRED
BUCK ALBERT WILLIAM
BUCK FREDERICK CHARLES
BAKER F.N.
BAKER G.
BALAAM HAROLD
BANKS WILLIAM C.
BANKS H.J.
BANKS EDWARD
BASS ALICK
BASS A.I.
BASS GUY
BILARD FREDERICK
BLOOM A.I.
BLOOM FREDERICK
BLOOM R.
BLYTH RUPERT
BOXALL MAURICE
BRIGHT EVAN
BRIGHT MAURICE
BRIGHT D.G.
BRADFORD ERNEST
BRADFORD JOHN W.
BROWN THOMAS JOHN
BROWN WILLIAM
BROWN ROBERT G.
BEARY T.W.
BONNEY CHARLES
BONNEY JAMES

BONNEY ALBERT E.
BONNEY GEORGE W.
BOYDEN LEONARD
BULL WALTER
BURLES JOSEPH
BURTON HENRY DENNIS
BUSH JAMES TIMOTHY
BUSH ALFRED R.
BUTTERY WILFRID E.
BUTTERY HAROLD A.
BAYFORD PERCY
BROWN W.
BARRETT G.
BUNTING W.A.
BRAND C.
BRADFORD CHARLES
BALL C.
BRIGHT PERCY
BULL FRANK
BUSH JESSE
COTTEE PERCY
CAMP E.G.
CARTER GEORGEHENRY
CARTER JOHN
CHESHAM W.STANLEY
CHESHAM ERNEST
CHURCH PERCY
CLARK A
CLARKE TIMOTHY
CLARKE S.S.
CRICK BERTIE JAMES
CHILDS WILLIAM
CHILDS JOHN
CHILDS A. HENRY
CHILDS JOSEPH
CHILDS CHARLES
COOPER EDWIN
CARUTHERS DONALD
CARUTHERS ROY
CAVILL HERBERT FREDERICK
CHAPMAN HENRY W.
CARTER CHARLES
CROCKFORD ALBERT
CROCKFORD J.WALTER
CANNON G.A.

BUTTERS REGINALD
BUTTERS EDGAR
DAY HARRY
DIXON HERBERT H.
DIXON SIDNEY LOUIS
DIXON THOMAS A.
DENNISON ALEXANDER
DEDMAN J.H.
DOWNHAM JOSEPH
DOWNHAM ERNEST
DOCKERELL J.F.
DALE LEWIS
DIXON ARTHUR
EVERITT ERNEST JOHN
EVERITT W.G.
EVERITT W.G.
ENDERSBY S.
EGLINTON S.
FLACK CORNELIUS
FLOREY SAMUEL
FLOREY A.B.
FOTHERGILL JOHN
FOTHERGILL JOSEPH
FOTHERGILL THOMAS
FROST ALFRED THOMAS
FRANCIS LEWIS
FYSH FRANK R.
FELSTEAD ERNEST
FELSTEAD ARTHUR
FELSTEAD FREDERICK
FRANCIS WILLIAM
FINCH PERCY FREDERICK
FINCH HERBERT JOHN
FELSTEAD ISAAC JOSEPH
GATES JOHN
GIBBS STANLEY
GIBBS LOFTUS
GIBBS EDGAR
GOLD ARCHIE
GOLD CHARLES
GOLD LESLIE
GOLD DONALD
GOLD NORMAN
GRIGGS CHARLES
GRIGGS GEORGE

GRIGGS W.G.
GRIGGS CECIL
GRIGGS THOMAS
GRAY JAMES
GRAY WALTER F.
GRAY FRANCIS A.
GRAY ARTHUR
GREEN CHARLES HARRY
GOODEY W.T.
GRAY WILLIAM
GOWERS LESLIE GORDON
GOODEY EDWARD G.
GROVER ALFRED G.
HEADLAM PHILIP C.
HAGGERWOOD FRANK
HAGGERWOOD FRED
HAGGERWOOD WILLIAM G.
HAGGERWOOD CYRIL
HAGGERWOOD JOSEPH
HAGGERWOOD JAMES
HARBRIDGE WILLIAM
HARBRIDGE E.
HAYNES HAROLD SIDNEY
HARVEY ERNEST A.
HARVEY WILLIAM HENRY
HARVEY SIDNEY
HARVEY PERCY G.
HARVEY FREDERICK H.
HARVEY HAROLD
HERINGTON WILLIAM
HERRINGTON HARRY
HERINGTON HENRY
HERRINGTON ERNEST
HERRINGTON WALTER
HERRINGTON GEORGE R.
HART CHARLES
HILL JOHN
HUDGELL JAMES N.
LEVEY ROBERT
LEVEY G.T.
LEVEY THOMAS W.
LEVEY GEORGE S.
LIVESEY JOHN S.
LIGHT FRED
LONG H.

LONG A.C.
LUBBOCK CHARLES
LUCKY ERNEST
LIVINGS ETHELBERT
LIVINGS JAMES H.
LAMBERT
LITTLE
LAW WALTER ALBERT
LAW ARTHUR SIDNEY
LIVINGS HARRY
FULLER-MAITLAND W.A.
FULLER-MAITLAND R.E.
MASCALL RICHARD
MASCALL THOMAS
MATHEWS ERNEST EDWARD
MAYHEW WALTER
MILTON ARTHUR
MILTON HUBERT
MONK JAMES
MONK HARRY
MONK DAVID
MONK WILLIAM T.
MONK A.M.
MORETON ALBERT
MORTON JAMES
MUMFORD HARRY W.
MUMFORD J.E.
MATTHEWS WILLIAM E.
MACKARNESS ALBERT E.
MILLBANK EDWARD W.
MILTON CHARLES
MILTON FREDERICK
NEWELL ARTHUR
NASH ABRAHAM
NIXON CHARLES FULLER
NUNN FRANK
NORMAN ROLAND
HICKLING DONALD
HICKLING GEORGE HERBERT
HICKLING CHARLES
HUTLEY WILLIAM
HUTLEY REGINALD
HUTLEY ERNEST
HUTLEY WALTER
HAMMOND LAWRIE

HAMMOND R.W.
HAMMOND L.C.
HAMMOND G.W.
HICKS THEODORE
HAGGERWOOD CHARLES
INGOLD GEORGE
JACKSON THOMAS DARE
JACKSON GEORGE JULIUS
JACKSON CLAUDE STEWART
JACKSON RUSSELL
JARVIS HORACE
JOHNSON ALBERT E.
JOHNSON WILLIAM G.
JOHNSON CHARLES THOMAS
JOHNSON THOMAS
JORDAN ALFRED
JORDAN ARTHUR
JORDAN GEORGE T.
JACKSON A.H.
JOHNSON CHARLES
JACKSON STANLEY
KING RICHARD
KETTERIDGE L.
LAIRD WILLIAM
LAIRD ALFRED LEWIS
LAIRD EDWARD
LAW HORACE DAVID
LAW CHARLES WILLIAM
LAW H. JAMES
LAW REUBEN
LOW WALTER K.
LEACH CHARLES W.
LEACH G.S.
LEVEY ARTHUR
PATMORE CHARLES
PATMORE ARTHUR
PATMORE FRANCIS E.
PATMORE ALFRED W.
PATMORE ARCHIBALD
PATMORE SIDNEY LEWIS
PATMORE F.G.
PATMORE HERBERT
PATMORE ROBERT
PATMORE ALBERT JOHN
PAGE CHARLES SAMUEL

PEACHY ARTHUR
PHILLIPS HARRY
PHILLIPS CHARLES
PHILLIPS CLIFFORD I.
POLAND ROBERT
POOLE HORACE REGINALD
POOLE HENRY ALFRED
POOLE PERCY FREDERICK
POWELL LEONARD
POWELL FRED
POWTER A.W.
PITTKIN
PRATT WILLIAM E.
PRIOR FRANK
PRIOR HENRY WALTER
PERRY HERBERT ERNEST
POOLE CLIFFORD
POOLE LEONARD
POOLE STANLEY
POOLE VICTOR VALENTINE
PLAYER WILLIAM JOHN
POOLE G.S.
RATCLIFF WALTER G.
RATCLIFF WILLIAM JAMES
RATCLIFF WILLIAM THOMAS
RATCLIFF JAMES LEONARD
RAMSEY E.
RAWLINGS HARRY
REED GEORGE
RICHARDSON ARTHUR
RIVIERE HENRY GILBEY
RIVIERE GEORGE GILBEY
RIVIERE PHILLIPS GILBEY
ROBINSON CHARLES
ROBINSON BENJAMIN
ROBINSON REGINALD
ROBINSON PERCY D.
ROBINSON LAWRENCE
ROBINSON C.W.
ROOME CLAUDE STEWART
RUSHDEN PERCY
RUDLAND ALFRED J.
RUDLAND ALBERT
RUDLAND CHRISTOPHER
RUDLAND WILLIAM R.

RUDLAND HENRY
RUST FREDERICK
REEVE EDWARD JOHN
REEVE JOHN CHRISTIAN
REEVE REGINALD AUSTIN
SAGGERS ERNEST WALTER
SAGGERS FRANK
SAMPFORD CYRIL
SAPSFORD THOMAS J.
SAPSFORD WILLIAM ALBERT
SANDERS ALFRED
SAVORY FREDERICK
SAVORY JAMES
SAVILLE HERBERT E.
SAVILLE BERTIE CHARLES
SAVILLE SIDNEY
SAYER ERNEST R.
SAYER FRANK
SEAMER FREDERICK
SEAMER FRANK
SEAMER ARTHUR
SHEPHARD WALTER
SHEPHARD ALFRED
SMITH LEORNARD
SMITH E.K.
SMITH C.V.
SMITH CHARLES HAROLD
SMITH MAURICE J.
SMITH PHILIP H.
SMITH REUBEN
SNOW ERNEST
SNOW PERCY
SNOW STANLEY
SNOW STEPHEN
SNOW HENRY WALTER
SNOW F.GEORGE
SPEED AUGUSTUS J.
SPALDING WALTER H.
SPALDING JOHN
STACKE JOHN
STACKE THOMAS
SOMERFELDT CHARLES
SOMERFELDT FREDERICK
SUGARS ARTHUR
STANSFIELD CHARLES

SMITH ARTHUR
SWAN W.
STAINES STEPHEN STANLEY
SIMMONDS F.H.
SNELLING THOMAS
SURRIDGE DANIEL G.
SNOW NELSON
THURGOOD HERBERT DORRINGTON
TUCKER HENRY JAMES
TUNBRIDGE HERBERT
TUNBRIDGE MAURICE
TURNER FREDERICK JOSEPH
TURNER ALFRED
TURNER FRANK P.
TURNER JOHN
TURNER T.E.
TURNER FREDERICK C.
TURNER FRANCIS W.
TURNER THOMAS
TURNER ARCHIBALD
TURNER HARRY
TURNER HERBERT J.
TURNER GEORGE
TURNER ERNEST C.
TURNER FREDERICK
TURNER ARTHUR
TURNER GEORGE
TABOR CHARLES
TABOR R.
VERNON HENRY
WATSON A.F.
WATSON G.B.
WATERMAN RONALD W.
WATERMAN JAMES
WARNER FREDERICK
WARNER BERT
WARWICK PETER
WARWICK HENRY
WARWICK WILLIAM
WARWICK ARTHUR
WARWICK CHARLES W.
WARWICK JAMES
WATTS H.W.
WATTS WALTER W.
WHALL GEORGE

WHALL SIDNEY
WHITE GEORGE
WHITE HARRY
WHITE WILLIAM
WINDER HORACE
WREN ERNEST JAMES
WREN J.GEORGE
WREN CHARLES
WRIGHT HERBERT
WENN ERNEST JAMES
WELCH JOHN D.
WIFFEN W.
WELLS ARTHUR G.
WELLS CHARLES F.
WILKINS W.
WYATT S.
WARD H.E.

THE END

My Grandfather, Edwin (Ned) Martin, who fought for our freedom and was one of the fortunate ones who came home.
Not a Stansted lad but from nearby Bishop's Stortford, the town of my birth which I intend to be my next book.